MINDING AMERICAN EDUCATION

Reclaiming the Tradition of Active Learning

MINDING AMERICAN EDUCATION

Reclaiming the Tradition of Active Learning

MARTIN BICKMAN

Teachers College, Columbia University
New York and London

Published by Teachers College Press, 1234 Amsterdam Avenue,
New York, NY 10027

Library of Congress Cataloging-in-Publication Data

Bickman, Martin, 1945–
    Minding American education : reclaiming the tradition of active learning /
Martin Bickman.
      p. cm.
    Includes bibliographical references (p.   ) and index.
    ISBN 0-8077-4352-6 (paper : alk. paper) — ISBN 0-8077-4353-4 (cloth :
alk. paper)
    1. Active learning—United States.   2. Progressive education—United
States—History. I. Title.
LB1027.23.B53 2003
370'.973—dc21   2002041615

ISBN 0-8077-4352-6 (paper)
ISBN 0-8077-4353-4 (cloth)

for Louise

I cast away in this new moment all my once hoarded
knowledge, as vacant and vain. Now for the first time,
I seem to know any thing rightly. The simplest words,
—we not know what they mean, except when we love.

—Ralph Waldo Emerson

Contents

Acknowledgments

This book comes out of both individual reflection and participating with others in educational projects, out of a few years of focused research and a lifetime of being a student and teacher. My debts to others, then, would be too long, but a highly elliptical list would include various gratitudes to: Ron Billingsley, John Bryant, Howell Chickering, Evans Clinchy, Brian Ellerbeck, Samantha Harvey, Mary Klages, Steve Kurzban, Ron Miller, Wes Mott, Mary and Fred Resh, Jeffrey Robinson, Mary Ann Shea, and my fellow President's Teaching Scholars. My greatest debt is recorded in the dedication; Louise is my muse and mentor, believing in the transformative possibilities of mind and love even when my own faith sometimes wavered. One of our great satisfactions has been to watch our children grow into reflective and compassionate teachers themselves, Sarah as a physics instructor and Jed as a teacher of inner city middle schoolers. All these people have taught me more than I have learned from books and more than I can say.

Introduction:
Children in the Concrete

Teaching demands thoughtfulness. There simply is no way to become an outstanding teacher through adherence to routine, formula, habit, convention, or standardized ways of speaking and acting. Thoughtfulness requires . . . a willingness to look at the conditions of our lives, to consider alternatives and different possibilities, to challenge received wisdom and the taken for granted, and to link our conduct with our consciousness.

—William Ayers

THE MINISTER had just given a delightful sermon, a Wordsworthian paean on the wonder and innocence of childhood, and was now bidding farewell to his parishioners on the church steps. Suddenly he saw out of the corner of his eye some children playing in freshly poured cement on a few squares of new sidewalk that were ineffectually fenced off with yellow tape. He rushed over, red in the face, and began scolding them, as close to the verge of profanity as someone in his profession could come. One woman who was particularly shocked at the outburst said, "Why, Reverend, you just told us how much you love children!" The minister answered, "I love children well enough in the abstract, but not in the concrete."

The aim in this book is to reverse this attitude and bring the history and philosophy of American education into closer conjunction with what we actually do in the classroom. While courses in these subjects are usually required for teaching in public schools, the textbooks and syllabi that form their core often leave the experience of students and instructors in the dust of an abstract language and an antiquarian approach. Such courses are usually sealed off from more practical ones such as teaching methods with only the vague hope that these future teachers might someday make their own connections. But more often than not, we professors as well as our students are isolated behind the walls of our own academic specializations and can think only in units of course credits instead of reaching out for relation and synthesis. This situation is a microcosm of American education as a whole, another symptom of its failure to integrate the conceptual and symbolic with the perpetual flow of our lives.

In this book I will reconstruct a countertradition that is the antidote to this problem, a current in American thought the very goal of which is to relate the abstract to the concrete, contemplation to action. I call this confluence the tradition of active learning—without capitalization, because I do not want to reify or memorialize it. Although the tradition encompasses a diverse group of writers and educators over the span of 180 years, I argue for its ultimate coherence both as a theoretical framework and a set of practices. In a modest way, this book itself is an attempt to close the gap between thinking and doing by being at once an intellectual adventure and a call to action.

This will not be a thorough and detailed exposition of the history of American education as much as a reconceptualizing of it. The history of our schools can be reconstructed as a tension between those who want to put the act of thinking at the center and those who let other priorities override this, priorities such as socialization and the need to compete economically. But it has been said that there are two kinds of people in the world—those who say there are two kinds of people in the world and those who don't. Not to put myself too firmly in the former camp, I want to stress that I see an understanding of this tradition as a way of reconciling opposing tendencies in current school reform movements, in mediating between conservative and progressive approaches. The tradition of active learning envisions a necessary dialogue between individual experience and cultural symbols, between self-expression and teaching the basics. Too often, warring factions in educational reform have seized upon only a part of the cycle that generates real learning and urged it upon us as the entire solution. We can learn from and transcend their errors.

This book can be explained further by contrasting it with another that has recently had some play in the press, Diane Ravitch's *Left Back: A Century of Failed School Reforms* (2000). Ravitch convincingly shows how what went under the name of progressive reform movements was anti-intellectual and uneducative. She rightly deflates movements such as "scientific" curriculum-making and life-adjustment studies. But she tells only half the story, for the traditionalism and conservatism she does not critique have been at least as anti-intellectual and uneducative. Receiving what some consider the apogee of classical education in a public system, I attended Boston Latin School, and I found that institution at least as hostile to the life of the mind as was any offshoot of progressivism. The Latin language was treated more as a collection of datives and ablative absolutes through which to "build character" than as a medium of cultural and literary power. Although in my senior year we translated the first four books of the *Aeneid*, it was not until college that I learned it was indeed a poem. But worse than Ravitch's partiality is her negativity; she offers no positive program, partly because she does not appreciate how harmful the very division between progressives and traditionalists that she is perpetuating is, and that this division is itself part of the problem. We are oppressed by our educational past, but we can also see beneath its most obvious contours a hidden, vital current that offers us seeds of hope from groups often marginalized or co-opted.

This narrative begins with one such group, the New England Transcendentalists, in the 1830s and 1840s. For these transformative intellectuals, ideas were valuable only to the extent that they were realized, put to work in our lives. They did not all adhere to a single party line—Margaret Fuller said of them that they were a group of the like-minded in that no two of them thought alike—but shared an interest in creating a new education that would not only transmit the previous ideas of a culture but also create new ones. They saw in education a way to respect both the continuities and metamorphoses of a rapidly changing society and to give its democratic ideals the kind of institutional support they had often lacked. They envisioned a schooling in which the power of thought would triumph over privilege, prejudice, and habit.

Although their actual educational experiments were few and small—Bronson Alcott's Temple School: Margaret Fuller's Conversations with the women of Boston; the academy run by the John and Henry David Thoreau—I give the Transcendentalists what may seem like a disproportionate amount of attention. But the full story of Transcendentalist education has never been fully told; these figures have been relegated to the past, where they are often viewed as otherworldly and naive dreamers. At best they are read as exemplars of certain developments in the history of ideas or literary taste; at worst, they become fodder for exam questions, factoids of cultural literacy. That they could actually speak to our current dilemmas is rarely considered.

But if one aim of this book is to rescue the Transcendentalists from the restricted realm of belles lettres, another is to reverse the process and see what insights literary studies can bring to our educational thinking. Prose writers such as Ralph Waldo Emerson and Herman Melville and poets such as Robert Frost have solved within their works issues of the relation of openness to form that are relevant to how we can restructure education. Sometimes they make this relevance explicit, in which case we can ferret out and organize these statements; where it remains implicit we can draw out the implications ourselves through close analysis. Further, the field of literary criticism itself has its own pedagogical relevance, and while rarely have literary critics written about education with enough specificity and clarity to be helpful, they need only refocus the same scrutiny they use on texts to their own classrooms to make their efforts fruitful. This book represents my own attempt to make my experiences as a literary critic, a teacher, and an educational activist converge in ways that might be of use to others.

This book does not contain the promise of any quick fixes or provide ready-made blueprints for reform. Quite the opposite, it insists that fresh thinking be constantly applied every moment of our teaching lives, that "no method nor discipline can supersede the necessity of being forever on the alert" (Thoreau, 1854/1971, p. 111). If in this book I reach into the past, as the preceding sentence does, for words to move us in this direction, I do so to begin to create a community of thinking that links us with people and events in our educational history as well as with others in the present who are willing to share this vision.

While I took great care in arranging this material, I also want to be true to the spirit of active learning and encourage readers to approach this text in a proactive way. Some readers more interested in educational activism— precisely those readers I most want to reach—may prefer to skip over the second chapter and the first half of the third, both of which go into more depth on matters of philosophy and intellectual history than some would like. Some readers may also want to begin with the last chapter for a sense of the immediate applications of the ideas advocated here before going into their history and rationale. To further this interactive spirit, I am hoping that readers will contact me at *bickman@colorado.edu* with their reactions and questions.

CHAPTER 1

The American Scholar vs. American Schools:
Ralph Waldo Emerson
and Horace Mann

It is well, when the wise and the learned discover new truths; but how much better to diffuse the truths already discovered, amongst the multitude! . . . Diffusion, then, rather than discovery, is the duty of our government.

—Horace Mann

Colleges, in like manner, have their indispensable office,—to teach elements. But they can only highly serve us, when they aim not to drill, but to create; when they gather from far every ray of various genius to their hospitable halls, and, by the concentrated fires, set the hearts of their youth on flame.

—Ralph Waldo Emerson

A T A TIME when there is such an urgency to bring the act of thinking more fully into our schools, it may seem pedantic or superfluous to detour through the 19th century. Yet American education was given its basic form at this time and the petrified hold of the past will keep us in its grasp as long as its assumptions remain unexamined and unchallenged. Until we see the specific historical conditions under which our system arose, we will accept it as natural and inevitable, as what school essentially is. But if its rigidity, anti-intellectualism, and authoritarianism are legacies of the mid-19th century, so too are our best tools for challenging this system and creating alternatives.

Of course, any historical narrative is necessarily a fiction. Not quite a lie, it is more accurately a construction, shaped by choosing out of a vast set of persons and incidents a few to weave together with links of chronology and causality. The story I am about to construct is not the one exclusive truth about American educational history, but it does reveal previously unnoticed patterns. On another level, the narrative can be taken as an allegory for understanding any given moment in the act of teaching as one in which we can either respond openly and reflectively to the immediate situation or unthinkingly lapse into the habitual. We begin with one of these crucial moments when American education could have taken either of these paths.

On the afternoon of August 31, 1837, a young, relatively unknown alumnus delivered the annual Phi Beta Kappa address, "The American Scholar," to the graduating class of Harvard College. Ralph Waldo Emerson had not been elected to Phi Beta Kappa when he was a senior at the college 16 years earlier, and even now he was second choice. Having resigned from his post as minister in the Second Church of Boston, he preached only occasionally as an itinerant and up to this time had written only one thin book, *Nature,* published the previous year. Just as there was no reason to expect anything extraordinary from the speaker, the occasion itself hardly augured a break from the past. Commencement speeches are more likely to be moments when traditions are affirmed rather than questioned, where the young are exhorted to follow in paths society has already worn. So when the 215 members of the Phi Beta Kappa Society marched at noon from Harvard Yard to the First Parish Church, they were not expecting a speech that would challenge the very foundations of their own education. Perhaps only the location itself, the site of the log meetinghouse where 200 years earlier Anne Hutchinson was tried for antinomianism, hinted at any radical possibilities.

Late in his life, Emerson wrote, "There are always two parties, the party of the Past and the party of the Future; the Establishment and the Movement" (1883, p. 325), and certainly the Establishment dominated the audience. Present as Harvard faculty were Edward Tyrrel Channing, who taught rhetoric to both Emerson and Thoreau, and Edward Everett, himself a former Phi Beta Kappa orator, as well as Eliot Professor of Greek Literature. But the Movement was also present, in a group of upstarts becoming known even then as Transcendentalists, most of whom had the same Unitarian backgrounds as their Establishment elders, but were flirting with an idealism exported from Germany that had begun to undermine the prevailing materialism of Boston-Cambridge culture. Several of these young people, including Bronson Alcott, Margaret Fuller, and Elizabeth Peabody, also were to congregate at Emerson's house the next day for one of their irregular discussion meetings. Henry David Thoreau was a member of this Harvard graduating class of 1837, but there is no evidence for either his presence or absence; he may have even returned to his native Concord while Emerson was journeying in the opposite direction. Later, Thoreau was to read the address and embody its central ideas in his own living more fully than any of his Transcendentalist friends, including Emerson himself.

The member of the audience who was to have the widest influence on American education fits comfortably into neither group but was on the margins of both. On the Transcendentalist side, Horace Mann had befriended Elizabeth Peabody and was later to marry her sister, Mary. On the Establishment side, he was an influential member of the Massachusetts State Senate, although his humble birth on a farm and his own involvement in idealistic reform made him an outsider to the most prominent social circles. Mann had just resigned his senate seat two months earlier to become the first secretary of the Massachusetts Board of Education, an office that he as a legislator was instrumental in creating. Many of his friends felt that he had foolishly interrupted a promising political career for a dead-end assignment. Before this appointment, he had had little experience in the schools, but he threw himself into the position with the same kind of committed energy he had shown previously in other causes, such as temperance and abolitionism. The previous night he had just returned to Boston from Worcester, where he had delivered his first two speeches as education secretary.

In what turned out to be a 12-year tenure in this position, Mann proved to be an effective reformer in many ways, reflecting liberal and humane impulses. He advocated better school buildings and less use of corporal punishment. He widened the reach of public schooling and elevated the status of the teaching profession through training institutions. But without fully realizing it, Mann set in motion forces that would lead to increasing bureaucratization and social control. In confronting an anarchic stew of various kinds of school organizations and disorganizations, he initiated a tendency toward homogeneity and standardization that would develop as a force in its own right, far beyond his intentions or even perhaps his imagination. As David Tyack (1967) has put it, "The school reformers of Horace Mann's generation hoped to create system where they saw chaos. . . . The quest for educational uniformity began as individual agitation, gained momentum as others joined the cause, and finally became fixed by law or institutional custom—thus becoming a self-perpetuating pattern of institutional behavior" (p. 31). When Mann's successor, Barnas Sears, said in 1880, "I think we may fairly regard the year 1837 . . . as the commencement of the modern epoch of education in this country" (Katz, 1968/2001, p. xl), he did not realize how prophetically ominous his words were.

Mann helped to establish what Tyack in a later book written with Larry Cuban (Tyack & Cuban, 1995) terms the "grammar of schooling," which has established itself in the minds of generations of Americans as synonymous with school itself. As these historians point out, any school reform that challenges this grammar meets resistance: "Most Americans have been to school and know what a 'real school' is like. Congruence with that cultural template has helped maintain the legitimacy of the institution in the minds of the public" (p. 9). The central irony here is that the institution in our society most explicitly charged with encouraging thought has become the most impervious to reflective, unbiased thinking about its own workings; it has been running on automatic pilot for the past 2 centuries.

The elements of this grammar of schooling have structured our experiences so thoroughly that we have trouble thinking of them as having been created at a certain point in history. In brief, these elements are the following: the grouping of students by age in self-contained classrooms with a single teacher; the division of knowledge into "subjects"; the use of textbooks to teach these subjects; the exclusive reliance on paper-and-pencil tests to measure knowledge; and the production of regular report cards to disseminate these measurements. Tampering with more than any one of these will meet with opposition on the part of teachers, students, parents, administrators, or all of the above.

Most of this grammar was constructed by the changes that Mann set in motion and have been detailed by his biographer, Joseph Messerli (1972). Despite his admiration for his subject, Messerli sees the confining effect of Mann's reforms as well as their advantages: "To create an educational ecology of formalism was to risk sacrificing many of the imaginative, spontaneous, poetic, and aesthetic indigenous lessons to be experienced in the emerging American culture" (p. 346). In other words, Mann never analyzed some of the ways in which order and uniformity by their very nature discourage genuinely educative possibilities. For example, the separation of students into "grades" of one-year units with corresponding egg-carton physical plants to house them creates several further separations, most of them invidious, as Messerli points out:

> Mann never envisioned that graded instruction could also mean a mind-numbing regimentation as repressive as anything accomplished by the Boston masters, nor did he expect that children would spend one-sixth of their lives, and some of their most formative years, in an environment of cells and bells. Although he would laud the new Hancock and Quincy schools in Boston with their monotonous individual classrooms and long corridors as his "idea of a perfect school edifice," he did not recognize that these secure, prison-like structures would become prototypes for a thousand others. Neither did he understand that such buildings could isolate children and wall them off from direct and vital relationships with their physical and cultural environment, surrounding them instead with two-dimensional symbols and abstractions carefully and tastefully packaged to ensure a growing consumership, even if this meant a competence of mediocrity. (p. 347)

This division of students into age-segregated sequential grades encouraged the division of knowledge into a systematic and uniform curriculum, dictating what should be taught at each level. The system has an undeniable convenience, but it also straitjackets processes of discovery, as Messerli notes:

> It was necessary for subjects to be subdivided into lessons of bits and pieces of information, then reorganized, classified, labeled, and given some hierarchy of values. In this way, the chasm between ignorance and learning would not be negotiated only by the insightful leaps of a talented few. It would be filled in with hundreds of textbooks, thousands of assignments, and an infinitude of words, numbers, and facts, so that the multitudes could cross over in lockstep fashion with less intellectual effort, albeit with far more drudgery and boredom. (p. 341)

Knowledge, then, was predigested and structured by someone other than the learner, whose mastery of the material was often measured by only the ability to repeat the words of the textbook instead of by any operational knowledge. Any productive encounter with uncertainty and difficulty, with that shifting but instructive edge between the known and the unknown, was foreclosed. This attitude toward knowledge is as persistent a feature of the grammar of schooling as any institutional structure.

Of course, the imposition of order on chaos is a crucial feature of any cultural endeavor. But the stance of American education since Horace Mann is to impose order prematurely, too neatly and complacently, so that it becomes a confining box rather than a door or window. We then mistake the shape of this box for the shape of the universe. A mother once told me about a conference with her daughter's kindergarten teacher, who was concerned that the child did not color within the lines on her handouts. The mother was a little puzzled, since she knew her daughter to be a good artist for her age, so she queried the child at home. The daughter said, "But a bear doesn't stay inside the lines—it's shaggy." Schools have acquired a knack for smoothing out the shagginess of reality and arresting its flux with nice clean lines that have more to do with our rage for order than with our actual experience of the world.

Herbert Kliebard (1992) has conceptualized the problem well. He notes that teachers are asked to perform two functions, to keep order and to instruct, both of which seem to be compatible in theory. But in practice the first almost always trumps the second: "The injunction to keep order has become so supreme that it simply swamps the teaching function" (pp. 103–104). Kliebard generalizes that "educational reforms involving changes in teaching practice fail with such monotonous regularity because enlightened reform rhetoric and the generosity of spirit that impels people to attempt to change things for the better come into direct conflict with institutional realities" (p. 104).

With all this separating students into grades, knowledge into lessons and textbooks, days into fixed periods, the school system stands as a monument to rigid stability in a world of variety and novelty. But Mann did not so much introduce a new epistemology into American education as disseminate the view of knowledge already implicit in thousands of classrooms across the country. As Barbara Finkelstein (1989) notes in a study that includes schools from the beginning of the nineteenth century:

> Teachers proceeded as though they believed that all knowledge, from reading to arithmetic, comprised collections of fact—absolute, unchanging, true. They did not seem to regard knowledge as provisionally held and progressively realized, as constantly changing and as subject to creative manipulation. The task of the student was to learn the material. The task of the teacher—essentially moral, rather than intellectual—was to make students learn. For these teachers, the cultivation of intellect and the development of character proceeded in the same mechanical, orderly and controlled manner. (p. 137)

What Mann did was to reinforce these attitudes and create for them a habitation—a set of school systems and training institutes—that particularly resists constructive scrutiny or imaginative revision. Paradoxically, in Mann's drive to create a more encompassingly democratic system of schooling, he helped build one of our most stratifying and hierarchical institutions. We want to ask, then, What was Horace Mann thinking on that sunny Wednesday afternoon of August 31, 1837, when he heard Emerson delineate a conception of American education diametrically opposed to the one he helped foster?

❦   2   ❧

As we read Emerson, we should not only be asking what Mann was thinking but also what is "thinking" itself? Should our thinking be directed toward the immediacies of our own lives or something beyond it? Do the conditions of American life provide ways of rethinking the relations between present experience and previous cultural achievements? How should education function in a fluid, democratic culture? These are some of the questions Emerson addressed in his speech but that Mann generally ignored. It is unfair, though, to single out Mann for blame here, since generations of American educators have used Emerson's speech as just another text on which to quiz students or to pigeonhole as "our American intellectual declaration of independence," to use the phrase coined by Oliver Wendell Holmes.

Emerson is less concerned with nationalism than with distinguishing between the true scholar and the false one in any country: "In the right state he is *Man Thinking*. In the degenerate state, when the victim of society, he tends to become a mere thinker, or, still worse, the parrot of other men's thinking" (p. 54). "Man Thinking," as the present participial construction suggests, is always in process. "Thinker," by contrast, is a static noun, a label that can remain affixed after the actual act of thinking has past. But even worse than the thinker, Emerson goes on to say, is the parrot, the ersatz scholar who merely repeats unreflectively the remnants of other people's thinking. That traditional education produces such people is not its failure but the logical result of its methods and attitudes.

Emerson extends and develops these ideas on the influences on the scholar, which are, first, nature; second, the mind of the past, especially in the form of books; and third, action. It is tempting to oversimplify by saying that he argues for the first and the third at the expense of the second, but it is more accurate to view him as searching for a working dialectical relation among all three. Emerson considers "nature" to be "the first in time and the first in importance of the influences on the mind" (p. 55), yet it gets the shortest treatment. One reason is that his book, *Nature*, already took the relations between mind and nature as its main subject.

Another reason for the brevity of this first section is that as soon as one starts writing about nature, one is no longer in that realm but immediately enters that of culture. The very word *nature* is necessarily other than nature, is rather part of our universe of human symbols. A description of this process begins the next section on "the mind of the Past": "The scholar of the first age received into him the world around; brooded thereon; gave it the new arrangement of his own mind, and uttered it again. It came into him life; it went out from him, truth. It came to him, short-lived actions; it went from him, poetry. It was dead fact; now, it is quick thought" (p. 56). The very shape of these sentences, with their balanced antitheses, their repeating rhythms, their aphoristic monosyllables, suggest a complementary and dynamic balance between the mind and nature. Emerson's depiction of knowing departs from the Lockean model of the mind as a blank slate passively receiving and being shaped by sense impressions from outside. This Lockean, or sensationalistic, view of the mind, modified some through Scottish Common Sense philosophy, was hegemonic at Harvard College both when Emerson was a student and when he gave this address. It was taught explicitly in philosophy classes and was the basic assumption behind the actual practice of instruction, with its primary mode of the "recitation," in which, as Emerson's sentence about "the thinker" implies, the students mechanically parrot back knowledge poured into them from passively reading their texts. Frederic Henry Hedge, who attended Harvard College along with Emerson, said the attitude of the Harvard faculty was, "Hold your subject fast with one hand, and pour knowledge into him with the other. The professors are task-masters and police officers, the President the Chief of the College Police" (Wells, 1943, p. 141).

By contrast, the new paradigm that Emerson introduced to his Harvard College audience can be characterized as constructive and transactive. The mind is not passively shaped by reading or the outside world but actively creates knowledge in an interactive process in which the world is not only observed but also shaped. To use his own terms, there is a kind of productive rhythm between "the world" and "the arrangement of his own mind," between "life" and "truth," between "actions" and "poetry," between "fact" and "thought." The scholar takes in each first term to give back to the world the second term as knowledge, as formulations, as words and images. But once this knowledge is constructed, there is a danger in merely accepting and dwelling in it, instead of constantly refashioning and reconstructing it:

> Each age, it is found, must write its own books; or rather, each generation for the next succeeding. The books of an older period will not fit this. Yet hence arises a grave mischief. The sacredness which attaches to the act of creation—the act of thought—is transferred to the record. The poet chanting, was felt to be a divine man: henceforth the chant is divine also. The writer was a just and wise spirit: henceforward it is settled, the book is perfect; as love of the hero corrupts into worship of his statue. Instantly the book becomes noxious: the guide is a tyrant. (1983, pp. 56–57)

The imagery and diction reinforce the meaning, as the "hero," a living actor in the world, becomes frozen as a "statue" of cold, inanimate stone—Emerson elsewhere refers contemptuously to statues as "stone dolls" (p. 438). Our "love," potentially a mutual relation between equals, degenerates into the self-abasing and one-way attitude of "worship." "The poet chanting," a participial phrase that emphasizes action in the present tense, is turned into a static noun, just as "Man Thinking" turns into an inert book. What was in process now becomes settled, fixed, lifeless.

Even more than individuals, institutions constantly commit this error through canonization and through organizing knowledge into static blocks of curricula and textbooks:

> The sluggish and perverted mind of the multitude, slow to open to the incursions of Reason, having once so opened, having once received this book, stands upon it, and makes an outcry, if it is disparaged. Colleges are built on it. Books are written on it by thinkers, not by Man Thinking; by men of talent, that is, who start wrong, who set out from accepted dogmas, not from their own sight of principles. Meek young men grow up in libraries, believing it their duty to accept the views, which Cicero, which Locke, which Bacon, have given, forgetful that Cicero, Locke, and Bacon were only young men in libraries, when they wrote these books. (p. 57)

Later, William Butler Yeats was to epitomize similar insights in a poem titled "The Scholars," perhaps with an allusion to the title of Emerson's address: "Bald heads, forgetful of their sins, / Old, learned, respectable bald heads / Edit and annotate the lines / That young men, tossing on their beds, / Rhymed out in love's despair / To flatter beauty's ignorant ear" (1933, p. 139). Emerson goes further in this vein:

> Books are the best of things, well used; abused, among the worst. What is the right use? What is the one end which all means go to effect? They are for nothing but to inspire. I had better never see a book, than to be warped by its attraction clean out of my own orbit, and made a satellite instead of a system. The one thing in the world, of value, is the active soul. . . . The book, the college, the school of art, the institution of any kind, stop with some past utterance of genius. This is good, say they—let us hold by this. They pin me down. They look backward and not forward. (1983, pp. 57–58)

No one before Emerson had so clearly articulated this process by which once the act of writing is completed, its effects can be undone by dwelling in the result. As he said in an earlier lecture, troping an image from the Bible: "Thought is like manna, that fell out of heaven, which cannot be stored. It will be sour if kept; and tomorrow must be gathered anew" (1959–72, vol. 2, p. 93). These would be extraordinary words anywhere, but in the setting of a college graduation they are a particularly courageous indictment of how institutions of knowledge block knowing, how they turn thinking into having once thought, the act of writing into texts that have become fetishes rather than incitements. The paradox of school is that by not viewing the symbolic constructs of the past as only one point in a dynamic process, by isolating them from the experiences they distill and rearrange, we are in danger of inhibiting and stunting such efforts in the future. Emerson's solution, though, is not to abolish the institution of schooling but to widen its conception and activities. He concedes that one function of colleges is to transmit the accumulated learning of history, "but they can only highly serve us, when they aim not to drill, but to create; when they gather from far every ray of various genius to their hospitable halls, and, by the concentrated fires, set the hearts of their youth on flame" (1983, p. 59). The college is not merely to pass along the rays of knowledge but to stimulate its students to bring them to bear on some Promethean act of fiery creation, as a lens converges sunbeams. In other words, colleges should be places not just where culture is transmitted but where it is created and transformed, personally inflected and negotiated.

Colleges should not ignore the record of the past, but approach it in a less overawed, more critical and active spirit: "There is then creative reading as well as creative writing. When the mind is braced by labor and invention, the page of whatever book we read becomes luminous with manifold allusion" (p. 59). Emerson's vision is consonant with our best current thinking on reading, that meaning is created in a transaction between the reader and the text. If Emerson seems to emphasize the role of the reader, it is because the kind of education to which he himself was subjected overemphasized the importance of the text in a way that discouraged original thought: "Undoubtedly there is a right way of reading, so it be sternly subordinated. Man Thinking must not be subdued by his instruments. Books are for the scholar's idle times" (p. 58). Reading supplants and preempts the possibilities of new writing and reading, or as Emerson puts it, "Genius is always sufficiently the enemy of genius by over influence. The literature of every nation bear me witness. The English dramatic poets have Shakespearized now for two hundred years" (p. 58). Elsewhere Emerson says, "These books should be used with caution. It is dangerous to sculpture these evanescing images of thought. True in transition, they become false if fixed." (1959–72, vol. 2, p. 134).

The third resource of the scholar is "action," not so much a separate influence as a way of relating mind to world: "It is the raw material out of which the intellect moulds her splendid products. A strange process too, this, by which experience is converted into thought, as a mulberry leaf is converted into satin" (1983, p. 60). We are constantly thinking about and articulating what we have lived through, and, conversely, we can become aware of our subliminal, subconscious mental workings when we see them resulting in physical actions: "The preamble of thought, the transition through which it passes from the unconscious to the conscious, is action." (p. 60). One way to keep the process of learning, the activity of the scholar, from hardening into narrowness is to make sure new symbolic structures are created from the experience of living and working in the world, not from other books; we should be less like the bookworm than the silkworm. In turn, these new structures have meaning only as they are turned back into the world of action for clarity and refinement. "So much only of life as I know by experience, so much of the wilderness have I vanquished and planted, or so far have I extended my being" (p. 60). Or, as Zora Neale Hurston has one of her characters say in another vernacular, "Yuh got tuh *go* there tuh *know* there" (1937, p. 285).

On one level, Emerson may seem to be extolling a well-rounded life, balancing intellectual work with physical work. But at a deeper level he is deconstructing the fundamental oppositions between the abstract and the concrete, mind and body, thinking and labor, by viewing them as complementary opposites that undulate into each other as rhythmically as "the inspiring and expiring of breath" (1983, p. 62). In envisioning a continuing dialectic between knowing and acting, Emerson initiates America's major contribution to philosophy: pragmatism. More fully and technically formulated later in the century by William James and John Dewey, pragmatism reverses the overemphasis on being and knowing at the expense of becoming and acting. Plato extolled the idea over the thing, putting the former on a greater plane of reality. He used mathematics as a central metaphor—a perfect circle can exist in the mind as a concept but can never exist in the physical world—and preferred this fixity of concept over the fleeting and confusing chaos of immediate existence. Even Aristotle, who was less radically dualistic, exalted mental work over physical work by imagining his god as the Unmoved Mover, who leaves the dirty work of dealing with matter to lesser forces.

Dewey will later historicize this Greek separation of the theoretical from the practical as that of a slave society, and Emerson attempts to heal these deleterious splits in an epistemology for a more democratic culture in which the majority participate in physical work. In making his formulations, Emerson is perhaps not so much the inventor as one who makes explicit certain tendencies already present in American life. Several historians have noted a particularly American stance toward knowing that grew up with the conditions of settling the country, living and working in a "new" world, unmapped and uncategorized. As Daniel Boorstin (1958) has described it:

> The haze which covered the New World in that age probably covers no part of the world today; America was one of the last places where European settlers would come in large numbers *before* the explorers, geographers, and professional naturalists. . . . We sometimes forget how gradual was the "discovery" of America; it was a by-product of the *occupation* of the continent. To act, to move on, to explore meant also to push back the frontiers of knowledge; this inevitably gave a practical and dynamic character to the very idea of knowledge. To learn and to act became one. (p. 159)

Related to this emphasis on immediate experience as the source and measure of knowledge, Emerson speaks later in the address of the value of applying intelligence and extracting wisdom from the minute particulars of our quotidian life: "What would we really know the meaning of? The meal in the firkin; the milk in the pan; the ballad in the street; the news of the boat; the glance of the eye; the form and gait of the body" (p. 69). He moves from external objects to our very modalities of knowing and experiencing. To read Emerson's words as simply a plea for a distinctively American literature is to miss its vision of an education that at once radically departs from the entire Western tradition of schooling and at the same time reunites the sundered aspects of that tradition in ways that ultimately affirm and complete it.

❦ **3** ❧

If Horace Mann had fully grasped the implications of what Emerson was saying, there would be no need to write this book. Some conventional histories of education see Emerson and Mann as more aligned than opposed. It is true that Mann often shared ideas with his sister-in-law, Elizabeth Peabody, an important Transcendentalist educator, and that there were other, less personal affinities among all these New England reformers. But from the beginning both sides recognized the deep divisions between them. For example, Bronson Alcott records in his journal that for a teacher's institute in 1847, Mann "deemed it unsafe to introduce me to the teachers, and, on pressing my desire to give them the benefit of my experience as an educator, I was informed that my political opinions were esteemed hostile to the existence of the State" (1938, vol. 1, p. 195). And on being asked to donate money for a commemorative monument to Mann, Thoreau, continuing in the same vein of Emerson's dislike of statues, said: "I declined, and said that I thought a man ought not any more to take up room in the world after he was dead. We shall lose advantage of a man's dying if we are to have a statue of him forwith" (1906, vol. 12, p. 335). But it was Emerson who saw earliest, in 1839, the petrifying effects of Mann's work:

> Yesterday Mr Mann's Address on Education . . . Sad it was to see the death-cold convention yesterday morning as they sat shivering[,] a handful of pale men & women in a large church, for it seems the Law has touched the business of Education with the point of its pen & instantly it has frozen stiff in the universal congelation of society. (1969, pp. 237–238)

Emerson notes that the educational system being constructed is more concerned with social control than with individual development: "I notice too, that the ground on which eminent public servants urge the claims of popular education is fear: 'This country is filling up with thousands and millions of voters, and you must educate them to keep them from our throats'" (1983, p. 600). Emerson perceptively detected that underlying the rhetoric of liberal democracy were anxieties over class struggles and mob rule. What the journal passage is most clear about is how Mann's moves toward overorganization and bureaucratic structuring are a threat to the very play of mind Emerson wished to make the center of the educational process.

It is not quite accurate, though, to see the differences between Mann and the Transcendentalists as a simple divergence of philosophy, since Mann seemed far less interested in theory than in institutional practice. His biographer writes:

> Theoretical discussions made him impatient. Such things he thought unnecessary. Thus when Elizabeth Peabody attempted to be the conduit between Emerson and Mann and raised some theoretical questions concerning the common school reform movement, Mann replied with a not too carefully concealed irritation:

> Oh my dear lady! If a tough question were before a District Sch. Meeting about doing something for the school;—or before a Town Meeting about helping any side or limb of humanity forward, how think you, your oracle [Emerson] would lead or manage the minds of his people, which we call great by country! Oh these Reformers and Spiritualizers who can do everything well on paper! They can tell exactly how a road ought to be laid between here and New Orleans, but can they lay it? (Messerli, 1972, p. 336)

As with many school administrators, there was an anti-intellectual edge to Mann, an intuition that to conceptualize education might create divisive ideological positions, that some things are best left unexamined and unarticulated. Yet there was a kernel of insight in Mann's remark that helps explain why his version of American education won out over Emerson's.

For Emerson so valued the self-reliant individual and was so distrustful of any kind of institutional action that he shied away from offering an educational alternative, even in his mind. In a later essay, "Education," he says:

> I confess myself utterly at a loss in suggesting particular reforms proposed in our modes of teaching. No discretion that can be lodged with a school-committee, with the overseers of visitors of an academy, of a college, can at all avail to reach these difficulties and perplexities, but they solve themselves when we leave institutions and address individuals. (1883, pp. 156–157)

In this quotation we see an essential paradox: the institution of school must be changed by the engaged mind acting on it; in current jargon, reform can be only from the bottom up. Yet unless the institution is changed, individual thought within that framework can be increasingly stifled.

It seems that in the end Emerson can propose only retaining the traditional grammar of schooling but with an openness and spontaneity quite at odds with it. In the rest of the paragraph he goes on to say:

> I advise teachers to cherish mother-wit. I assume that you will keep the grammar, reading, writing and arithmetic in order: 't is easy and of course you will. But smuggle in a little contraband wit, fancy, imagination, thought. If you have a taste which you have suppressed because it is not shared by those about you, tell them that. Set this law up, whatever becomes of the rules of the school; they must not whisper, much less talk; but if one of the young people says a wise thing, greet it, and let all the children clap their hands. . . . Of course you will insist on modesty in the children, and respect to their teachers, but if the boy stops you in your speech, cries out that you are wrong and sets you right, hug him! (pp. 157–158)

Emerson's stance here is similar to that he held toward the institutions of religion, as when in "The Divinity School Address" the following year he advises the new ministers to avoid establishing yet another "Cultus," but "rather let the breath of new life be breathed by you through forms already existing" (1983, p. 81). Emerson may have been observant enough to see where education was going if it followed Mann's directions, but even he underestimated the pervasiveness and destructiveness of the forms that did evolve. He did not see that even small movements toward thinking, toward basic human decency and common sense, could be cut off before they begin in such an atmosphere. On one level, he was right to put the onus on the single individual in the classroom as opposed to institutional decree, but it is too often an uneven match. Mann's top-down bureaucracy can perpetuate and replicate itself so well because that is its main goal.

❦ 4 ❦

Thus we see two conceptions of education beginning at the same time and developing side by side. Mann projected a network of schools that would transmit existing knowledge efficiently and uniformly to passive recipients, while Emerson's speech is the keynote for a tradition of active learning. In short, this tradition views knowledge as provisionally constructed by the mind in perpetual interaction with the world. The end results of this process are cultural artifacts such as ideas, classifications, and formulas, works of litera-ture—basically a body of knowledge that has been organized and divided as the curriculum. The worst mistake of conventional education is to over-value and fetishize only these end products, and merely hand them over ready-made instead of involving students in the entire process of reconstruct-ing the world for themselves, of engaging in dialectical movements between experiencing and conceptualizing, acting and thinking, practice and theory. It is a practice and a philosophy that we would now term more constructivist, more student-centered, more metacognitive, engaging students more as culture-creating agents than as simply conduits for the transmission of cul-ture. It is wholistic, focusing not on developing the intellect solely but on integrating knowledge with the body and the feelings.

The present volume is an alternative history of alternative ways of think-ing about schooling, ways that focus on the mind continually creating a re-lationship with the world. It traces a coherent tradition of re-forming schooling itself to align it more with the ways in which we actually learn. This tradi-tion always seems to be in a losing conflict with the forces of inertia, of systemization, of mindless self-replication. We have to be careful, though, not to simply view the situation as the forces of good against those of evil. For school reform itself is not immune to the process Emerson describes of thinking becoming frozen in lifeless cultural artifacts. As Emerson writes elsewhere: "The first act, which was to be an experiment, becomes a sacrament. The fiery reformer embodies his aspiration in some rite or covenant, and he and his friends cleave to the form, and lose the aspiration" (1983, p. 749). John Holt has said, "A conservative is someone who worships a dead radical" (Jervis & Montag, 1991, p. ix), and indeed Emerson himself, like Horace Mann, has become something of a statue. When I was a student at another of his alma maters, Boston Latin School, I used to occupy myself during boring assemblies by reading the names of famous alumni etched in gold on the frieze, Emerson's name among them. At Harvard, I later took my philosophy of education course in Emerson Hall, ironically named because Emerson had been disinvited from the campus for thirty years after he delivered his "Divinity School Address" in 1838. The building showcased a hefty bronze statue of Emerson as the Sage. I was not assigned to read anything by Emerson in either institution.

To give another example, we can look at what happened to Bronson Alcott's innovations. Unlike in traditional schools where the main student utterances were recitations of textbook materials, at his school, Alcott had his young students actually giving their own ideas to the reading through journals and open discussions. Wishing to spread the word of his methods and to affirm the innate wisdom of children, he had transcripts and descriptions published in a series of books. Hiram Fuller, an entrepreneurial young man who opened the Greene Street School in Providence in 1837, was taken with Alcott's methods—so taken, in fact, that instead of trying to replicate the kinds of discussions Alcott reported, he simply read to his own students each day long passages from these books. Similarly, in teachers colleges, students have been asked to memorize large portions of John Dewey's book *How We Think* (1910), one of the main purposes of which was to argue against such recitations. By themselves these incidents are small in scope, but they are paradigmatic of what so often happens in school reform: the educational hero becomes a statue, the spirit becomes the letter, the act of mind becomes a text. But I do not see a tragic inevitability to the story. Becoming aware of exactly how this process happens, of how vision turns into method and liberation into oppression, is the first step in breaking the cycle.

CHAPTER 2

Romantic Wholism:
Education as Reintegration

Philosophy is really homesickness, an urge to be at home everywhere.

—Novalis

This separation necessarily calls forth a longing for a reunion with that which has been lost—especially after the masculine heroic quest has been pressed to its utmost one-sided extreme in the consciousness of the late modern mind.

—Richard Tarnas

ANOTHER CRUCIAL aspect to which Emerson's "American Scholar" address introduces us is embodied in its opening parable:

The gods, in the beginning divided Man into men, that he might be more helpful to himself; just as the hand was divided into fingers, the better to answer its end. . . . there is One Man,—present to all particular men only partially, or through one faculty; and that you must take the whole society to find the whole man. Man is not a farmer, or a professor, or an engineer, but he is all. Man is priest, and scholar, and statesman, and producer, and soldier. In the *divided* or social state, these functions are parceled out to individuals, each of whom aims to do his stint of the joint work, whilst each other performs his. The fable implies that the individual, to possess himself, must sometimes return from his own labor to embrace all the other laborers. But unfortunately, this original unit, this fountain of power, has been so distributed to multitudes, has been so minutely subdivided and peddled out, that it is spilled into drops, and cannot be gathered. The state of society is one in which the members have suffered amputation from the trunk, and strut about so many walking monsters,—a good finger, a neck, a stomach, an elbow, but never a man. (1983, pp. 53–54)

This parable suggests a vision in which education shapes society through individual self-realization rather than society shaping education for its own immediate needs. Further, it embodies a paradigm for thinking about the role of education in individual and cultural development, a paradigm at once ancient but also "ever new and sublime" (p. 53), of immediate relevance to a young nation in the process of creating its schools.

In pursuing this line of thought, we will sometimes leave the confines of the classroom, branching off through boulevards and bypaths in the history of consciousness. But just as the paradigm is often embodied in the image of a circular journey that takes us away from our origins only to return us to them with more insight, so this excursion will return us to the classroom with a better sense of its wider contexts and deeper potentials. As we examine these contexts, the notion of a particularly American tradition will recede as we see the entire movement in broader European contexts, particularly that of international Romanticism. This larger context only reminds us that the United States is part of the intellectual history of the West—its westernmost extension—and becomes the cutting edge of reconceptualizing the entire philosophical enterprise in the 19th century.

Emerson's parable takes its place in this wider European perspective as what some would call a mythic archetype and others a cognitive paradigm: the sequence of unity-division-reintegration—or the One, the Many, and a return to the One. In it a primal whole becomes split, but the fragments retain the desire for and promise of later reunification. Often the growth of the individual and the ability to function in society require a separation of systems, a lopsided development of capacities that creates divisions within the individual—splits between thought and feeling—and parallel divisions between the individual and nature, the self and society. While this splitting is necessary, the process often acquires a momentum of its own and the divisions become impermeable barriers even after they have ceased to be developmentally helpful. A deliberate effort, then, has to be made to heal the splits and create a balance.

Viewing Emerson's fable through this paradigm, we can see that the "unknown antiquity" includes not only arcane and sometimes occulted sources such as the philosophy of Empedocles, the Logos of the Neoplatonists, and the Adam Kadmon of the Cabala, but also the central myth of our culture, the biblical story of the Garden of Eden, as inflected through a particularly Romantic worldview. This reading of the myth has been elaborated by two major critics of Romanticism, M. H. Abrams and Northrop Frye. Abrams (1971) notes both the symmetry and the prospective character of the design of biblical history: "It begins with the creation of the heaven and the earth and ends with the creation of 'a new heaven and a new earth'; the history of man begins with his felicity in an earthly paradise and ends with his felicity in an equivalent paradise, first on earth, then in a heavenly city which will reproduce the conditions of Eden" (p. 370). Both Abrams and Frye view the Romantics as introjecting this cosmic and religious myth into individual mind:

> What corresponds to the older myth of an unfallen state, or lost paradise of Eden, is now a sense of an original identity between individual man and nature which has been lost. It may have been something lost in childhood, as in Wordsworth's *Ode on Intimations of Immortality*. . . . but it haunts the mind with the same sense of dispossession that the original Eden myth did. The context of what corresponds to the "fall," or the myth of alienation, changes accordingly. Man has "fallen," not so much into sin as into the original sin of self-consciousness, into his present subject-object relation to nature, where, because his consciousness is what separates him from nature, the primary conscious feeling is one of separation. The alienated man cut off from nature by his consciousness is the Romantic equivalent of post-Edenic Adam. (Frye, 1968, pp. 17–18)

As Emerson remarks of this original sin of self-consciousness: "It is very unhappy, but too late to be helped, the discovery we have made that we exist. That discovery is called the Fall of Man" (1983, p. 487). This feeling of separation creates a dualism between the self and the outside world, as we look at it through lenses that do not converge: "The ruin or blank, that we see when we look at nature, is in our own eye. The axis of vision is not coincident with the axis of things, and so they appear not transparent but opake. The reason why the world lacks unity and lies broken and in heaps, is, because man is disunited with himself" (p. 47).

While Emerson's version of the myth has a peculiarly American coloring, we must note his debt to German Romantics, who also saw in education the promise of healing our split psyche and restoring a psychic Eden. Especially pertinent was Friedrich Schiller, who wrote in *On the Aesthetic Education of Man*:

> Enjoyment was separated from labour, means from ends, effort from reward. Eternally chained to only one single little fragment of the whole, Man himself grew to be only a fragment; with the monotonous noise of the wheel he drives everlastingly in his ears, he never develops the harmony of his being, and instead of imprinting humanity upon his nature, he becomes merely the imprint of his occupation . . . the lifeless letter takes the place of the living understanding, and a practised memory is a surer guide than genius and feeling. (1795/1965, p. 40)

Schiller and other German Romantics were particularly attracted to education after what most of them reluctantly came to see as the failure of the French Revolution. The revolution in its violent and totalitarian phases convinced them that political change is not enough to create a free republic, that the people must be ready to accept this freedom. The German thinkers centered their visionary hopes on the concept of *Bildung,* which means at once "culture," "learning," and "personal growth." *Bildung* understood in this widest sense would reconcile what are sometimes viewed as competing educational goals—the self-realization of the individual and the health of the community; sympathetic feelings and the use of reason; and the artistic and the cognitive. In articulating their underlying assumptions, Frederick Beiser (1998) gives us what can also be read as a gloss on Emerson's fable:

> The romantics' aim was to *reunify* man with himself, nature, and others, so that we would once again feel at home in his world. According to the romantic philosophy of history, early man had been at one with himself, with others, and with nature; the unity was purely natural, given to him by no efforts of his own. Inevitably and tragically, however, this primal harmony had been torn apart by the development of civilization. Man had become alienated from others as a result of the increasing competition of civil society; he had become divided within himself with the rise of the division of labor; and he had become estranged from nature after the sciences had demystified it, making it into an object to be dominated and controlled for human benefit. The task of modern man was to *recreate* on a self-conscious and rational level that unity within ourselves, others and nature that had once been given to early man on a naïve and intuitive level. (pp. 294–295)

For these Germans and Emerson, what education has done, education can undo and redo. The "American Scholar" address links Emerson's vision of education as a path to re-creation and integration with a view of cultural forms as temporary constructions whose hold on the mind must be relaxed for further development. Emerson suggests that we can give children the symbolic tools they need to navigate in the world without alienating them from their own psyches and experiences, and that what education puts asunder through the analytic understanding, it can also draw back together through joining our immediate experience with these symbols.

 2

Although they are often put in philosophical or theological terms, these ideas are rooted in the immediacies of the human psyche. The divisions are not simply cognitive conundrums or epistemological quandaries but part of our most direct experience. As Mircea Eliade (1962/1965) reminds us, it is our "deep dissatisfaction . . . with what is called the human condition" that creates the very motive for metaphor and concept: "Man feels himself torn and separate. . . . It is as a result of such existential experiences caused by the need

to transcend the opposites, that the first theological and philosophical specu-
lations were elaborated" (p. 122). We should not so much try to explain our
lives through religion or philosophy as do the reverse, to search for the psychic
roots of our religions and philosophies. For example, Dewey writes that what
attracted him to Hegel's philosophy was an "inward laceration," "the sense
of divisions and separations" that were "a consequence of a heritage of
New England culture, divisions by way of isolation of self from the world,
of soul from body, of nature from God" (1930, p. 19). We will follow Dewey's
development later, but let us now explore the experiences of two other
New Englanders, both teachers and writers, Margaret Fuller and Henry
Adams. Like Dewey, they experienced an early sense of alienation, and
also like him they moved toward wholeness in ways that have implications for education.

As we turn first to Margaret Fuller, there is a jarring irony in Eliade's
first word, *man*, which parallels Emerson's use of the "One Man," since it
unconsciously perpetuates oppositions by taking only one side of the male-
female duality as the whole. For the primary way Fuller experienced this
sense of division was in terms of gender roles and associations. In a brief
autobiographical fragment, Fuller depicts her parents—and the ways they
became internalized within her own psyche—as both source and symbols
for a set of warring dualisms. Her father, turning his disappointment that his
firstborn was a girl into the challenge of making her a child prodigy, took
her education into his own hands. Yet his instruction in language and literature seemed bereft of the very reasons for which we read literature. Margaret writes: "My father was a man of business, even in literature" (1992, p. 26);
and more broadly, "To open the deeper fountains of the soul, to regard life
here as the prophetic entrance to immortality, to develop his spirit to per-
fection,—motives like these had never been suggested to him" (p. 24). In
writing, especially, he comes to embody the Enlightenment values of order,
clarity, and rationality. Margaret recalls being told that "you must not express a thought, unless you can give a reason of it, if required; must not
make a statement, unless sure of all particulars"; "such were his rules. 'But,'
'if,' 'unless,' 'I am mistaken,' and 'it may be so,' were words and phrases
excluded from the province where he held sway" (p. 28). While the daughter sees these goals as perhaps valuable in themselves, she also realizes that
their emphasis leaves developed only a small part of the psyche, ignoring
or actively repressing potentials within herself that she feels are particularly
powerful and particularly her own:

> He made the common prose world so present to me, that my natural bias was
> controlled. I did not go mad, as many would do at being continually roused
> from my dreams. I had too much strength to be crushed,—and since I must put

on fetters, could not submit to let them impede my motions. My own world sank deep within, away from the surface of my life; in what I did and said I learned to have reference to other minds. But my true life was only the dearer that it was secluded and veiled over by a thick curtain of available intellect, and the coarse, but wearable stuff woven by the ages,—Common Sense. (p. 28)

By contrast, Margaret depicts her mother as embodying the qualities most like those of her own inner nature and complementary to her father's attitudes:

She was one of those fair and flower-like natures, which sometimes spring up even beside the most dusty highways of life—a creature not to be shaped into a merely useful instrument, but bound by one law with the blue sky, the dew, and the frolic birds. Of all persons whom I have known, she had in her most of the angelic,—of that spontaneous love for every living thing, for man, and beast, and tree, which restores the golden age. (p. 25)

Where the father is utilitarian, the mother appreciates beauty and becomes associated with that natural, harmonious world in which she lives. Indeed, the Romantic, pastoral imagery blends with the recovery of the paradisal state of both Christian and classical mythology, as suggested by "angelic" and "the golden age," before intellect and emotion have been separated. Further, the mother becomes associated with a literal garden that she creates and appreciates, a natural realm behind the house itself that is a truer and richer "home" to the child Margaret: "Our back door opened . . . into a little garden, full of choice flowers and fruit-trees, which was my mother's delight, and was carefully kept. Here I felt at home" (p. 31).

So we see a series of related dichotomies—father/mother; house/garden; intellect/emotions; duty/enjoyment—between which Margaret Fuller experienced her own psyche as the battleground. Either side was partial, and each seemed hostile to the other, as Eve Kornfeld (1997) summarizes the situation: "Neither of her parents could guide her from her isolation and agony to a whole life; her father's assertive intellect and lack of grace were no more attractive alone than her mother's physical weakness and intellectual uncertainty" (p. 12). A society of increasing gender differentiations (the cult of domesticity was growing rapidly at this time), combined with a particularly dichotomized family situation to both, cause and symbolize these splits. In her private journals, Fuller records her frustrating sense of self: "A man's ambition with a woman's heart is an evil lot" (1852, vol. 1, p. 229). And in a letter, she writes: "One should be either private or public. I love best to be a woman; but womanhood is at present too straitly bound to give me scope. At hours, I live truly as a woman: at others I should stifle" (1983–1994, vol. 6, pp. 143–144).

Henry Adams saw his life as fiercely divided as Fuller did hers, but he expressed these divisions more in the time and space coordinates of what he saw as his double life. His early memories are structured by the opposition of summers at his grandparents' rural estate near the ocean and winters in the city of Boston. In his autobiography, significantly titled *The Education of Henry Adams*, he describes the series of oppositions as does Dewey as inherent in the very act of coming to consciousness in New England:

> The chief charm of New England was harshness of contrasts and extremes of sensibility—a cold that froze the blood, and a heat that boiled it. . . . The violence of the contrast was real and made the strongest motive of education. The double exterior nature gave life its relative values. Winter and summer, cold and heat, town and country, force and freedom, marked two modes of life and thought, balanced like lobes of the brain. Town was winter, confinement, school, rule, discipline; straight, gloomy streets piled with six feet of snow in the middle; frosts. . . . Town was restraint, law, unity. Country, only seven miles away, was liberty, diversity, outlawry, the endless delight of mere sense impressions given by nature for nothing and breathed by boys without knowing it. (1983, p. 727)

Much is communicated through the imagery, rhythms, and syntax of the prose itself here. The first sentence, for example, enacts some of these opposite extremes—the alliterative, seemingly idyllic opening, "chief charm," is undercut by opposite intensities of fire and ice; such Latinate words as "sensibility" are contrasted and balanced after the dash with a run of Anglo-Saxon monosyllables. As the passage proceeds, an inner rift is imaged in parallel outer rifts: underlining the cyclical progression of extreme seasons, the boy alternates geographically with as well, with winters in the city, summers in Quincy. The pleasure principle of immediate gratification, of sensual apprehension—of simply living, in short—is at odds with the reality principle of what it takes to prepare for and organize life in the future. But at another level, the conflict is epistemological, with immediate experience contrasted with symbols and concepts.

There is no question that Adams's emotional sympathies are with the second terms of the parallel binaries: against winter, town, force, confinement, school, rule, discipline, restraint, law, and unity; for summer, country, freedom, outlawry, and diversity. Yet he knows we cannot remain forever in this latter world, for to do so, as this language implies, is to not grow up, to remain, like the original Adam, regressively in the realm of the pleasure principle, excluded from the act of knowing itself. As with Emerson, Adam wonders how to give young people language and concepts, the tools they need to make order in the world and yet continue to live physically within it, enjoying their immediate sensuous apprehension. How do we turn the world into symbols without destroying the rich, concrete realities from which these symbols are derived and of which they are often anemic ghostly versions? Adams writes a few pages later: "From cradle to grave this problem of running order through chaos, direction through space, discipline through freedom, unity through multiplicity, has always been, and must always be the task of education, as it is the moral of religion, philosophy, science, art, politics and economy" (p. 731). Yet this necessary ordering of freedom, this unifying of multiplicity, has to be done with the utmost sensitivity and tact, for "a boy's will is his life, and he dies when it is broken, as the colt dies in harness, taking a new nature in becoming tame" (p. 731).

Adams continues to see these opposites as perpetually at odds, and that any educational scheme that tries to ignore or oversimplify them is a sham: After decades, schoolteachers still serve for him as symbols of those who oversimplify to the point of falsification the immediate experience of consciousness:

> The bearing of the two seasons on the education of Henry Adams was no fancy; it was the most decisive force he ever knew; it ran through life, and made the division between its perplexing, warring, irreconcilable problems, irreducible opposites. . . . From earliest childhood the boy was accustomed to feel that, for him, life was double . . . and the man who pretended they were not, was in his eyes a schoolmaster—that is, a man employed to tell lies to little boys. (pp. 728–729)

Yet Adams was pragmatic, and the entire book is a search for ways to bring together these opposites, to bring some kind of saving but not distorting unity to this multiplicity, some kind of healing harmony.

 3

Before suggesting some of the ways in which Margaret Fuller and Henry Adams tried to integrate these splits in a movement toward wholeness, it will be helpful to sketch out Carl Jung's theory of development. This is not because Jung's psychology has more claims to absolute truth than others' but because it is squarely in the Romantic tradition we have been tracing and, though it jumps ahead some years, provides a version that is at once more analytic and closer to the experience of consciousness. Jung divests elements in this tradition of much of their philosophical and theological status and reattaches them to the original feelings from which they were first abstracted. He internalizes its metaphysics as a theory of human development and adopts its worldview as a psychological drama rather than a description of the cosmos.

In Jung's thought, the individual psyche begins in a state of complete, undifferentiated unconsciousness, a primordial wholeness that exists prior to and encompasses all opposites. This state is analogous to the paradisal situation, but also correlates with the state of chaos that exists before creation in both the biblical myth and other cosmologies. Out of this realm emerges what Jung calls the "ego" a psychic complex that serves as the center of consciousness, a core around which a personal identity is constructed. As the ego develops, it tends to separate itself from the rest of the psyche, setting up barriers between consciousness and what becomes unconscious. This process is accompanied by the creation of other dualities, such as inner/outer, subject/object, light/darkness, masculine/feminine. Although this development is necessary for functioning in what we call everyday reality, it creates an imbalance in the "self," the entire psychic unit, and leaves a person divided, with only a fragment of his or her potential realized.

Later in life, this unrealized potential beckons toward a rejoining of the ego with the rest of the self in a fuller integration of personality. The ego comes to recognize that it is not an autonomous entity, but part of a larger unity, within which it must establish a working harmony. For Jung the unconscious is not merely what we have personally experienced and then repressed as it was for Freud, but a world of unrealized dispositions and potentials. Jung sees a teleological development of human life toward integration and unity, from a merely personal ego toward a more inclusive humanity, an ultimate wholeness that "gathers together what is scattered and multifarious, and exalts it to the original form of the One, the Primordial Man" (1969, p. 265).

We can broaden this model by applying it to the movements of Western culture, especially to its philosophical tradition. Just as in the development of the individual, the separation of the ego from the rest of the psyche is the equivalent of the Fall, so Western culture since the ancient Greeks has lopsidedly emphasized a consciousness standing apart from nature in an almost aggressive and rapacious mode. Richard Tarnas (1991) generalizes with a Jungian slant on this development, restoring some of the gender differences that informed Margaret Fuller's experience: "The evolution of the Western mind has been driven by a heroic impulse to forge an autonomous rational self by separating it from the primordial unity with nature" (p. 441).

This tendency became particularly pronounced at the beginning of modern philosophy in the West with Descartes's positing of his own ego as the foundation upon which to rebuild all our knowledge. Disclaiming all previous authorities, he began with what came to be known as the cogito—"I think, therefore I am"—as the most certain of certainties. He was unaware that the structure of European languages, requiring a subject as well as a verb for every sentence, constructs the thinking "I" more than any ontological necessity. The philosophical formulation converges with the linguistic one to exacerbate the subject/object dichotomy that Frye mentions, with the ego separated from the rest of the world, which becomes only the object of the "knowing," in contrast with the more interactive and constructive relations that Emerson will posit.

The Romantic vision of wholism that Emerson shares can be seen as a reaction, a compensatory movement to this vector in Western philosophy. While some intellectual histories talk about the Romantics favoring emotion over intellect, passion over rationality, their real goal is to heal the splits between them. Tarnas follows Jung in suggesting that an entire culture can correct its lopsidedness:

> As Jung prophesied, an epochal shift is taking place in the contemporary psyche, a reconciliation between the two great polarities, a union of opposites: a *hieros gamos* (sacred marriage) between the two long-dominant but now alienated masculine and the long-suppressed but now ascending feminine. . . . *For the deepest passion of the Western mind has been to reunite with the ground of its being.* The driving impulse of the West's masculine consciousness has been its dialectical quest not only to realize itself, but also finally, to recover its connection with the whole, to come to terms with the great feminine principle in life: to differentiate itself from but then rediscover and reunite with the feminine, with the mystery of life, of nature, of soul. (p. 443)

Of course, this development will not happen by itself but will take conscious effort and humane vision, to move our culture in the direction that Tarnas describes; we cannot simply go with the flow of some impersonal zeitgeist. But these perspectives from Jung and Tarnas can help us contextualize in psychological and cultural terms what our nineteenth-century figures often expressed in religious or philosophical languages.

❦   4   ❧

We are now in a better position to understand the movements that Margaret Fuller and Henry Adams made to heal the wrenching dichotomies they experienced. Fuller's first recorded experience of peace from these rifts within herself is described in her journal in an entry written when she was twenty-one. She was forced to go to church on Thanksgiving, when she felt a particularly acute sense of separation from the congregation and the preacher. "Wearied out with mental conflicts, and in a mood of almost childish, childlike sadness" (1852, vol. 1, p. 139), she left the church to wander in the dark, cold natural landscape, when suddenly the sun broke out, and she found herself along a stream and then beside a pool, in an outer landscape that suggests also a journey into her own unconscious sources.

> I saw there was no self; that selfishness was all folly, and the result of circumstance; that it was only because I thought the self real that I suffered; that I had only to live in the idea of the ALL, and all was mine. This truth came to me, and I received it unhesitatingly; so that I was for that hour taken up into God. In that true ray most of the relations of earth seemed mere films, phenomena. (vol. 1, p. 141)

What Fuller calls the "self" here we have seen Jung term the "ego," and what she calls the ALL, Jung terms the "Self," or the entire psychic whole. In other words, Jung gives an intrapsychic reading to this kind of visionary experience in which the oneness of the universe is registered and symbolized in the harmony of the mind. The experience of being taken up into God can be read at this level as a numinous experience of the entire psyche and not merely its narrower ego identity. This moment was not an immediate and permanent nirvana for Fuller, but it did open up spiritual and psychological possibilities that would always be for her a comfort and a goal: "Since that day I have never more been completely engaged in self; but the statue has been emerging slowly from the block. Others may not see the promise even of its pure symmetry, but I do, and am learning to be patient. I shall be all human yet" (vol. 1, p. 142).

This retreat from civilized life into nature, from the fixities of culture to the flux of a landscape with water and wind, from society to solitude, to integrate with larger sources, is a prototypical Transcendentalist scene. Fuller's experience has all the elements of the one Emerson will later describe at the beginning of *Nature*, where he becomes, notoriously, a "transparent eyeball": "Standing on bare ground,—my head bathed by the blithe air, and uplifted into infinite space,—all mean egotism vanishes" (1983, p. 10). The ego dissolves into something larger, both within the psyche and in the outside world: "I am nothing; I see all; the currents of the Universal Being circulate through me; I am part or particle of God" (p. 10). While these experiences seem to owe much to German Romanticism, there is a crucial difference in that the Americans take the visionary experience itself as a foundation for action and thought instead of trying to erect a philosophical system.

Fuller adds another dimension to that of the male Transcendentalists. As we have seen, her individual psychology was shaped and experienced through gender oppositions, so we should not be surprised to find that her image of God, the key symbol of psychic reintegration, was androgynous. In a letter to Frederic Henry Hedge, she writes, "I have no confidence in God as a Father" (1983–1994, vol. 1, pp. 224); and in a poem, she protests against those "who separate the eternal light / In forms of man and woman, day and night; / They cannot bear that God be essence quite" (1859, p. 391).

Not only is God encompassingly androgynous, but Fuller works her way to seeing each human as such. Like Jung, she views the mind as being composed of elements that are psychologically both masculine and feminine and believes that in the ideal version of each gender, the balance would be nearly equal, tipped only a slight bit toward relevant biological sex, as she states in *Woman in the Nineteenth Century*, originally published in 1845:

> In so far as soul is in her completely developed, all soul is the same; but in so far as it is modified in her as Woman, it flows, it breathes, it sings, rather than deposits soil, or finishes work. . . . But it is no more the order of nature that it should be incarnated pure in any form, than that the masculine energy should exist unmingled with it in any form. Male and female represent the two sides of the great radical dualism. But, in fact, they are perpetually passing into one another. Fluid hardens to solid, solid rushes to fluid. There is no wholly masculine man, no purely feminine woman. (1992, pp. 309–310)

Flux, movement, and song are associated with the female, and order, permanence, and form with the male, but Fuller does not essentialize them as much as view them as complementary opposites in everyone's psyche. This vision of the androgynous mind runs through European Romanticism, but Fuller with justification traces it back to Plato: "Plato sometimes seems penetrated by that high idea of love, which considers man and woman as the two-fold expression of one thought" (p. 301).

Despite the use of metaphor here, Fuller's expression of opposites is still basically conceptual, as it is throughout the entire book, but the preface presents the reconciliation of these opposites in visual form. The drawing (Figure 1) portrays two superimposed interlocking triangles, one pointing down, the other up, one dark, the other light, suggesting the union of the earthly and spiritual, male and female. Surrounding the triangles is a circular design created by a snake with its tail in its mouth, a version of what mythographers call the *ouroboros*, suggesting both the primordial unity out of which all arose and a final illuminated reconciliation of time and eternity. A poetic version of this emblem is rendered in one of the poems Fuller wrote the previous year, 1844, the title of which describes the drawing—"Double Triangle, Serpent and Rays":

> Patient serpent, circle round
> Till in death thy life is found,
> Double form of godly prime
> Holding the whole thought of time,

FIGURE 1

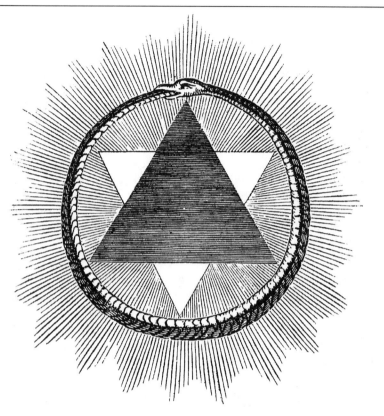

When the perfect two embrace,
Male & female, black & white,
Soul is justified in space,
Dark made fruitful by the light;
And, centred in the diamond Sun,
Time, eternity, are one. (1992, p. 233)

Both the drawing and the poem are what Jung calls symbols of transformation, or mandalas, in that they do not merely represent or stand for a
striving for wholeness but are the means and medium of this psychological
work. The very act of creating—of drawing and writing—moves the process
of individuation further along. For real integrative gains to be made, the subject

has to construct such symbols—merely reading or looking at those created by others will not do, a point crucial for the tradition of active learning.

These symbols of transformation pervade a series of poems Fuller wrote in 1844, which form a personal mythology of wholeness that yet borrows freely from pagan and Christian mythic images. Particularly prominent are female figures such as Isis, Euridice, and Mary, grieving for lost partners who at one level represent their own hidden masculine aspects. The fulfillments of these quests appear in images of wholeness such as jewels, flowers, suns, and moons. That this symbol-work was psychologically successful is registered by the fact that Fuller did not continue to ceaselessly delve into her own psyche but was able to emerge from the writing to embrace social and political activism, both as a reporter on Horace Greeley's *New York Herald Tribune* and as a partici-pant in the Italian revolution of 1848. As Jeffrey Steele (2001) notes:

> In *Woman in the Nineteenth Century*, we see only the outcroppings of myths that Fuller was detaching from private contexts and transposing into the realm of public discourse. However, in Fuller's 1844 poetry, we can discern more clearly the ways her mythmaking facilitated a profound model of personal and social transformation in which the reshaping of the self depends upon the remapping of the ideals defining human accomplishment. Fuller's 1844 poems thus represent the workshop where she transposed personal insight into the domain of political aspiration. (p. 168)

This movement from inner exploration to outward action is registered in a poem of this time, "Winged Sphinx," in which the speaker solves the riddle by turning from "the wizard spells / Drawn from intellectuals wells, / Cold waters where truth never dwells" to "seek her in common daylight's glow" (Fuller, 1992, p. 234). Fuller had to reconcile the warring parts of her own being to reach her peak of effectiveness as a feminist writer and public fig-ure. In the first half of the 19th century, she was enacting the cultural shift Tarnas sees only in the 20th century, and creating a feminist consciousness where the personal is indeed the political.

Like Margaret Fuller's, Henry Adams's moves toward healing psychic splits involved a reconciliation of gendered opposites in imagery infused with religious resonances. One way of reading the *Education* is to see it against the larger cultural background that Tarnas provides, as a story of a boy raised to share the same masculine, rationalistic ways of acting and perceiving as did Fuller's father and his own eminent patriarchal ancestors, but who finds these ways insufficient in the world into which he grows. Jackson Lears (1983) provides a helpful orientation for this interpretation:

> Early ingrained with male ego ideals, he was increasingly attracted toward "feminine" values. . . . Committed to active engagement, he was nevertheless

a sensitive boy who detested "the strife of the world" and longed for a quiet
literary life. He alternated between manic ambition and depressive withdrawal.
The "feminine" realm of nurturance and repose, idealized in the cult of domesticity, grew more attractive as Adams grew older. . . . he began to create a
personal mythology centering on an archaic feminine principle. (pp. 262–263)

Adams does much of his searching for the feminine in *Mont Saint Michel
and Chartres*, published a year before the *Education*, and serving as a "study
of thirteenth-century unity" that was complementary to the *Education*'s "study
of twentieth-century multiplicity" (Adams, 1983, p. 719). In *Chartres*, Adams
sees the quest for unity as the mainspring of all human desire: "Man is an
imperceptible atom always trying to become one with God. If ever modern
science achieves a definition of Energy, possibly it may borrow the figure:—
Energy is the inherent effort of every multiplicity to become unity" (p. 649).

But *Chartres* is primarily a historical study of medieval art and literature, and Adams finds that his approach can bring him no closer to the feminine in an emotionally healing way: "The scientific mind is atrophied, and
suffers under inherited cerebral weakness, when it comes in contact with
the eternal woman,—Astarte, Isis, Demeter, Aphrodite, and the last and greatest deity of all, the Virgin" (p. 523). This list of goddesses is close to Margaret Fuller's genealogy of the feminine principle, but while Fuller uses them
as symbols to explore and integrate her own psyche, Adams seems only to
be able to analyze this force from the outside as it results in artworks. Adams
laments that the rediscovery of the feminine "owing to some revival of archaic
instincts" is "perhaps the mark of the artist alone, and his solitary privilege.
The rest of us cannot feel; we can only study" (p. 52). In the *Education*,
Adams makes even clearer that he speaks not only for himself but for all of
American masculine culture: "The true American knew something of the facts,
but nothing of the feelings; he read the letter but he never felt the law"
(p. 1071). He and his countrymen can begin to understand the forces that
built Chartres but not share in them. The energy of love seeking unity has
irrevocably been converted into statues that we can now observe but cannot equal with our own creations.

It is no wonder, then, that the *Education* does not move toward unity
but rather toward an ineluctable multiplicity. Increasingly as his life goes
on, Adams cannot accept a uni-verse, only a multi-verse. For the overarching
theories of the closing chapters—titled "A Dynamic Theory of History," "A
Law of Acceleration"—Adams significantly uses the indefinite article *a* rather
than *the*; in the very act of putting these theories forward he concedes their
inadequacy. The orders of history and science are nothing but a series of
mistakes, and the only saving grace that Adams can envision is to acknowledge that they are mistakes, as he implies in the last sentence as he imag-

ines his friends "allowed to return together for a holiday, to see the mistakes of their own lives made clear in the light of the mistakes of their successors" (p. 1181).

Just as Adams indicated at the beginning, we find at the end that life indeed consists of "irreducible opposites," with only schoolmasters pretending otherwise. As Lears says, "Ultimately he sought not to banish tension but to endure it. Dialectic became the fundamental principle of his late work. Intelligence and instinct, Dynamo and Virgin, appeared and reappeared in the ferment of his imagination" (p. 263). Adams's increasing tendency to view life as a spectator sport is both a symptom and a cause of his inability to make the kind of integration that Fuller eventually attained through a creative journey of great personal pain and discovery.

This having been said, we must also acknowledge that the *Education* remains one of the great American books on the subject of its title. It brilliantly describes the lived experience of an acceleratingly changing reality always outrunning whatever formulations we give the young in the name of education. "Nothing in education is so astonishing as the amount of ignorance it accumulates in the form of inert facts" (Adams, 1983, p. 1066). Yet his critique remains primarily negative. As a young Harvard professor, Adams detested the lecture system, "which was very much that of the twelfth century" (p. 995) and moved toward creating student-centered structures: He "frankly acted on the rule that a teacher, who knew nothing of his subject, should not pretend to teach his scholars what he did not know, but should join them in trying to find the best way of learning it" (p. 996). But Adams never seems to have enjoyed teaching, and he significantly titles the chapter that closes out this episode of his life "Failure." Yet this same chapter contains the sentence "A teacher affects eternity; he can never tell where his influence stops" (p. 994). Ultimately, his negative view of education implies its opposite, that an education should teach people not facts or subjects but how to learn: "No doubt the world itself will always lag so far behind the active mind as to make a soft cushion of inertia to drop upon, as it did for Henry Adams; but education should try to lessen the obstacles, diminish the friction, invigorate the energy" (p. 1007).

❧ 5 ❦

We can better consolidate the notion of education as integration by examining Emerson's treatment of Plato in *Representative Men*, which is a later unpacking and elaboration of the One Man parable with which we began this chapter. As the book's title suggests, Emerson does not see a radical gap between men of genius and ourselves; rather, they only represent potentials in all of us. Plato in particular is seen as the ideal paradigm for the development of consciousness both in the individual and in larger cultural movements. Emerson begins the essay by setting out a kind of algebra of consciousness:

> Two cardinal facts lie forever at the base; the one and the two.—1. Unity, or Identity; and, 2. Variety. We unite all things by perceiving the law which pervades them; by perceiving the superficial difference, and the profound resemblances. But every mental act,—this very perception of identity or oneness, recognizes the difference of things. Oneness and otherness. It is impossible to speak, or to think, without embracing both. (1983, p. 637)

Emerson then goes on to align related dualities along this unity/variety opposition in ways that recall Adams's bifurcated universe: "If speculation tends thus to a terrific unity, in which all things are absorbed, action tends directly backwards to diversity. . . . These two principles reappear and interpenetrate all things, all thought; the one, the many. One is being; the other, intellect; one is necessity; the other, freedom" (p. 639). Thinking can become either too abstract and general or too scattered and fragmentary if it remains at either end of this opposition too long: "A too rapid unification, and an excessive appliance to parts and particulars, are the twin dangers of speculation" (p. 640).

There has to be, then, mediation and interaction between these extremes, but what exactly should the relation be? Using Plato as a living embodiment of the solution, Emerson sketches an ideal progression that is congruent with the Jungian pattern of individuation and Tarnas's congruent one for Western philosophy. After noting that "this first period of a nation, as of an individual, is the period of unconscious strength," he points out that Plato has studied in Asia, where minds are inclined "to dwell in the conception of the fundamental Unity": "The Asia in his mind was first heartily honored,—the ocean of love and power, before form, before will, before knowledge, the Same, the Good, the One; and now, refreshed and empowered by this worship, the instinct of Europe, namely culture, returns; and he cries, Yet things are knowable!" (p. 645). Unity, then, precedes multiplicity ontologically, in the development of culture and in the growth of human consciousness. Knowledge, intellect, the ability to distinguish the one as many, is in some ways a higher, more distinctly human faculty, yet it remains subsumed by oneness.

The movement of cultural development from Asia to Europe toward a synthesis that subsumes both, then, encompasses and is mirrored in the arc of an individual life. But further within that individual life are smaller parallel spiral movements from unity to multiplicity to a higher unity that happen on a daily basis and are the foundation of the larger reintegrations of self and culture. Emerson moves the locus of unity from the metaphysical to the aesthetic and psychological, from something we discover in the universe to something we create from moment to moment. And it is here that the two main themes of "The American Scholar" converge, education as integration and education as the continual deconstruction and reconstruction of cultural forms. Before we see how this vision is extended beyond Emerson himself, we must go behind him to sources such as Samuel Taylor Coleridge and to educators such as James Marsh and Bronson Alcott who tried to put this notion of a unifying education into practice even before Emerson's 1837 address.

CHAPTER 3

Philosophy Descending:
James Marsh and Bronson Alcott

The soul as a living and life-giving principle, could not be satisfied with abstractions, nor its hollow cravings be stilled with unsubstantial shadows and barren formulas. The great question with him was not alone what is truth? but, what is that which imparts to truth its living reality; which connects knowing with being.

—Joseph Torrey on James Marsh

Philosophy and Religion, descending from the regions of cloudy speculation, must thus become denizens of our common earth, known among us as friends, and uttering their saving truths through the mouths of our little ones. . . . We must deal less in abstractions; depend less on precepts and rules.

—Bronson Alcott

EMERSON'S "American Scholar" address is a convenient starting point, but behind it were other beginnings. Just as Emerson suspected that Walt Whitman's sudden blazing forth in the 1855 *Leaves of Grass* "yet must have had a long foreground somewhere" (Miller, 1969, p. 1), so his own formulations of 1837 had their precedents and provocations. Would Emerson have been so deeply interested in a theory of American education if his new friend Bronson Alcott had not just been pilloried in the Boston press for his experimental Temple School? And would Emerson have had the intellectual tools to forge such a theory without the editorial work of James Marsh, the main conduit for introducing the thought of Coleridge and therefore much of European philosophy to American readers?

Both Marsh and Alcott were crucial figures behind the paradigm shift registered in Emerson's address. As Barbara Packer (1995) puts it: "If the German philosophers were right about the mind's structure and relation to the world, then the prevailing system of education was hopelessly and radically wrong. Rote learning, drill, and coercion were all cruel and wasteful ways to teach children. True education should be a coaxing out or an un-folding of the mind's intuitions, not a cramming session in which unrelated facts are stuffed into empty and recalcitrant heads" (p. 372). While Emerson's words ring with a clarity and eloquence beyond the talents of either Marsh or Alcott, these two men put active learning into practice before the address, remaining true to its spirit by embodying it as well as formulating it. In this chapter I will examine their contributions in enacting the implications for education in the shift from Locke to Kant and in the growing attraction to wholism discussed in the preceding chapter.

James Marsh's most important contribution is publishing in 1829 the first American edition of Samuel Taylor Coleridge's *Aids to Reflection*, prefacing it with his own "Preliminary Essay," which foregrounds what he felt were its most relevant ideas. Robert Richardson (1995) says Marsh's edition of Coleridge "more than any other single volume catalyzed the synthesis be-tween the new ideas Emerson was finding in Sampson Reed and the new importance of the old ideas he found in Plato, Plutarch, Montaigne, and the seventeenth century" (p. 93). When John Dewey, a later figure in the tradi-tion and a graduate of the University of Vermont, was presented late in life with a copy of Marsh's book, he remarked: "I admired Marsh as a teacher and philosopher; he had a big influence on me, and this book . . . revealed to us that spirit is not a substance but a kind of life. This was for me an emancipation" (Schneider, 1974, p. 542).

With these testimonies to its liberating effects ringing in our ears, it is a little disappointing to turn to *Aids to Reflection* and find it not exactly a light-ning bolt. It is a collection of snippets, mainly from the writings of a 17th-century divine, Robert Leighton, archbishop of Glasgow, whose "aphorisms" are intermixed with others by Coleridge himself, as well as the latter's often rambling, tangential editorial comments. Even more strangely, this key event in American intellectual history is also Coleridge's apologia for the Church of England. Further, Marsh himself was a conservative religious thinker, an orthodox Calvinist who turned to Coleridge to restore what he felt were more traditional aspects of Christianity that had been undermined by Enlighten-ment thought. Marsh later came to look with suspicion at the major school of thought that his own work had helped create. To understand, then, why the American *Aids to Reflection* should have such a radical effect on educa-tional thought in spite of Marsh's own dispositions will take an act of the historical imagination.

Marsh was born in rural Vermont in 1794 and attended Dartmouth Col-lege, an opportunity that was opened to him when his older brother, Roswell, too embarrassed to take along with him to this institution a leg of mutton as partial payment for tuition, ran away from home. Dartmouth at this time was in a state of political and religious upheaval over control of the college that eventually resulted in the famous case that Daniel Webster argued before the Supreme Court. Amid this chaos, the students often found they had to educate themselves, and Marsh read and discussed books with a close circle of friends: John Wheeler, Joseph Torrey, and Rufus Choate, the first two of whom were to eventually succeed Marsh in the presidency of the University of Vermont. After Dartmouth, Marsh studied divinity at Andover Theological Seminary, which had been founded to counteract the dangerous Unitarian turn that Harvard Divinity School had taken at the beginning of the century. Around 1815, he seems to have had a spiritual crisis, precipitated by a doing a proof in Euclid, when Marsh found himself staring into the abyss of a mechanistic universe bereft of human will: "As I proceeded in the demonstration, all my faith in things invisible seemed to vanish, and I almost doubted the reality of my own existence" (Torrey, 1843, p. 20). He was able to get through this crisis by finding an inner faith that served as the basis for his journey toward reconciling his intellect and his religion.

As Marsh studied theology he became vexed that in the religious quarrels of the day both the Unitarians and the Congregationalists, the liberal and the orthodox Christians, used John Locke's theory of knowledge as their foundation. This epistemology viewed the mind as a tabula rasa, a blank slate at birth, on which sense impressions imprint images that are then combined to form more general ideas. The model is basically materialistic in that thought is seen as a succession of shadows cast by the outside world on the walls of mind, a ghostly epiphenomenon of the solid reality of the physical objects. Locke's philosophy also tilts toward determinism, since so much of the mind's workings are a function of what it happens to take in through the senses, and it is atomistic in that there is no prior unity or identity to the mind, which becomes merely the sum total of its sensory impressions. Most distressingly for Marsh, Locke's philosophy had no room for both heaven and earth; it provided no ontological basis for direct religious experience, no way of moving from matter to spirit. For both camps, religious doctrines had to be accepted on the basis of the authority of the Bible, which only deferred the question of where that authority came from in the first place.

Marsh turned to a number of sources to find a way out of this Lockean labyrinth, such as the works of Saint Paul and of a group of English Renaissance writers who came to be known as the Cambridge Platonists. The Christianized Neoplatonism of these writers was yet another version of the unity-division-reintegration paradigm already discussed, beginning with the world as a fallen emanation from the One to which the devout and enlightened mind could finally return. Marsh, though, was interested less in their metaphysics and more in their stance toward spiritual knowledge, as he says:

Their minds were raised above the narrow peculiarities of a speculative system by a more habitual contemplation of the great fundamental truths of reason and revelation. They had formed themselves, and aimed to form others, to the habit of intense and earnest *reflection* upon their own moral and spiritual being. They retired inward in order to ascend upward. (Wells, 1943, p. 20)

Marsh considered creating an anthology of their writings for an American audience, but around the same time, he encountered Coleridge, first in the *Biographia Literaria* and then in *Aids to Reflections*. While Pauline pietism and English Neoplatonism did not have to refute Enlightenment rationalism and Lockean materialism, Coleridge did so and the weapons he used were the latest developments in German philosophy. Gottfried Wilhelm Leibniz had responded to Locke's assertion that there is nothing in the mind that was not put there by experience by saying, "Nothing, but the mind itself." Immanuel Kant elevated this response into a systematic theory of knowing by positing a series of mental categories that he termed a priori through which experience itself is known. Since these shaping organizations exist before and beyond sensory experience, they are *transcendent,* but Kant did not intend to ascribe any divine or supernatural aspects to them. We both half create and half perceive the world we experience, as Wordsworth was later to put it. Although this philosophy provided a more complex and sophisticated account of how we know the world, it was still dualistic in its separation of a material world known by an immaterial mind. Further, for Kant direct knowledge of physical or spiritual realities, the *Ding an sich* (thing in itself), was impossible because we can know only through the inescapable categories of the mind. Later German philosophers such as Johann Fichte, Friedrich von Schelling, and Georg Wilhelm Friedrich Hegel tried to philosophically vault above these barriers separating mind from matter and knower from known by attributing not only a shaping but also a constituting power to the mind. They stood Lockean materialism on its head in positing that matter is an emanation or embodiment of mind and that the nature of the mind itself was initially and ultimately a unity, not only within the individual but also in the larger sweep of the cosmos. These post-Kantian philosophers created in its broadest outlines yet another version of the paradigm of biblical history and Neoplatonism, as M. H. Abrams delineates it:

In this philosophical context the Christian history of the creation, fall, and redemption was translated to the realm of human consciousness as stages, or "moments," in its evolving knowledge. In the initial act of self-conscious knowledge which separates the knower from the known consists both the creation of a world conceived as external to the knowing mind and also the fall of man from his primal innocence (equated with self-unity) into the knowledge of evil (equated with self-division and conflict). But if knowledge is initially analytic and divisive, it is also in its higher manifestations, unifying and integrative; for the mind, when it fully succeeds in grasping and comprehending the thing it knows, assimilates that thing and makes it its own. (1971, pp. 188–189)

The only remedy for knowing, then, is to know more and know reflectively. For example, Coleridge, in examining the workings of his own mind from the Lockean perspective, noted that more general ideas are really built up not from the senses but from our previous ideas distilled from the senses and stored already in the mind, and that the distinctions we make between things and the mind are imposed on a prior unity. While reading idealist philosophers can point the way, what is crucial is adopting a self-reflective turn in one's own thinking, a figure-ground reversal in which the entire mind views itself in its dialectical workings instead of focusing merely on its contents per se.

What was crucial, then, for Marsh in Coleridge's work was the personal intensity and importance of self-monitoring as discovery. He did not need to go to Coleridge to learn about the new German philosophy, for he had read Kant and the post-Kantians in the original and was to become a translator himself of key German texts. What attracted Marsh to the British writer was not only the synthesis of ancient spiritual wisdom with the latest philosophy, but also his approach to knowledge, which is actually closer to American ways of thinking than European. While Coleridge borrowed—some would say plagiarized—widely and freely from such writers as Fichte, Schelling, and Friedrich Schlegel—he was too pure an embodiment of what Emerson would call "Man Thinking" to ever rest comfortably in any one of their systems. As Gerald McNiece (1992) puts it, an urge toward systematizing in Coleridge's mind is constantly in conflict with its opposite in the name of honesty and vitality: "He searched for a vital knowledge which would connect thought to the facts and pressures of actual existence. . . . For such minds truth is both provisional and progressive, drawing direction and energy from conflict and contradiction" (p. 5). This description of Coleridge's thinking can serve well as a definition of the tradition of active learning, which approaches philosophical structures only as mediate, as tools for further encounter with the world. Coleridge envisioned a "Dynamic Philosophy," in which seeming opposites such as concrete and abstract, particular and universal, unity and plurality, are poles or end points of a single continuum along which his own work moves in dialectical undulations. As with Emerson's ideal scholar and the context of American thinking that Boorstin (1958) has delineated, thinking is more important than system building. This stance toward knowledge helps explain why Coleridge's work at first was more favorably received in America than in his home country. Before his death, Coleridge suggested to two young friends that they go to the United States: "I am known there. I am a poor poet in England, but I am a great philosopher in America" (Reid, 1890, vol. 2, p. 432).

This stance is foregrounded and emphasized in *Aids to Reflection*'s first three aphorisms, all written by Coleridge (1829):

> I. It is the prerogative of Genius to produce novel impressions from familiar objects: and seldom can philosophic genius be more usefully employed than in thus rescuing admitted truths from the neglect caused by the very circumstance of their universal admission. . . . Truths . . . are too often considered as *so* true, that they lose all the power of truth, and lie bed-ridden in the dormitory of the soul.
>
> II. There is one sure way of giving freshness and importance to the most *common-place* maxims—that of *reflecting* on them in direct reference to our own state and conduct, to our own past and future being.
>
> III. To restore a common-place truth to its first *uncommon* lustre, you need only *translate* it into action. But to do this, you must have *reflected* on its truth. (p. 1)

Coleridge's book immediately confronts one of the paradoxes of its own existence. As merely set of verbal formulations, it cannot penetrate the reader's consciousness, no matter how "true" in the abstract it may be. The reader must "reflect" on it not only through more abstract thinking but also by linking these truths directly with immediate experiences; formulations, which originally arose from the writer's experience, must be reinstated into the experience of the reader, the word made flesh again. Further, for the reader to fully apprehend their truth in an operational sense, testing both their power and their limits, they must be translated into action. Marsh, as a writer with particularly American concerns, emphasizes in his "Preliminary Essay" these reflective and experiential dimensions of Coleridge's work. Marsh appreciates and even revels in the fact that this is not a straightforward exposition of doctrine but instead a complex book that foregrounds the acts of reading, interpreting, and reflection: We see Marsh interpreting Coleridge interpreting Leighton, with no attempt at systematizing or securing any ultimate truth. The reader has to make his or her own connections between the various fragments, connecting these elliptical passages with concrete, personal experience. For those who try to read otherwise, Marsh issues a preemptive warning: "To those, whose understandings by long habit have become limited in their powers of apprehension, and as it were identified with certain *schemes* of doctrine, certain *modes* of contemplating . . . it may appear novel, strange, and unintelligible" (1829, p. xi). Stating the situation positively, underscoring the significance of the title, Marsh writes:

> It is important to observe that it is designed, as its general characteristic, to aid REFLECTION, and for the most part upon subjects, which can be learned and understood only by the exercise of *reflection* . . . It is not so much to teach a

speculative system of doctrines built upon established premises . . . as to turn the mind continually back upon the premises themselves—upon the inherent grounds of truth and error in its own being. (1829, p. viii)

In other words, the reader's own mind is the initial and ultimate source of knowledge, the sun at the center of what Kant himself called a Copernican revolution in thinking. As Marsh goes on to say, even more radically:

It is by self-inspection, by reflecting upon the mysterious grounds of our own being, alone, that we can arrive at any rational knowledge of the central and absolute ground of all being. It is by this only, that we can discover the principle of unity and consistency, which reason instinctively seeks after, which shall reduce to a harmonious system all our views of truth and of being, destitute of which all the knowledge, that comes to us from without, is fragmentary. (p. ix)

Not even the Bible, the revealed word of God, has the spiritual authority of what one finds in looking into one's own soul. Unity comes not from the coherence of an external system but from perceiving as a whole person and rejoining the various parts of one's own psyche through this kind of self-consciousness.

Marsh uses the word "Reason" as the faculty that seeks and creates this unity, and the term, if somewhat misleading, is not arbitrary. It relates to what Emerson and other Transcendentalists took from Marsh and Coleridge as their central conceptual breakthrough, the distinction between the Reason and the Understanding. In an excited letter of 1834 to his brother, Edward, Emerson explains and elaborates:

Philosophy affirms that the outward world is only phenomenal & the whole concern of dinners of tailors of gigs of balls whereof men make such account is a quite relative & temporary one—an intricate dream—the exhalation of the present state of the Soul—wherein the Understanding works incessantly as if it were real but the eternal Reason when now & then he is allowed to speak declares it is an accident a smoke nowise related to his permanent attributes. Now that I have used the words, let me ask you do you draw the distinction of Milton Coleridge & the Germans between Reason & Understanding. . . . Reason is the highest faculty of the soul—what we mean often by the soul itself; it never *reasons*, never proves, it simply perceives; it is vision. The Understanding toils all the time, compares, contrives, adds, argues, near sighted but strong sighted, dwelling in the present the expedient the customary. (1939, vol. 1, pp. 412–413)

For Coleridge, Marsh, and Emerson, the Understanding consists of what the Lockeans considered the sum total of the mind's capacities: the ability to take in sense impressions, combine and generalize upon them, and produce "ideas" from them through rationality. Reason subsumes Understanding as a part of its total powers, since it includes the capacity of the mind to observe its own workings and perceive itself as whole. It also intuits, from the direct act of perception, spiritual truths that are above and beyond sensory data, and is the locus of our volition, lifting us above the passivity inherent in the Lockean model.

Rather than try to salvage Lockeanism by simply adding to it another capacity, a universal moral apprehension analogous to our sensory apprehension as the Scottish Common Sense philosophers attempted, Marsh realized that a new model of mind was necessary to reconcile philosophy and religion. As the very first aphorisms of *Aids to Reflection* imply, there are crucial implications for education. While there are lower faculties that work in ways Locke described, a more genuine and deeper knowledge is created when the mind can watch itself going through these operations. It sees at once the nature of the outside world but also the part the mind itself has in half perceiving, half creating it. Reason sees truth not as something to be arrived at once and for all, but as a continual process and as something individually constructed. As Marsh emphasizes, Coleridge sees thought and action as forming a bipolar unity, a dynamic whole. A. D. Synder (1929) quotes Coleridge as saying, "Thinking can go but *half* way. . . . To know the *whole* truth we must likewise ACT" (p. 16) and then provides the following summary of his legacy for education:

> It was Coleridge's concern for himself and for others that they should have knowledge of the truth, but his even greater concern that they should have the experience of knowing. So it was that a large part of Coleridge's educational work consisted in distinguishing, by one means or another, between thinking that was dynamic, imaginative, and fertile, and the relatively passive thing that often went by its name. He tried method after method of bringing the distinction home, contrasting now *thought* with mere *attention*, now the *imagination* with the *fancy*, and again, and more frequently, the *reason* with the *understanding*. For the experience of knowing involved, Coleridge insisted, the "total man," not simply the "understanding." (p. 12)

Marsh could be said to follow Coleridge's own thinking here more faithfully than Coleridge himself in actually trying to translate it into educational realities. As soon as Marsh became president of the University of Vermont, he launched a critique of traditional education and, more important, put forth an alternative vision to it that he tried to enact. In his critique, he emphasized how rote methods and external coercion were in the long run self-defeating:

> Practically there is far too little of actual teaching and too much is left to de-
> pend on the textbook. The scholar for the most part is required merely to
> exercise his talents in apprehending the ideas of others instead of having his
> mind brought in contact with those of his instructors and freely employing his
> own powers of thought and judgment. . . . There is not enough of . . . the actual
> trial of the scholar's powers to give the habit of applying them with prompti-
> tude and effect in the business of life. (1973, pp. 59–60)

Further, the traditional system is too uniform and homogeneous, treating all
minds alike, pacing them in lockstep fashion; it "has too much the appearance of a predetermined and established routine" (p. 60). Yet even with this
predetermined aspect, it is incoherent; it replicates the atomist Lockean psychology in that the various separate courses are not seen as part of a larger
whole. As Peter Carafiol says of Marsh, "He believed that true system of
knowledge must reflect the unity and order of divine reason, and he opposed those which simply divide that unity into unrelated parts to make it
easier to examine" (1982, p. 152).

Marsh created, in contrast to this hodgepodge, a curriculum that was at
once more flexible and more unified and that was loosely based on Coleridge's
"Preliminary Treatise of Method," with a progression from the natural to the
spiritual, from the Understanding to the Reason. This progression was reca-
pitulated in a course on philosophy in the senior year that began with "crys-
tallography" and ascended through vegetable and animal life to higher forms
of organization, such as psychology and metaphysics. John Wheeler, who
succeeded Marsh in the presidency, put the general rationale as follows: "It
seeks to give a coherence to the various studies in each department so that
the several parts shall present, more or less, the unity, not of an aggregation
nor of a juxtaposition, not of a merely logical arrangement, but of a *development and a growth*, and therefore, the study in it, rightly pursued, should be
a growing and enlarging process to the mind of the student" (Marsh, 1973,
p. 7). Marsh reconceptualized the curriculum in terms of the development
of the student rather than the role he should play in society. Anticipating
Emerson's parable, he writes:

> The legitimate and immediate aim of education, in its true sense, is, not by the
> appliances of instruction and discipline to shape and fit the powers of the
> mind to this or that outward condition in the mechanism of civil society, but
> by means corresponding to their inherent nature, to excite, to encourage, and
> affectionately to aid *the free and perfect development of those powers themselves*.
> (Torrey, 1843, p. 589)

A related reform is Marsh's minimizing of the huge role of rote memo-
rization in classrooms through substituting monotonous recitations with semi-

nars along the lines being developed at the new German universities. These small, discussion-based classes often met in half-day blocks to allow "more constant and familiar intercourse between the mind of teacher and learner" (p. 80). This was not simply a new structure but a new conceptualizing of knowledge as personal and constructive.

Marsh insisted that knowledge must be applied and embodied to fulfill itself. As J. J. Duffy (Marsh, 1973) says, "Resisting the temptation to leave Reason to operate in the realm of pure speculation, and thus significantly modifying Kant, Marsh argued that Reason must terminate in action" (p. 23). Marsh took to heart Coleridge's first thesis in the *Biographia Literaria*: "Truth is correlative to being. Knowledge without a corresponding reality is no knowledge. . . . To know is in its very essence a verb active" (Coleridge, 1817/1997, p. 157). To make education more immediately amenable to practice, Marsh put more emphasis on the study of English literature and modern languages as opposed to the classics and developed a separate curriculum for those students who planned to enter avenues other than the customary ones for college graduates—law, divinity, or medicine.

Marsh's story makes clear that the tradition of active mind is not exclusively that of educators whom one would call liberal or progressive. He created a more student-centered, interactive learning structure not out of a liberal ideology but because his study of philosophy and his observations of schooling led him to believe that people learn better this way. Despite his ultimately conservative goals and temperament, the consequences not only of his thinking but also of his pedagogical practice were radical in the context of his times. This paradox can be partly explained by his courageous thinking against the grain, his challenging of the dominant Lockean paradigm, and his putting forth a more complex and inclusive view of how the mind works, his envisioning of new possibilities for education. As Emerson says, "Beware when the great God lets loose a thinker on this planet. Then all things are at risk" (1983, p. 407). The thrust of Marsh's thinking was to deepen the act of thinking itself through reflection, through the mind's turning back to examine its own workings. He was instrumental in the chain of events that in 1834, the year after Marsh resigned from his presidency, would lead a young child in Bronson Alcott's classroom to write in her journal, "I never knew I had a mind before" (Peabody, 1835, p. 217).

&*ep* 2 *ep*

When James Marsh became president of the University of Vermont, he had already formed his vision of a wholistic, reflective Coleridgean education and was able to implement it from a position of credentialed power. By contrast, Bronson Alcott had only a few years of education in a country school, belonged to no particular denomination, and developed his educational philosophy only gradually and unsystematically. By the time his reputation grew strong enough to have the leading families of Boston send their children to his Temple School, his attitudes and methods would become so controversial that the enterprise soon collapsed and Alcott was never to have his own classroom again. Alcott's lessons for us, then, are both positive and negative; he was the first person in the tradition of the active mind to create a school that fully enacted its principles, but he was oblivious enough of social realities beyond the classroom to either sustain this school or spread its ideas further. His long life span, from 1799 to 1888, makes him a valuable lens through which to witness some important vicissitudes of American education.

Amos Bronson Alcott was born on a bleak, windy farm in Wolcott, Connecticut. His best friend in childhood was his cousin and neighbor William Andrus Alcott, with whom he attended a school typical of American rural education. As Bronson Alcott (1866) describes it: "The schoolhouse stood near the centre of the district at the junction of four roads. The spot was peculiarly exposed to the bleak winds of winter; nor were there any shade trees near, to shelter the children from the scorching rays of the summer's sun during their recreations" (p. 130). Around three sides of the single, small room were desks for the older children facing the teacher's desk on the fourth side, on which rested a rod and a ferule. In front of the teacher's desk were the benches for the youngest students. The little ones, being closest to the large fireplace, were the most likely to get cooked and smoked by the burning of this soggy wood and the older students seated in back were usually chilled; the two temperatures available were too hot and too cold.

The physical discomfort, however, shrank in comparison to the impoverishment of the mental environment. The primary instructional method, just as at Harvard, was the recitation, in which it was the student's task to commit material to memory and then stand and deliver in front of the teacher, who corrected such performances. In the article already quoted, Alcott describes the teaching of spelling, which emphasizes the learning of isolated words instead of seeing them in context: "To teach spelling, a lesson was assigned, consisting of a certain number of columns of words arranged in alphabetical order. . . . No faculty was called into exercise but the memory" (p. 132). In reading, there was no better correlation of marks and meanings, as "the instructor . . . made the corrections. These extended no farther than the right pronunciation of the words" (p. 133).

In reaction to these methods, when Alcott began teaching in 1823 in the country schools near Wolcott, he declared that the teacher's task was "to invite rather than to compel attention; to awaken thought rather than to load the memory; and in one word to develop the whole mind and heart, rather than a few of the properties of either" (McCuskey, 1940, p. 135). The first thing he did was redesign the classroom, creating desks with backs and ensuring that each student would have private writing space. This would seem a small enough innovation, yet it took someone with Alcott's vision to confront the obvious: "The Yankee ingenuity which had designed the Windsor and Hitchcock chairs was satisfied to let children bend their spines as they sat for hours like so many birds perched on a backless pine bench" (Messerli, 1972, p. 291). Alcott arranged these desks in a semicircle around the walls, leaving an open central space for games and other activities. He decorated his classrooms with pictures, engravings, and cypress branches and encouraged his students to bring in flowers and other ornaments for their desks.

In his teaching, Alcott reversed the customary order, often moving from the concrete to the abstract. He began the study of geography by having the students make maps of the schoolyard and taught arithmetic through physical objects: blocks, cubes, and beans—what we would now call math manipulatives. In reading he carefully taught his students the sounds of the letters but also used pictures to have them identify whole words, anticipating the word recognition method. His spelling words were taken from the students' reading, not from lists. Instead of repeating sentences from a copybook, the students wrote and shared their own thoughts in journals.

During this period of teaching 5 years in four different Connecticut schools, Alcott did not read widely in philosophy. His main influence was the Swiss educator Johann Pestalozzi, whose ideas Alcott absorbed second-hand through reading the *American Journal of Education,* founded in 1826 by William Russell, later to become a friend and collaborator. Pestalozzi believed that human nature was basically good and could be perfected through education; his epistemology was Lockean, having students begin with observing and discussing physical objects in the classroom. As Alcott's thought and practice developed, he went beyond the limitations of this system to place more emphasis on cultivating active thinking. In a letter of 1827, he stresses "the production and original exercise of thought. I found that whatever children do themselves is theirs; and besides the advancement of the intellectual progress, tends to produce strength, and ability to encounter more severe trials" (F. B. Sanborn & W. T. Harris, 1893, p. 73). From the start of his teaching, Alcott had an intuitive sense that thinking can best be fostered not by external impositions but by observing and following the child's own tendencies:

> The province of the instructor should be simple, awakening, invigorating, directing, rather than the forcing of the child's faculties upon prescribed and exclusive courses of thought. He should look to the child to see what is to be

done, rather than to his book or system. The Child is the Book. The operations of his mind are the true system. (1938, vol. 1, p. 12)

As Alcott's schools became more widely known, partly through articles written by his cousin William and himself in the *American Journal of Education*, they attracted the attention of a young Unitarian minister in Brooklyn, Connecticut, Samuel May, who was convening a school reform convention in Hartford. Alcott was invited to May's house, where, in the minister's absence, he was hosted by his sister, Abby, whom Alcott later married. May helped arrange for Alcott to start a charity infant school in 1828 in Boston, then the hub of reform movements.

Alcott's experiences in Boston led to his first book, *Observations on the Principles and Methods of Infant Instruction* (1830). The immediate occasion of its writing was a contest for $100 offered by the Pennsylvania School District for the best essay on running a school for children under 5. After noting that " the child is essentially an active being" (p. 5), Alcott maintains, "The claims of animal nature in infancy are primary and paramount to all others; and it is not till these are anticipated and relieved by unrestrained movement, that the intellect can be successfully addressed" (p. 5). Play and exercise are not simply a preliminary to intellectual instruction but create a context to which intellectual instruction leads back: "Instruction, unless connected with active duty, and expressed in character, can be at best but a doubtful good" (p. 7). Further, instruction should never be solely intellectual but should be connected with emotions, with the immediate contexts of a child's life: "Mechanical recitations, wordy lessons, dissociated from the intellect, are to be wholly avoided" (p. 24). Foreshadowing his chief method in the Temple School, he says: "Affectionate and familiar conversation is the chief avenue to the infant mind. . . . This is the powerful spring which puts the young heart in action" (pp. 7–8). While Alcott felt that education should be moral, he knew that this aspect could not take the form of abstract precepts separated from concrete situations. The book ends with a summary that can serve as an epitome for future child-centered education:

Infant education when adapted to the human being, is founded on the great principle, that every infant is already in possession of the faculties and apparatus required for his instruction, and that, by a law of his constitution, he uses these to a great extent himself; that the office of instruction is chiefly to facilitate this process, and to accompany the child in his progress, rather than to drive or even to lead him. (p. 27)

Alcott's entry did not win first prize but attracted the notice of Robert Vaughn in Philadelphia, who invited him and William Russell to set up a school in Germantown. This school and similar attempts in Philadelphia itself never attracted a wide enrollment, and Alcott used the ensuing leisure to study the infant development of his first two daughters, Anna and Louisa, and to begin reading widely and deeply in philosophy. He reread Locke and moved on to Plato, Aristotle, and Francis Bacon. Then in September 1832 he read Coleridge's *Aids to Reflection* in James Marsh's edition. Alcott said that this book "formed a new era in my mental and psychological life" (Dahlstrand, 1982, p. 95), read it five times within the first 4 years of his discovery, and for the following 50 years kept it on his list of annual reading. Specifically, Alcott looked at Coleridge and Marsh as providing a more supple and complex basis for education: "I was looking around for the origin of the human powers. . . . It was Coleridge that lifted me out of this difficulty" (1877, p. 47). Reading *Aids* did not cause Alcott to jettison Locke but to see his epistemology as only one faculty of the mind, the Understanding, while the higher and more encompassing function of Reason allowed the mind to apprehend the spirit in the same way that the senses did for matter. Further, Reason, reflecting on all the workings of the mind, could create a growing, unified, active self.

Still unable to attract students in Philadelphia, Alcott returned to Boston. There he met Elizabeth Peabody, herself a teacher as well as being an unpaid secretary to William Ellery Channing, the founder of American Unitarianism. Peabody was so impressed with Alcott's teaching that she helped organize the Temple School, which opened in September 1834. With the backing of the influential Channing, she was able to recruit thirty children between the ages of 3 and 12 from some of the city's most elite families. Further, she served as Alcott's assistant, teaching areas in which Alcott was weak, such as Latin and arithmetic.

We are fortunate to have a detailed picture of this school from *Record of a School, exemplifying the General Principles of Spiritual Culture* (1835, 1836), a book published under her name. Peabody also transcribed discussions on Christ's life, titled *Conversations with Children on the Gospels, Unfolding the Doctrine and Discipline of Human Culture*, published in two volumes in 1836 and 1837 under Alcott's name. As the full titles of each suggest, the books are attempts to discover general propositions about education and the nature of the child through the close examination of particular students in a particular school. These books are the first extensive descriptions of an American school for two reasons. First, Alcott and Peabody were probably the first teachers to acknowledge that children might have anything valuable to say on their own, that their utterances were worth listening to in the classroom and then setting down in writing. Second, since the principles and methods of the school were based on interactive processes with the students, there was no way to convey a sense of these principles and methods through the more usual channels of abstract philosophical exposition, curriculum guides, or textbooks. These books tell the story of a single classroom as a way of getting to the heart of educational issues and as such are the first in a genre of American writing that did not fully blossom until the 1960s and 1970s.

While both books attempt to relate the general to the particular throughout, they also each begin with statements of principles; Peabody writes an extensive "Explanatory Preface" to the second edition of *Record*, and Alcott prefaces *Conversations* with an essay, "The Doctrine and Discipline of Human Culture." In these statements Peabody and Alcott expound a thoroughly Transcendentalist and idealist view of education. They see conventional education as facing in the wrong direction by turning outward to the natural world, which can only reflect the spirit less directly then the child's own mind. This emphasis on external fact, Peabody suggests, runs counter to the students' own inclinations and aptitudes:

> There has been proof enough, that this common plan is a bad one, in the universally acknowledged difficulty of making children study those things to which they are first put . . . —also in the absolute determination, with which so many fine minds turn aside from word-knowledge and dry science, to play and fun, and to whatever interests the imagination or heart;—finally, in the very small amount of acquisition. . . . In most cases, the attention has been bewildered, discouraged, or dissipated by a variety of objects; and in the best cases, the mind has become onesided and narrow. (p. iv)

In contrast to this proliferation of external facts through separate subjects and textbooks, Peabody and Alcott propose a more wholistic education based on the children examining and articulating their own consciousness, engaging in a juvenile version of the act of spiritual reflection as proposed by Coleridge and Marsh. The external world is indeed used, but primarily as "imagery, to express the inward life" (p. v), and tendencies toward egotism and self-absorption can be checked by contemplating one's spirit as the particularization of an infinite God.

The most obvious objection here is that the Temple School is founded upon a particular metaphysic that has few adherents now and that this vision becomes the hidden agenda of the school. It is an objection not easily disposed of, but it had been anticipated by the teachers. Peabody notes that the very methods Alcott adopts—his beginning with students' own perceptions, through journals and Socratic discussions—work against any kind of indoctrination: Alcott "is so successful in arousing the activity of the children's own minds, and he gives such free scope to their associations, that his personal peculiarities are likely to have much less influence than those of most instructors" (p. vii). She points out that there can be less objection to Alcott's working with student definitions of vocabulary words than to Johnson's dictionary, for in the former's approach, "the manner in which the words are studied and talked about in school is such that the children must be perpetually reminded, that nothing connected with spiritual subjects can be finally settled into any irreversible formula or doctrine" (p. vi), a fluidity that extends to the entire biblical text:

> Having read the lesson for the day, he asks for their own associations with words, their impressions of events, the action of their Imagination, and the conclusions of their Reason upon them. All sides of every subject are presented by the various children. . . . He does not wish the children to think, that the meaning of Scripture is a matter of authority; and this is the chief reason why he does not decide in favor of particular views, dogmatically. (p. xi)

The conception of spirit at the Temple School was not as a fixed entity but metamorphic, always in process, so that it created a kind of transitoriness and incompletion for any single verbal formulation.

This appreciation of the constructed and provisional nature of any verbal creation lies behind some of the best teaching moments. For example, in their conversations throughout the first year, the class had formulated a table of certain human attributes such as "aspiration," and "imagination"—abstractions that the students then went on to explore and define in terms of their own experiences. On the last day of class, Peabody records the following:

> Mr. Alcott then recurred to the blackboard, and said he would read the scale. This diagram had been altered many times during the quarter. It was intended merely to systematize the conversations in a degree; and never was presented to the children as a complete map of the mind. Some have objected to these diagrams, as if they would be fetters on the minds of the children. But their constant renewal and changes preclude the possibility of their being regarded as any thing but what they are. After having read the scale through, he began at the end asking the meaning of each word, and as they were defined, he obliterated them, until all were gone. (1836, p. 167)

The diagram here is not offered as a detached and self-contained truth, but as a tool to help the students probe, order, and articulate their own experience. As Peabody points out, the scheme is treated as mediate in the light of that experience, subject to reconsideration and revision. In a final flourish, Alcott even erases the scheme after each term is used to emphasize that the verbal construct should be not be abstracted from the lesson, taken away as product, but rather that the entire process is crucial.

This emphasis on process, on the making of knowledge, also helps explain the centrality of the discussion method. For Alcott, Jesus was a great teacher not because of what he said but for how he engaged his listeners: "Instead of seeking formal and austere means, he rested his influence chiefly on the living word, rising spontaneously in the soul. . . . Speech comes unbidden. Nature lends her images. Imagination sends abroad her winged words. We see thought as it springs from the soul, and in the very process of growth and utterance" (1836, vol. 1, p. xxxvi). At about this time, Alcott noted in his journal: "Education is not merely the diffusion of knowledge already attained; but it is that agency which so unfolds the soul, and whets its powers, as to put new provinces of nature and spirit within its reach; and is full of prophecies of discovery" (Carlson, 1981, p. 80). Indeed, one of Alcott's crucial achievements is that he grasped in an immediate, operative way the liberating potential of classroom conversation:

> Certainly the best we can do is to teach ourselves and children how to talk. Let conversation displace much that passes current under the name of recitation; mostly sound and parrotry, a repeating by rote not by heart unmeaning sounds from the memory and no more. Good teaching makes the child an eye-witness, he seeing, then telling what is seen, what is known, or comprehended; a dissolving of the text for the moment and a beholding in thought as through a glass. . . . So taught the masters: Plato, Plutarch, Pythagoras, Pestalozzi, so Christianity was first published from lovely lips; so every one teaches deserving the name of teacher or interpreter. Illustration always and apt; life calling forth life; the giving of life and a partaking. (1861, pp. 9–10)

With all this in mind, we should listen to some passages from the transcripts to see how the process worked. Alcott initiates the conversations on Gospel passages thus:

> The best thoughts do not lie on the surface of our minds. We have to dive under for them, like pearl fishers. This morning I am going to ask some questions, that I may prove to you, by your own answers to them, that you are capable of thinking on this subject; and of having thoughts come from your minds, which will interest all,—teaching yourselves to know yourselves, and teaching me. (1836, vol. 1, p. 2)

Alcott warns the students that they will learn the most by going as fully as they can into their own minds, searching for both emotional depth and strenuous thinking, as suggested by the pearl-diving metaphor. Further, their thinking has to be their own in an intellectually self-reliant way, not just a replication of what either teacher or students have learned in the past: "I do not know all I am going to say, for I shall have new thoughts, that I never had before. Still less do you know all you are going to say. . . . But if we all think, and all say what we think, not repeating the words and thoughts of others, we shall teach each other" (vol. 1, p. 2).

In the second conversation in the series, Alcott suggests that a close consideration of both nature and scripture proves the existence of spirit, but as usual the doctrinal point recedes and the play of mind over the ideas becomes crucial in itself:

> MR. ALCOTT: Do smaller things prove greater things, or greater things smaller things? How many do not understand me? (*Several held up their hands.*)
> Does an acorn prove there has been an oak, or an oak prove there has been an acorn? (*Some said one and some the other, as they did also to the next question.*)
> MR. ALCOTT: Which was first in time, an acorn or an oak?
> GEORGE K: Sometimes one is first and sometimes the other. In the woods, oaks grow up wild; and you can plant acorns and have oaks.
> SAMUEL R: I think God made oaks first, and all the other oaks there have ever been, came from the acorns of those first oaks.
> MR. ALCOTT: Does light prove darkness, or darkness light?
> SEVERAL: Each proves the other. . . .
> (*He then asked questions about many things, among the rest a brook and the ocean, the cradle and the grave, and similar answers were returned. He remarked that their answers showed which minds were historical and which were analytic.*) (vol. 1, pp. 12–13)

Alcott's first question here is probably unanswerable, and in any case he does not seem to have a particular answer of his own that he wants the children to adopt. Instead of trying to adjudicate among students as to which is the best answer, he makes what we would now call a metacognitive, reflective move, suggesting that how we answer might depend on how we approach thinking itself, not on which way is objectively "true." Without trying to have this somewhat playful discussion bear too much weight, we might say that Alcott here initiates the students in post-Kantian thinking—if we cannot produce ontological statements that are certain, we can at least set our minds to a task and then observe and reflect upon its workings.

In a later conversation, after reading a passage from Luke about John the Baptist in the desert, Alcott begins the discussion by asking, "Now what came into your minds while I was reading?"

> JOSIAH: The deserts seemed to me a great space covered with sand, like that in the hour-glass. The sun was shining on it, and making it sparkle. There were no trees. John was there alone.
> EDWARD J: I thought the deserts meant woods, with paths here and there.

> LUCY: I thought of a space covered with grass and some wild
> flowers, and John walking about.
> CHARLES: I thought of a prairie.
> ALEXANDER: I thought of a few trees scattered over the country, with
> bees in the trunks.
> GEORGE K: I thought of a place without houses, excepting John's; and
> flowers, trees, and bee-hives. (vol. 1, p. 61)

This interaction is more affective and imaginative than the previous passage, engaging the students in what we might now call creative visualization. The first thing to notice here and throughout all the conversations is the long run of uninterrupted student responses without any intervening teacher remarks to praise, blame, or correct. Alcott declines the customary teacher role of central switchboard—verbally acknowledging each student comment before sending it back out to the class. By contrast, Alcott allows here a rich display of divergent thinking, that yet has its convergent aspect, as when the responses build on one another when George K. brings together in his comment previous images of flowers, trees, and bees.

One way to consider discussions like this is to see them as early experiments in reader response criticism. We can see before us how the children, given a biblical narrative very sparse in details, fill in the picture with their own visualizations and concrete details. This is not so much simply adding to the text but is rather an intrinsic part of reading, and it is this very process of active construction that makes it such a pleasure. Our memories and imaginations supply vitality and plenitude. Of course, the individual reader feels that he or she is simply reading the text, and it takes an experience such as that in Alcott's classroom to see that one's own interpretation is just that, one way of apprehending it. Here is another example from the same conversation:

> ANDREW: I thought, one night, as Elisabeth was sleeping, an angel
> brought her a child, and made her dream she had one, and she
> awoke and it was lying at her side.
> WILLIAM B: I think he was born like other children except that
> Elisabeth had visions.
> GEORGE K: I thought God sent an angel to give her a child. It cried as
> soon as it came and waked up its mother to give it something to
> eat.
> LUCIA: When John was first born, his mother did not know it, for he
> was born in the night; but she found it by her side in the
> morning. (vol. 1, p. 62)

The text Alcott had read to them at the beginning of the session simply says: "Now Elisabeth's full time came that she should be delivered: and she brought forth a son." The children themselves fill in the narrative gaps left by this bare, laconic account in ways similar to the ways in which they fill in the gaps of their own lack of knowledge about childbirth.

> ALEXANDER: Birth is like the rain. It comes from heaven.
> LUCIA: I think it is like a small stream coming from a great sea; and it runs back every night, and so becomes larger and larger every day, till at last it is large enough to send out other streams.
> LEMUEL: Lives streamed from the ocean first; now smaller streams from the larger ones, and so on.
> SAMUEL R: Birth is like the rising light of the sun; the setting is death. (vol. 1, p. 63)

Again we see the students responding divergently but also building on one another's responses, as when Lucia takes the image of rain and expands it to streams and seas, which in turn Lemuel elaborates, all in ways that resemble the use of analogies to stimulate creative thinking. One of Alcott's main goals here is to help the students establish their own personal, imaginative relations to reading that are the opposite of the decontextualized and mechanical methods with which he was taught. The connections his own students make will help make their reading a more voluntary activity as well as a more actively cognitive one.

All this should be kept in mind as we confront the most frequent criticism of Alcott's teaching, which we have already noted—that he manipulates the students. Some of this is surely going on at both the conscious and unconscious levels. Just as Freudian patients tend to come up with Freudian dreams, and Jungian patients with Jungian dreams, so Alcott's students often seem particularly idealistic and Wordsworthian. While Alcott's vision helped set the parameters of discussion and dictated his own line of questioning, as he taught it became more of a framework, just like the diagram he first uses and then erases. As Frederick Dahlstrand (1982) puts it:

> Alcott's paradigm gave the children a means of exercising their minds. It served as a structure on which they could build ideas. In one sense the paradigm limited them, but in another important way it freed them—it freed them from the tyranny of disorganization. It time they could cast away the paradigm, but the thought processes it helped them develop could stay with them forever. Alcott may not have made his students more spiritual, nor awakened in them the truth of spiritual things, but he did make them think. Almost despite himself, his methods succeeded. (p. 127)

Barbara Packer (1995) takes a similar view of the effect, suggesting that Alcott's success in getting his students to think and imagine was his primary aim:

> As a way of collecting a new set of Christian evidences, Alcott's pedagogy would seem to fail miserably, because the children can never be persuaded to adopt his beliefs and indeed argue back to him more and more. . . . Yet Alcott seems as pleased with their resistance as their concurrence. On the first page of the book itself is an illustration showing Alcott's classroom—Alcott at a desk, and the children ranged rather stiffly around in a semicircle at some distance from him. At the end of both volumes is another illustration, this time of the boy Jesus teaching the elders in the Temple. Between these two emblems occurs the education in self-reliance that finally comes to seem the real message of the book and gives it its power and its innocence. (p. 390)

Indeed, Alcott himself in his introduction to *Conversations* says: "It is a work, intended rather to awaken thought; enkindle feeling; and quicken to duty; than to settle opinions, or promulgate sentiments of any kind" (vol. 1, p. xiii). And he wrote in the *Dial* for January 1841: "The true teacher defends his pupils against his own personal influence. He inspires self-trust. He guides their eyes from himself to the spirit that quickens him" (Myerson, 2000, p. 304). In these statements, as in the teaching itself, he emphasizes education as a dialectical activity in which the energy of the process is always more crucial than any single end point.

As if true to its appreciation of flux and the fleeting usefulness of any cultural creation, the Temple School did not last long. Its downfall was initiated, paradoxically, by the very attempt of Alcott and Peabody to preserve in these books the work of the school and bring it to wider notice. Elizabeth Peabody had anticipated problems when she extracted some passages that were unusually candid about childbirth. Alcott agreed to these excisions, but then naively published them as notes in an appendix, providing the prurient and the hostile with easy reference. The reaction by the Unitarian establishment after the publication of the second volume of *Conversations* was swift and unambiguous. Joseph T. Buckingham, editor of the *Boston Courier*, suggested that if Alcott "be either honest or sincere, he must be insane or half-witted, and his friends ought to take care of him without delay" (Carlson, 1988, pp. 453–454). Andrews Norton, a leading professor at Harvard Divinity School, and sometimes called the Unitarian Pope, said of the *Conversations*: "One third was absurd, one third was blasphemous, and one third obscene" (p. 453).

In most accounts of the Temple School the prudery of these proper Bostonians is given as the main source of outrage. But for these individuals, what they saw as prurience was only the most obvious part of the school's real offense, which was to completely reverse the normal direction of education from adult to child, from institution to individual, and from the text-book to the mind. That Alcott clothed the endeavor in Christian rhetoric and that he used as his epigram "Except a Man be converted and become as a little Child . . . he cannot see,—nor enter into,—the kingdom of Heaven" (1836, vol. 1, p. i) only exacerbated matters. Nathan Hale, editor of the *Daily Advertiser*, most fully tips his hand when he complains that Alcott's main abuse of his students was "to accustom them to trifling and irreverent habits of reflection upon the most grave and solemn subjects . . . and to impress them with a degree of self-esteem, quite unfavorable" (Carlson, 1988, p. 408). It is not so much any particular subject matter as the process of reflection, stimulated by writing and talking, that opens a Pandora's box out of which only Alcott and his fellow Transcendentalists could discern anything called Hope.

Although defended in print by Emerson and James Freeman Clarke, Alcott found the enrollment in his school soon dwindling, and by the summer of 1837 there were only 11 students. As it became impossible to continue the school, Emerson tried to console Alcott with the prospect of writing for a future audience that might be more sympathetic to his views: "Write, let them hear or let them forbear—the written word abides until slowly & unexpectedly and in widely sundered places, it has created its own church" (Emerson, 1939, vol. 2, p. 75.) Emerson's advice was well intentioned, but inappropriate for Alcott in two ways. First, when Alcott wrote without the realities of his own classroom to anchor him, his writing became increasingly abstract, vaporous, confused. Unlike Emerson, Alcott himself paradoxically lacked the ability to use writing to clarify his thinking. The second reason Emerson's advice to retreat and write was inappropriate for Alcott is that the latter saw writing as only part of a larger process, incomplete without embodiment: "I desire to see my Idea not only a *written* but a *spoken* and *acted* word" (Carlson, 1981, p. 112). As he said of himself in an 1836 journal passage while the Temple School was at its height, "I am more successful, I apprehend, in the practical, than in the theoretic, exemplification, of my purposes. . . . As I go on, light will be shed down upon the details of practice, from the high sun of principles, and my own mind will be able to reflect this light, as it is" (Myerson, 1978, p. 28). Alcott's self-description of relating thought to action is exactly what Emerson articulated in the Emerson scholar, both the sense of using action to make the unconscious more conscious and the undulating dialectic between thought and action. At the height of the Temple School's success, Alcott wrote, "My actual life, my experiments, are coming more and more before the public. These are the true test of my theories. . . . So shall the testimony be authentic: the theory prove the practice, the practice be approved by the theory" (Carlson, 1978, p. 40).

Even after the circumstances surrounding Temple barred him from classroom work, he maintained his commitment to education. His attempt to found a utopian community called Fruitlands proved fruitless, but the conversations he conducted with adults were generally successful as educational events if not financially. One encounter related to these is particularly significant for our narrative. In March 1857 Alcott held a series of six conversations at Yale College. William Torrey Harris, a junior, was converted to Alcott's brand of idealism by the experience. Ten years later, Harris invited Alcott to St. Louis to meet with the group that came to be known at the St. Louis Hegelians. Harris went on to become a key figure in American education, exerting a conservative force, emphasizing the value of textbooks and the differentiated curriculum against innovations that were attempts to make education more experiential and wholistic. While Harris's conservatism should not be laid at Alcott's feet, the connection between the two does suggest that a vision is transformative only insofar as it challenges conventional habits. Idealism was innovative in the hands of a traditionalist such as James Marsh because it allowed him to see what the Lockean model missed. By Harris's time, idealism had become a rationale for existing educational practices and served as a defensive stance toward new weather in the intellectual climate, as signaled by such theories as Darwinism and pragmatic instrumentalism.

Even though Alcott's career as a classroom teacher occupied only the earlier years of a long life, it had a kind of literary reincarnation in the writings of his daughter Louisa May, especially in her novel *Little Men: Life at Plumfield with Jo's Boys* (1871). In this idealized version the author creates a portrait of what an Alcottian boarding school might look like: The children—despite the book's title, there are both boys and girls—are put in marvelously educative surroundings, where they have farm animals and crops to care for, plenty of books, and a museum to furnish and where they read to each other their essays on the exhibits. The problem boy is given his own cabinet, in which he can arrange and classify his natural history finds.

The Temple School represents the road not taken in American education. It was a place where imagination and intellect could flourish, unhampered by recitations and spelling tests. Its rapid demise was the fault of an uncomprehending public but also of a teacher who lacked the tact and the tactics to educate parents and the public as well as his students. But we are fortunate to have its record in such detail, not to treat as a sacred text as did Hiram Fuller, but as a spur to replicating its energies and openness in our own classrooms.

CHAPTER 4

Varieties of Transcendentalist Teaching:
Margaret Fuller and Henry David Thoreau

Thought works in the changing and becoming, not in the changed and became; all things sliding by imperceptible gradations into their contraries. . . . Nothing abides; all is image and expression out of our thought. So Speech represents the flowing essences as sensitive, transitive; the word signifying what we make it at the moment of using, but needing life's rounded experiences to unfold its manifold senses and shades of meaning.

—Bronson Alcott

ONE OF THE REASONS I regularly teach a course in the Transcendentalists to graduate students is that I see these figures as powerful role models who personify being an intellectual in America. Despite their reputation for otherworldly fuzziness—partly deserved, as when Elizabeth Peabody, after walking into a tree, said, "I saw it but didn't realize it"—they were committed, like Karl Marx, not just to understanding the world but also to changing it. Many present-day academics are content to define their radicalism by setting down in print views that they hope will be more extreme and witheringly skeptical than those of their colleagues; but as for living these ideas, their students can do that for them. The Transcendentalists felt that having ideas was the easy part and that unless these ideas were realized, they were incomplete, the sound of one hand yapping. As Thoreau said, "There are nowadays professors of philosophy, but not philosophers" (1854/1971, p. 14).

The Transcendentalists' work in education is important not just as a good example but also as offering a way to trace in detail the interaction between theory and practice. Moreover, this work is varied enough that we can see several different forms that a praxis based on the centrality of active learning could take in actuality. We have already seen, for example, the Temple School classroom, and we can view different if related educational structures in the later work of one of its two assistants, Margaret Fuller. The other assistant, Elizabeth Peabody, went on to make kindergartens a reality in American public schools, an achievement closely related to her Transcendentalism, but one that we do not have the room to trace here. Another Transcendentalist project that we can only mention is the innovative and successful school at the Brook Farm commune. Finally we will use as an epitome of the movement the work of the one of the latest Transcendentalists, Henry David Thoreau. Thoreau's official career as a teacher was short, but he continued to write about education throughout his life in a language that was more incisive and memorable than that of any of his peers. Passages from his extensive journal as well as the books published in his lifetime can be arranged to effectively summarize and embody not only Transcendentalist education but the entire tradition of active learning.

After the Temple School had closed, Alcott traveled the country offering conversational sessions for adults. In doing so, he was not only following the lead of Elizabeth Peabody and Margaret Fuller, but was also engaging in a particularly Transcendentalist mode. Lawrence Buell (1973) was the first scholar to write in detail on its centrality to the movement: "Transcendentalism can almost be said to have begun as a discussion group. Much of its internal ferment and a good deal of its external impact can be attributed to talkers like Alcott and Margaret Fuller; even its writing is largely oral literature, in the sense of having been composed originally for the pulpit or the lyceum" (p. 77). Conversations—whether as informal meetings among friends, as those of the Transcendentalist Club, or as public events for which Alcott and Fuller charged admission—were inherently democratic and spontaneous, thinking in motion rather than transfixed and fossilized. It is *continuing* education in the best sense of recognizing that no formulation is finally sufficient or permanent, that to be alive is to be a perpetual learner throughout life.

Emerson recognized these qualities of conversation as enacting his ideal of thinking when he wrote in his essay "Circles": "In conversation we pluck up the termini which bound the common of silence on every side. . . . When each new speaker strikes a new light, emancipates us from the oppression of the last speaker, to oppress us with the greatness and exclusiveness of his own thought, then yields us to another redeemer, we seem to recover our rights" (1983, p. 408). Talk tends to take on a life of its own; the insights are not so much the product of any one person but a kind of joint creation of an overarching mind, as Alcott describes it: "Good conversation is lyrical: a pentecost of tongues, touching the chords of melody in all minds, it prompts to the best each had to give, to better than any knew they had, what none claims as his own, as if he were the organ of some invisible player behind the scenes" (1868, p. 76). Further, conversations held the promise of surprise—a quality particularly valued by the Transcendentalists, as Alcott also noted: "All the beauty and advantages of Conversation is [*sic*] in its bold contrasts, & swift surprises; its large suggestiveness" (Dahlstrand, 1982, p. 217). It is a way not so much of exchanging what is already formulated but of discovering and creating new insights that in turn are further built upon in community with others: "Conversation is best when tentative, cumulative, & refuses the foreseen and determined passes, to have its own free and fearless way, opening out prospects which no foresight could command" (p. 217).

The most sustained and important of the Transcendentalist adult conversations was those of the series for women conducted by Margaret Fuller each winter and spring in Boston, from 1839 to 1844. One of the reasons for the success was that Fuller built on the skills and ideas she developed in her teaching for the previous 18 months at Hiram Fuller's Green Street School in Providence, Rhode Island. We have already seen Hiram Fuller engaged in the ironic practice of reading directly to his students from Alcott's books, but Margaret Fuller had worked in the Temple School itself, was close friends with Emerson and other Transcendentalists, and more fully comprehended their vision of education.

Most of Fuller's teaching involved the older girls in the school, whom she engaged in journaling and conversation and encouraged to think critically and reflexively. One student wrote to her parents that "it must not be our object to come and hear her talk for she could not teach us so, *we* must talk and understand our minds" (Johnson, 1910, p. 427). More pointedly, Fuller told her students: "A lesson is as far as possible from being learned by *heart* when it is said to be, it is only learned by *body*. I wish *you* to get your lessons by *mind*" (Fergenson, 1991, p. 83). Although she found that the daily grind of classroom teaching depleted her physically and left her no time for her own writing, she wrote toward the end of this period, "I am not without my dreams and hopes as to the education of women" (Fuller, 1983–1994, vol. 1, p. 354).

Fuller brought these hopes to the Boston conversations that she offered weekly in 12 sessions in the large front room of Elizabeth Peabody's bookstore and involved in their total span more than a hundred women, many from the top strata of society. Unfortunately, we do not have as extensive transcriptions for these conversations as we do for the ones Peabody and Fuller herself recorded for the Temple School, but we do have detailed notes taken by Elizabeth Peabody on the conversations in the first series, 1839–1840 (Simmons, 1994).

In the first of these conversations, Fuller said she wanted to provide for women the kind of outlet for articulating and consolidating their knowledge that was available to men in so many other spheres: "Is not the difference between education of women & that of men this—Men are called on from a very early period to *reproduce* all that they learn—. . . . This is what is most neglected in the education of women—they learn without any attempt to reproduce—The little reproduction to which they are called seems mainly for the purposes of idle display" (Simmons, 1994, p. 203). To stress the need for active, constructive learning, she told her participants that "those who do not talk will not derive the same advantages as those who openly state their impressions and consent to learn by blundering as is the destiny of Man here below" (Fuller, 1983–1994, vol. 2, p. 88). Women needed to bring to the task the kind of intellectual self-reliance Alcott asked of his children. Fuller said she was "not here to teach," but "to provoke the thoughts of others" (1852, vol. 1, p. 329).

Fuller did not only rely on speech but also asked her participants to write essays on the following week's topic, several of which are reproduced in their entirety in Peabody's notes. I suspect that it was this technique in large part that made Fuller's conversations so consistently successful, while Alcott's adult talks were only sporadically so. The essays ensured that every woman had already thought about the subject for the week and entered the session with something to say. The participants, then, were not simply talking spontaneously but had rehearsed and clarified their thinking in a form both they and Fuller could return to for further reference and rethinking. The very act of writing added to the activity a reflective dimension. Fuller does not use the ambiguity and insufficiency of language as an excuse for lapsing into silence before the ineffable, but rather challenges herself and the group to try for an even more exact discourse through their mutual efforts. Her critique of a week's essays is that they "were rather little poems about Beauty . . . than definitions of Beauty" (p. 210); she wants, rather, "to systematize thought" to "give a precision in which our sex are so deficient" (1983–1994, vol. 2, p. 87). In other words, she deliberately chooses to help develop what Jung will later call the contrasexual aspect of the psyche.

Charles Capper, the historian who has most thoroughly researched these conversations (1987, 1992), describes Fuller as "a most powerful advocate of an activism of the mind" (1987, p. 523) and views that activism as "historically critical":

> These ideas of "man thinking" and mind as activity were radical enough in early nineteenth-century America. But to apply them . . . to women, whose very intellectual identity and claim to cultural validation were defined by official culture as flowing precisely from their passive and therefore pure

absorption of common sense values and divine wisdom, was culturally subversive. (p. 522)

Thus the conversations themselves were enactments of the ideas in her later
political writings, following her own advice to her pupils "to build a life of
thought upon a life of action" (Fuller, 1983–1994, vol. 2, pp. 86–87). Fuller's
early death by shipwreck in 1850 was a tragedy not only for American femi-
nism but also for the notion of education as continuing and pervasive thinking.

∞ 2 ∞

Henry David Thoreau is a fitting figure with which to round off our discussion of the movement because he so well grasps its vision and articulates it
with flair. While he did not write a single work explicitly focused on education, a remarkably coherent and well-developed philosophy of education
runs through the entire oeuvre, especially in his masterpiece *Walden* (1854/
1971) and in the more than 2-million-word journal. In this section I will first
trace his brief career as a teacher and then present his lifelong engagement
with education through his writings, each of which illuminates the other.

As with the other figures in this tradition, Thoreau's relation to the existing
institutions of education has been problematic. He entered the teaching
profession early and left it a few years later, when he closed the private
school he conducted with his brother. Although there were external reasons
for this action, Thoreau's departure from teaching also resulted from disillusion with the conventional classroom, a growing sense that it prevented
learning rather than fostering it. Also, placing the focus where it really should
be, he came to feel increasingly that "it is strange that men are in such haste
to get fame as teachers rather than knowledge as learners" (1906, vol. 14,
p. 205). He spent the rest of his life learning and writing—the two were usually the same for him—but never lost his concern for teaching, both envisioning better ways to go about it and launching a powerful critique of the
way it was usually done: "What does education often do!—It makes a straight-
cut ditch of a free, meandering brook" (1981–1997, vol. 3, p. 130).

Thoreau began teaching before his own formal education was complete.
As a sophomore at Harvard College, he took advantage of a recent faculty
ruling that allowed students a leave of absence to teach school for up to 13
weeks. It is likely that Thoreau took this opportunity mainly for financial reasons, but he probably also wanted a break from an educational system he
often found diffuse, rigid, and superficial. He later said that Harvard taught all
the branches of learning but none of the roots (Albee, 1901, p. 31), and he
noted in *Walden* that he found he had been enrolled in a course called "Navi-

gation" that was so removed from nautical realities that he was unaware of having taken it. So in the fall of 1835, Thoreau applied to teach in Canton, Massachusetts, where he was interviewed by the young minister, Orestes Brownson. Little is known of this first teaching episode, except that whatever Thoreau's experience with his 70 students, he was not discouraged from teaching as a future career. Aside from what he learned about education, his development was probably fostered more by his study of German and his conversations with Brownson, the very model of an intellectual activist.

After graduating from Harvard College in the summer of 1837, Thoreau, now 20, began his shortest and most notorious teaching stint. In that year of financial panic he was fortunate enough to land a position in his native Concord as the teacher at the Center School, the main public school for college preparation. This post was traditionally offered to a recent Harvard graduate, but Thoreau, unlike many of his predecessors, was not just biding his time en route to becoming a lawyer or minister. Dick O'Connor (1996), who has most thoroughly studied Thoreau's brief tenure here, writes that he "had some ideas of his own about teaching that he was eager to put into practice. He fully intended to stay in teaching for several years, perhaps—after a year of public school experience and self-directed study—taking a position in a private academy" (pp. 153–154). But during his first few days, Thoreau was visited by Nehemiah Ball, one of the three members of the school committee. Ball found the activity and noise level of the classroom too high and instructed the young teacher to use corporal punishment more often. Stung by the criticism, Thoreau applied the ferule to six students, some chosen at random, some punished for minor infractions. That evening he turned in his resignation.

This act of uncivil obedience, like much of Thoreau's experience, was not as memorable or original in itself (Bronson Alcott had preceded him both in criticizing corporal punishment and in not paying his poll tax) as was his later verbal formulation of it; in seeking a new teaching job, he wrote to Brownson: "I have even been disposed to regard the cowhide as a nonconductor. Methinks that, unlike the electric wire, not a single spark of truth is ever transmitted through its agency to the slumbering intellect it would address" (Thoreau, 1958, p. 20). But more significant than this negative critique is his positive vision of schooling in the same letter:

> I would make education a pleasant thing both to the teacher and the scholar. This discipline, which we allow to be the end of life, should not be one thing in the schoolroom, and another in the street. We should seek to be fellow students with the pupil, and should learn of, as well as with him, if we would be most helpful to him. But I am not blind to the difficulties of the case; it supposes a degree of freedom which rarely exists. It hath not entered into the heart of man to conceive the full import of that word—Freedom. (p. 20)

Instead of any disillusion with teaching, Thoreau articulates an inspiriting philosophy that he was to apply to the rest of his educational work. He both looks back to his Transcendentalist antecedents and forward to John Dewey. Like Dewey, Thoreau chooses to see education as not simply a means, a preparation, for something else, but as intrinsically valuable. Both men assert a fundamental continuity between the schoolroom and the street, between the process of learning and the rest of experience. And both seek to go beyond the conventional dichotomy of teacher and student, suggesting that the teacher can learn with and from the student. Most centrally, both Thoreau and Dewey see education as crucial to democracy and vice versa; for democracy to be a living philosophy, it cannot occur only on election day but in every act of building community.

Soon after writing this letter, Thoreau made for himself an opportunity to embody these ideas in practice. After almost a year of unsuccessfully pursuing leads for other teaching positions, he decided to open his own school in June 1838. It began modestly in the family home with only four students. When Concord Academy, the private college preparatory school he had attended himself, looked as if it would fold, he was able to rent the building and take over the name. By the following winter, the school had enrolled enough students that Henry was able to bring in as a second teacher his older brother, John, who had been teaching on his own in Roxbury.

Although the brothers retained many features of conventional schooling, they supplemented these with a number of activities that moved education beyond the walls of the classrooms. There were frequent field trips, and not just to fields for nature study. The students were taken to the offices of a local paper to watch typesetting and to a gunsmith to watch the regulating of gunsights. In the spring each student had a small plot of plowed land to plant. In the fall of 1840, Henry brought in surveying instruments to teach his students yet another kind of fieldwork in organizing a survey of Fairhaven Hill. Surveying, as Thomas Pynchon was later to illustrate in his novel *Mason and Dixon* (1997), is a wonderful synecdoche for the imposition of human orders on the natural world, a way to explore the relation between mathematical concept and physical reality.

This account of a river trip was reported by F. B. Sanborn (1884), one of Thoreau's early biographers, who himself later ran a progressive school in Concord:

> Henry Thoreau called attention to a spot on the river-shore, where he fancied the Indians had made their fires, and perhaps had a fishing village. . . . "Do you see," said Henry, "anything here that would be likely to attract Indians to this spot?" One boy said, "Why, here is the river for their fishing"; another pointed to the woodland near by, which could give them game. "Well, is there

anything else?" pointing out a small rivulet that must come, he said, from a spring not far off, which could furnish water cooler than the river in summer; and a hillside above it that would keep off the north and northwest wind in winter. Then, moving inland a little farther, and looking carefully about, he struck his spade several times, without result. Presently, when the boys began to think their young teacher and guide was mistaken, his spade struck a stone. Moving forward a foot or two, he set his spade in again, struck another stone, and began to dig in a circle. He soon uncovered the red, fire-marked stones of the long-disused Indian fireplace; thus proving that he had been right in his conjecture. Having settled the point, he carefully covered up his find and replaced the turf,—not wishing to have the domestic altar of the aborigines profaned by mere curiosity. (pp. 205–206)

Thoreau helps his students read the natural landscape as carefully and closely as they would a page of Cicero. They are asked to not merely appreciate its beauty but to make logical inferences about its possible relations to the human world, to formulate hypotheses and test those hypotheses through further activity. Thoreau's own actions model an intellectual curiosity about the immediate world we move through, a willingness to take the risk of being proven wrong, and a respect for the past and other cultures.

On April 1, 1841, the brothers closed their school because of John's failing health from tuberculosis, the disease from which Henry was eventually to die also. Later, Henry tutored Emerson's nephew on Staten Island for a few homesick months in 1843. And informally he was a wonderful teacher to many of the children around him, as documented in detail by two of them, Edward Emerson in *Henry Thoreau as Remembered by a Young Friend* (1917) and Louisa May Alcott in *Little Men* (1871), where he is fictionalized as Mr. Hyde. He also became a pioneer in adult education through his work as both an organizer and a lecturer in the lyceum movement. But he was never to be a classroom teacher again. On the positive side he wanted to devote all his energies to his writing. On the negative side, he had a deep underlying suspicion of the whole activity of formal education. In his journal he writes: "How vain it is to teach youth, or anybody, truths! They can only learn them after their own fashion, and when they get ready" (1906, vol. 13, pp. 67–68).

Thoreau's subsequent involvement with education, then, was primarily as a writer. As noted, he did not write a separate single work on the subject, but as appropriate to one who saw education as continuous with all experience, he integrates his insights throughout the body of his work, side by side with natural history observations and reflections on his reading. Thoreau remained not only a learner but also a learner of how he learned, keeping in his journal a series of what we would now call metacognitive reflections. It is one of the most thorough and detailed records we have of what Emerson called "life passed through the fire of thought" (1983, p. 85), of productive alternations between living and writing.

If we simply read sequentially the passages on education, we might find at first some frustrating inconsistencies. Thoreau seems at times to scorn book learning and pedantry, but loves the study of the classics; he enjoins us to live in the here and now, but is fascinated with history; he sometimes values nature over human culture and sometimes not. This is in part the play of the active mind over time and circumstances, a willingness to follow a thought wherever it might lead. But at a deeper level, these inconsistencies are really phases of larger cycles of alternation, of the rhythms of learning. Just as Emerson sees learning as an undulating, rhythmic motion—"the mind now thinks, now acts" (1983, p. 62)—Thoreau writes equally rhythmically, "We have our times of action and our times of reflection" (1981–1997, vol. 1, p. 388), either of which alone soon becomes meaningless or sterile. Thoreau can praise the activity of classical study extravagantly as he does in the "Reading" section of *Walden,* and then begin the next chapter, "But while we are confined to books . . . we are in danger of forgetting the language which all things and events speak without metaphor" (1854/1971, p. 111). Even within a single sentence, Thoreau expresses the paradoxical interactions between knowing and unknowing: "At the same time that we are earnest to explore and learn all things, we require that all things be mysterious and unexplorable, that land and sea be infinitely wild, unsurveyed and unfathomed by us because unfathomable" (pp. 317–318). What seem like inconsistencies are most often different phases of a single process.

Since what Thoreau envisions is a continuous cycle, it is arbitrary to isolate a "beginning," but for the sake of exposition, we can first discuss the need to let go our past learning to be able to learn something new, to release ourselves from previous symbols, to put ourselves in the position for seeing the world freshly. Not even Emerson has written so well of the hardening effects of education, of how our very knowledge is sometimes bought at the price of less flexibility and responsiveness. In a more homely metaphor than that of the hero turning into a statue, Thoreau describes this process of intellectual rigor mortis: "It appears to me that at a very early age—the mind of man—perhaps at the same time with his body, ceases to be elastic. His intellectual power becomes something defined— & limited. He does not think as expansively as he would stretch himself in his growing days—What was flexible sap hardens into heartwood" (1981–1997, vol. 4, pp. 265–266). And elsewhere, he writes of those who go to Europe to "finish their education," pun intended: "Instead of acquiring nutritious and palatable qualities to their pulp, it is all absorbed into a prematurely hardened shell. They went away squashes, and they return gourds" (1906, vol. 5, pp. 344–345).

The worst effect of conventional schooling is to perpetuate and exacerbate this situation; as Emerson had written in his address to Thoreau's graduating class: "The book, the college, the school of art, the institution of any kind, stop with some past utterance of genius. This is good, say they,—let us hold by this" (1983, pp. 57–58). Thoreau uses a cluster of images for this process focusing on well-worn paths and ruts. In one journal entry he writes, "Every thought that passes through the mind helps to wear & tear it & to deepen the ruts which as in the streets of Pompeii evince how much it has been used" (1981–1997, vol. 3, pp. 289–291). Most poignantly, this figurative rut becomes literal as well in the path that Thoreau himself wears between his hut and Walden Pond:

> I had not lived there a week before my feet wore a path from my door to the pond-side; and though it is five or six years since I trod it, it is still quite distinct. It is true, I fear that others may have fallen into it, and so helped to keep it open. The surface of the earth is soft and impressible by the feet of men; and so with the paths which the mind travels. How worn and dusty, then, must be the highways of the world, how deep the ruts of tradition and conformity! (1854/1971, p. 323)

Even when the cultural artifact, then, is of one's own making, even when it is as supple and magnificent as a book like *Walden,* to remain with it is to get into a rut.

The antidote for this process is a kind of willed and cultivated ignorance, the last a word that Thoreau constantly battles to rescue from its negative connotations:

> I have heard that there is a Society for the Diffusion of Useful Knowledge—It is said that Knowledge is power and the like—Methinks there is equal need of a society for the diffusion of useful Ignorance—for what is most of our boasted so called knowledge but a conceit that we know something which robs us of the advantages of our actual ignorance. (1981–1997, vol. 3, p. 184)

In a particularly powerful passage in *Walden,* Thoreau writes about the experience of coming upon a well-known road during a snowstorm, and how the snow has changed it almost beyond recognition. It is the kind of experience he treasures, since it constantly renews the world and the mind:

> In our most trivial walks, we are constantly, though unconsciously, steering like pilots by certain well-known beacons and headlands . . . and not till we are completely lost, or turned round,—for a man needs only to be turned round once with his eyes shut in this world to be lost,—do we appreciate the vastness and strangeness of Nature. Every man has to learn the points of the compass again as often as he awakes, whether from sleep or any abstraction. Not

till we are lost, in other words, not till we have lost the world, do we begin to find ourselves. (1854/1971, pp. 170–171)

It is significant that "abstraction" is in parallel grammatical form with "sleep," since while the process of making generalizations is an active one, the abstraction itself is a world of vagueness from which we need periodically to awaken. The passage suggests that as we move through the world, we constantly make maps of it, which we need as heuristics to record what we have learned. Yet once we make a map, we sometimes mistake it for the world from which we have distilled it, losing some of its constantly changing freshness.

Our knowledge, then, has to be constantly refreshed and complemented by ignorance, so Thoreau continually tries to redefine the former word to engage and include the latter: "I do not know that knowledge amounts to anything more definite than a novel & grand surprise on a sudden revelation of the insufficiency of all that we had called knowledge before. . . . It is the lighting up of the mist by the sun" (1981–1997, vol. 3, p. 198). And in a Socratic vein, he writes, "In reference to important things, whose knowledge amounts to more than a consciousness of his ignorance? Yet what more refreshing & inspiring knowledge than this?" (vol. 3, p. 184). As we keep this in mind, we also have to remember that Thoreau himself was a surveyor, that he taught his students how to survey, and that it was he who created the map of the pond that appears in *Walden*. For as soon as one attains that Zen-like state of ignorance, one remains passive, stagnant, dumb, unless one can articulate what is learned from it, constructing new sounds and structures out of the silence.

From this sense of a dynamic and cyclical movement between experience and concepts come both Thoreau's positive, wholistic vision of education, and his negative critique of schooling, both of which are set out, often simultaneously: "To be a philosopher is not merely to have subtle thoughts, nor even to found a school, but so to love wisdom as to live according to its dictates a life of simplicity, independence, magnanimity, and trust. It is to solve some of the problem of life, not only theoretically, but practically" (1854/1971, pp. 14–15). In this passage, Thoreau goes directly to the etymology of *philosophy*, as *philos* (love) + *sophia* (wisdom), to invoke a tradition that precedes the forming of schools, one that hearkens back to the living dialogues of Socrates instead of the metaphysical system-building of Plato. Thoreau is not against the having of subtle thoughts, but only against keeping these thoughts untested and unrealized. This belief lies behind Thoreau's critique of how colleges are structured:

> The mode of founding a college is, commonly, to get up a subscription of dollars and cents, and then following blindly the principles of a division of labor to its extreme . . . —to call in a contractor who makes this a subject of speculation,

and he employs Irishmen or other operatives actually to lay the foundations. . . . I think that it would be *better than this*, for the students, or those who desire to be benefited by it, even to lay the foundation themselves. (1854/ 1971, p. 50)

Thoreau here gives a powerful series of examples of how we might end the schisms both created by and reflected in the division of labor that we have seen Emerson and Schiller lament:

How could youths better learn to live than by at once trying the experiment of living? Methinks this would exercise their minds as much as mathematics. . . . Which would have advanced the most at the end of a month,—the boy who made his own jack-knife from the ore which he had dug and smelted, reading as much as would be necessary for this,—or the boy who had attended the lectures on metallurgy at the Institute in the mean while, and had received a Rodgers' penknife from his father? (p. 51)

Thoreau's critique of the traditional curriculum, then, is not of the activities of reading, language study, and scholarship per se, but only as they have become sealed off from other life experiences.

Thoreau was acutely aware of the need to combine a certain goal-orientedness with openness to experience, to create a certain rhythmic alternation between self-abandonment and self-construction, creating interactions between the conscious and the unconscious: "Many of our days should be spent, not in vain expectations and lying on our oars, but in carrying out deliberately and faithfully the hundred little purposes which every man's genius must have suggested to him. . . . Both a conscious and an unconscious life are good" (1906, vol. 9, pp. 37–38). This integration of conscious and unconscious, purpose with openness, relates to Thoreau's emphasis on learning from physical labor: "We reason from our hands to our head" (1981–1997, vol. 4, p. 46). It is worth noting here that the amount and quality of Thoreau's writing was often equivalent to the length of his daily walks, as he suggests in another journal entry: "How vain it is to sit down to write when you have not stood up to live! Methinks that the moment my legs begin to move my thoughts begin to flow—as if I had given vent to the stream at the lower end & consequently new fountains flowed into it at the upper. . . . Only while we are in action is the circulation perfect" (1981–1997, vol. 3, pp. 378–379).

Through observation and monitoring his own thought processes, Thoreau anticipated our most recent knowledge on the physiology of thought that suggests the brain does not think alone but is part of the entire ecosystem of the body: "A man thinks as well through his legs and arms as his brain. We exaggerate the importance and exclusiveness of the headquarters" (1906, vol. 13, pp. 69–70). At another point in his journal Thoreau uses the phrase "thoughts which the body thought" (1981–1997, vol. 4, p. 170) and it is as an anthology of such thoughts, a living document as to how one learns through physical experience, that his major book, *Walden*, can profitably be viewed.

Thoreau's initial motivation in going to Walden Pond was to create a way of life that would allow him the most time for thinking, writing, cultivating spirit, and observing nature. But cutting trees for his hut, cementing bricks for its chimney, and hoeing beans became not so much means but ends in themselves, and Thoreau learns as much from these experiences as from the program of reading and writing he initially planned. He was, for example, "determined to know beans" (p. 161) and finally "came to love my rows, my beans. . . . They attached me to the earth, and so I got strength like Antaeus" (p. 155). In hoeing he experiences a visionary moment, where the barriers between subject and object lift: "It was no longer beans that I hoed, nor I that hoed beans" (p. 159).

This kind of earth-attached but profound knowing is seen also in the ice fishermen whom Thoreau meets on early winter mornings at the pond: "Here is one fishing for pickerel with grown perch for bait. You look into his pail with wonder as into a summer pond, as if he kept summer locked up at home, or knew where she had retreated" (p. 283). When Thoreau asks for an explanation, he finds out, "O, he got worms out of rotten logs since the ground froze, and so he caught them," inspiring the following reflection: "His life passes deeper in Nature than the studies of the naturalist. . . . The latter raises the moss and bark gently with his knife in search of insects; the former lays open logs to their core with his axe, and moss and bark fly far and wide" (p. 283).

Both this fisherman and Thoreau participate in a particularly American kind of knowing, described both in Emerson's address and in the passage from Boorstin quoted earlier in chapter 1, a knowing achieved through working directly in the world, free from preconceptions and prior constructs. Thoreau writes: "Fishermen, hunters, woodchoppers, and others, spending their lives in the fields and woods, in a peculiar sense a part of Nature themselves, are often in a more favorable mood for observing her, in the intervals of their pursuits, than philosophers or poets even, who approach her with expectation" (p. 211). The arc of the entire Walden experiment suggests that such fresh, embodied knowledge comes not from systematic study but as a by-product of living a life with responsive awareness.

Thoreau's vision of education is particularly important because it promises to resolve some of the false and self-defeating oppositions that have arisen between traditionalists and progressives, between the advocates of "basics" and those of openness and creativity. Some progressive educators make the mistake of thinking it is enough for students to have experiences; but experiences themselves are educative only if the students actively clarify, internalize, and reflect on these experiences through their own language-making. The corresponding mistake of educational conservatives is to assume that inert bits and pieces of culture committed to memory somehow constitute thinking. It is one of the many ironies of our current schooling that Thoreau's writings themselves have become fodder for exam questions instead of the "perpetual suggestions and provocations" (1854/1971, p. 100) he sought from his own reading; we should not so much venerate and memorialize Thoreau's writing as use it to spur our own: "Thought breeds thought. It grows under your hands" (1906, vol. 13, p. 145).

Thoreau himself frequently raises the question of how his own writings should be read. On the one hand, we cannot take them as literal prescriptions even if we could get beyond their apparent contradictoriness: "I would not have any one adopt *my* mode of living on any account; for beside that before he has fairly learned it I may have found out another for myself. I desire that there may be as many different persons in the world as possible; but I would have each one be very careful to find out and pursue *his own* way, and not his father's or his mother's or his neighbor's instead" (1854/1971, p. 71). But on the other hand, we cannot merely let this be a reading and thinking experience locked away within the mind. Thoreau said of what he considered a truly good book: "I must lay it down and commence living on its hint. : . . What I began by reading I must finish by acting" (1981–1997, vol. 1, p. 268). If some of the ideas of Thoreau and the other Transcendentalists seem visionary, seem like castles in the air, we must, to use Thoreau's metaphors, attach them to the earth and put the foundations under them.

CHAPTER 5

The Turbulent Embrace of Thinking:
Prose Style and the Languages of Education

> If he have not found his home in God, his manners, his forms of speech, the turn of his sentences . . . will involuntarily confess it.
>
> —Ralph Waldo Emerson

> Emerson's American Scholar is "man thinking," but so too are good scholars everywhere. In controversies about language since Plato the argument has always been made that it is incumbent upon us to release words from the posturing embrace of Thought so that they may enter the turbulent embrace of Thinking.
>
> —Richard Poirier

LOOKING AT BOTH teaching and writings about teaching, some people take the pervasive medium in which both are conducted—language—as invisible, as a transparency pointing only to something beyond itself. It is here that education can learn the most from literary criticism, which foregrounds language itself, tacitly accepting Marshall McLuhan's slogan that the medium is the message. The very sounds and shapes of our language, its syntax and texture, imply and create an emotional and philosophical stance that shapes the world as it grasps it. Language, "carved out of the breath of life itself" (Thoreau, 1854/1971, p. 102), is no more an extraneous and peripheral component to our lives than water is to that of fish. We will here consider how what prose writers such as Emerson, Thoreau, and Herman Melville do in literature can be transferred to the classroom, how the energies of art can unstiffen our teaching.

If we return once more to "The American Scholar," we see that one of the crucial services that action furnishes the scholar is to revitalize and re-create language:

> If it were only for a vocabulary, the scholar would be covetous of action. Life is our dictionary. . . . Life lies behind us as the quarry from whence we get tiles and copestones for the masonry of to-day. This is the way to learn grammar. Colleges and books only copy the language which the field and the workyard made. (Emerson, 1983, pp. 61–62)

What lies behind this paragraph is a theory of language that Emerson had expounded in a more systematic and detailed way the year before in _Nature_, where he sets out three related propositions:

1. Words are signs of natural facts.
2. Particular natural facts are symbols of particular spiritual facts.
3. Nature is the symbol of spirit. (p. 20)

In explaining the first, Emerson maintains that all language, no matter how abstract or "spiritual" it has become, was once concrete, sensuous in that its first use arose from an impression made on at least one of the senses: "Every word which is used to express a moral or intellectual fact, if traced to its root, is found to be borrowed from some material appearance" (p. 20). Tracing language back to its origins in physical reality is particularly important, because as the second proposition suggests, these "natural facts" are inherently meaningful in that they indicate spiritual facts. And as the third proposition says, all natural facts have both their origin and their ultimate meaning in spirit or mind, not in a separate God but in a consciousness that we all potentially share.

We need to constantly return to action, to direct experience, because language is inherently entropic—it tends to become worn out, increasingly abstract as it is detached from the concrete images from which it arises. To use examples Emerson himself gives, the more abstract notion of _right_, as in _correct_, comes from _straight_, _wrong_ from _twisted_. The psychological quality of being _supercilious_ comes from the physical action of raising the eyebrow. These concrete origins sometimes become etymologically concealed, as the Latin _cilia_ for eyebrow becomes buried in a longer word. But even if the evidence is right before our eyes, we tend to take the word as a conventional verbal counter and avoid the effort of imagining (creating a physical image), as in _skyscraper_, which has become through habit a dull, gray word, but is poetically vivid when reseen as a building touching the sky. Emerson describes with an economic metaphor this process of language losing the physical aspect that underwrites it: "New imagery ceases to be created, and old words are perverted to stand for things which are not; a paper currency is employed, when there is no bullion in the vaults. In due time the fraud is manifest, and words lose all power to stimulate the understanding or the affections" (pp. 22–23).

Thoreau was just as interested in returning to the origins of language and often recasts Emersonian ideas in his own images and wordplay, as in this *Walden* passage:

> It would seem as if the very language of our parlors would lose all its nerve and degenerate into *palaver* wholly, our lives pass at such remoteness from its symbols, and its metaphors and tropes are necessarily so far fetched, through slides and dumb-waiters, as it were; in other words, the parlor is so far from the kitchen and workshop. The dinner even is only the parable of a dinner, commonly. (1854/1971, pp. 244–245)

This passage comes immediately after Thoreau's countervision of a huge, primitive house that is all one great hall, where the visitor can see plainly and simultaneously its construction, the inhabitants, and the household tasks, such as washing and cooking. In the present paragraph, by contrast, we see the results of the increasing compartmentalization of our activities and our vocabularies. The "parlor," fulfilling its etymology in *parler,* becomes a realm of speech only—dull, polite chatter, or "palaver"—because we disconnect it from our physical work, where speech should actually be created, as the preceding "American Scholar" paragraph suggests. The processes by which living in the world is turned into language are hidden from us by walls of misplaced propriety and a self-defeating division of labor. "Dumb-waiters" suggests not only a kind of automatic, mechanical servitude but also a mute-ness and even stupidity imposed on what or who should be doing the speak-ing. The dinner, appearing mysteriously through this dumbwaiter, is discussed in self-contained parlor language by those to whom its preparation and even its immediate physical reality have become distant and obscured. We end up eating only our own words. The scholar here, unlike Emerson's heroic prototype, is trapped in a cocoon of his own spinning.

Thoreau, then, following Emerson's dictum for the American scholar, moves out into nature not simply to live a purer or simpler life but more specifically to regenerate the language. Using the same root pun on *parable,* Thoreau explains the real reason he planted and hoed beans: "Not that I wanted beans to eat . . . but perchance, as some must work in fields if only for the sake of tropes and expression, to serve a parable-maker one day" (p. 162). He wants to become one of those whom Emerson describes as "the primary writers of the country, those, namely who hold primarily on na-ture" to "fasten words again to visible things" (1983, p. 23).

Just as the entire "action" section of "The American Scholar" deconstructs the ancient Greek distinction between mental and physical labor, the view of language it contains reverses the ancient prejudice that values the ab-stract and general over the concrete and particular. Not that the Transcendentalists wished to return to some kind of primitive ur-language, but rather they realized that language becomes anemic, vague, and blunted if it leaves the specifics from which it was created too far behind. They saw the need to keep both the literal and the figurative, the natural fact and the spiritual fact, before the mind's eye in a kind of stereopsis that gives depth and precision. One does not write at the level of the solely physical, but uses the physical to simultaneously depict the metaphysical and psychological. As Thoreau writes, "It is an advantage if words derived originally from nature, it is true, but which have been turned (*tropes*) from their primary signification to a moral sense are used" (1906, vol. 13, p. 145). Indeed, this is a serviceable definition of poetry, of metaphor—a language that reveals the mental and spiritual through the visible image, the tangible texture, and the very rhythms of its words.

One can also say that the Transcendentalists seek a language that engages and integrates the mind and the body, thus aligning their project with the wholistic, integrative impulse of Romantic education. The entire tradition of active learning concurs in the necessity of making each single word the object of constant thinking and imagining. Taking a word or expression in both a literal and figurative way is a microcosm of the undulation between action and contemplation, the particular and general, that Emerson depicts in "The American Scholar." As an example we can take Thoreau's use of "far fetched" in the parlor passage. In our ordinary usage, the two words have become yoked so that we no longer see them separately but take the entire phrase as a single word, a description for the ridiculous. But Thoreau brings our sensory imagination into play by recontextualizing the expression, by having our metaphors fetched through actual space, through slides and dumbwaiters.

Walden particularly brims over with sentences and paragraphs that force us to fasten words again to physical things, such as "In any weather, at any hour of the day or night, I have been anxious to improve the nick of time and notch it on my stick too" (1854/1971, p. 17). As we first read "the nick of time," we take it as the worn expression that it is, almost a single compound word. But as we read "notch it on my stick too," we have to reconsider the phrase in terms of its component words, both because of a restored physical context, and because of its syntax—the pronoun *it* makes us subliminally return to the earlier clause. The rest of the sentence restores the physical meaning of *nick* as a small line: "to stand on the meeting of two eternities, the past and the future, which is precisely the present moment; to toe that line" (p. 17). Thoreau is able to polish the dusty, tarnished lamps of our most worn language to release the trapped but powerful genie of the physical already residing there.

&**2**&

This book begns with the suggestion that in every educational situation there is a conflict between the immediate workings of intelligence and the institutional structures that work against this very act of mind. The movement toward concretizing diction is just a special case within writing of an analogous conflict between the given, self-perpetuating forms of language and the process of new creation. Even the very structures an individual teacher or writer creates in one moment can overly dictate or restrain the same mind in the following moment or day. In his book on American fiction aptly titled *City of Words,* Tony Tanner expresses this tension:

> It is my contention that many recent American writers are unusually aware of this quite fundamental and inescapable paradox: that to exist, a book, a vision, a system, like a person, has to have an outline—there can be no identity without contour. But contours signify arrest, they involve restraint and the acceptance of limits. . . . Between the nonidentity of pure fluidity and the fixity involved in all definitions—in words or in life—the American writer moves, and knows he moves. (1971, pp. 17–18)

Just as Emerson stands at the beginning of our tradition in his awareness of this tension in education, he is the first and perhaps the foremost of our writers to wrestle with it in the turns of his own sentences, in the very way he shapes its formulation, as we can see in this passage from his essay "Circles":

> For it is the inert effort of each thought, having formed itself into a circular wave of circumstance,—as, for instance, an empire, rules of an art, a local usage, a religious rite,—to heap itself on that ridge, and to solidify and hem in the life. But if the soul is quick and strong, it bursts over that boundary on all sides and expands another orbit, on the great deep, which also runs up into a high wave, with attempt again to stop and to bind. But the heart refuses to be imprisoned; in its first and narrowest pulses, it already tends outward with a vast force, and to immense and innumerable expansions. (1983, pp. 404–405)

The passage is a more general meditation on what we have seen Emerson arguing in "The American Scholar," that cultural creations tend to limit the mind by stopping the onrush of thinking at particular formulations, institutions, customs, and systems. However, that energy can be dissipated, ungraspable both by others and ourselves, if it is not given definite form and clarity. It is crucial to see that Emerson not only states the conflicts but also dramatizes them in the ways he moves the reader from word to word and from clause to clause. Each of these sentences, but especially the second, seems to run on beyond the point at which our syntactic ear expects it to stop, piling phrase upon clause upon phrase, until we finally reach some kind of closure, both semantic and grammatical, such as "to stop and bind," a wonderfully appropriate way for the sentence to end. These four monosyllabic words reinforce the sense of closure implied by their meaning. Further, the initial sound of "bind" alliterates effectively with the powerfully onomato-poetic verb "burst," and with what is being burst, "boundary." The accretion of words in the passage such as "and," "also," again," along with the anomaly of two consecutive sentences beginning with "But," signal and foreground the mind's reflecting and turning upon itself.

Emerson's work in general and "Circles" in particular can be seen as an attempt to create verbal structures but ones with enough spaces for breath and for escape, forms that will not harden into fixed belief. Toward the end of "Circles," he writes: "I unsettle all things. No facts are to me sacred; none are profane; I simply experiment, an endless seeker, with no Past at my back" (p. 412), but from the very beginning of the essay this sense of movement and transition is created by the texture of the prose: "The eye is the first circle; the horizon which it forms is the second; and throughout nature this primary figure is repeated without end. It is the highest emblem in the cipher of the world. St. Augustine described the nature of the God as a circle whose centre was everywhere, and its circumference nowhere" (p. 403). The first sentence is really made up of three independent clauses, each drawing a circle around the one before it. Further thinking makes it even richer and more complex. For one thing, as we look into an eye, we see more than one concentric circle. The notion of the eye forming the horizon is a wonderful enactment of Transcendentalist philosophy—there is indeed no horizon per se in exter-nal reality but rather a curved line created only by the viewer's perspective. The third clause generalizes on the first two and seems to move us gracefully into the following sentence, although there is a tension between the words "without end" and their syntactic position at the end of the sentence. In the third sentence, the image of the circle in making its ascent turns into some-thing unvisualizable, hardly a form at all. This kind of move suggests the lim-its of language; God cannot really be described—only, perhaps, de-scribed, initially written only to be unwritten. Harold Bloom (1982) has characterized Emersonian prose like this as "voice and not text, which is why it must splin-ter and destroy its own texts, subverting the paragraph through the autonomy of sentences, the aggressivity of aphorisms" (p. 171). Or, as Emerson himself wrote: "No sentence will hold the whole truth, and the only way in which we can be just, is by giving ourselves the lie" (1983, p. 585).

"Circles" is one response to a set of problems that pervade Emerson's writing career: how to reconcile inspired vision with crafted structure, the perpetual open-endedness of truth with the satisfaction of some kind of temporary closure, individual perception and voice with the restraints inherent in language and other cultural patterns. As David Smith (1984) puts it, "It is not the mind's constructs or results that have value, in other words, but the mind itself in all its restless moments of awakening, expression, obsessive entrenchment, and eventual self-overcoming" (p. 387). Thoreau, a little more cryptically, writes in *Walden*: "The volatile truth of our words should continually betray the inadequacy of the residual statement" (1854/1971, p. 325). And Emerson himself said, "And of books it must also be said that they underlie the same defect as all attempts to preserve and perpetuate the past utterance of thought. In the moment when it is spoken it is alive; when you gather it up and write it in firm letters of black and white in vellum or on iron stereotypes it has already lost its best life" (1959–1972, vol. 3, p. 47). It is ironic that Emerson and Thoreau are sometimes viewed by radical academics as Dead White Males in an established canon, since they opposed the very idea of canonicity itself.

Even though most other American writers have not accepted what they took as the metaphysics of the Transcendentalists, they have followed with varying degrees of historical awareness their vision of language. In doing so, they have created a national literature of the first order and, as Tony Tanner suggests, negotiated brilliantly between fluidity and stasis, vitality and formalism. Since American education has not been as successful, it may be worthwhile to look at one more literary example, the first three paragraphs of the third chapter of *Moby Dick*. The narrator, Ishmael, like Herman Melville himself, has been a country schoolteacher, but an inner restlessness and impulses but half perceived impel him toward a whaling voyage. As he confronts his own anxieties in an unfamiliar situation, he becomes transfixed by the mystery of a painting in the first port of call for his voyage.

[1] Entering that gable-ended Spouter-Inn, you found yourself in a wide, low straggling entry with old-fashioned wainscots, reminding one of the bulwarks of some condemned old craft. [2] On one side hung a very large oil painting so thoroughly besmoked, and every way defaced, that in the unequal crosslights by which you viewed it, it was only by diligent study and a series of systematic visits to it, and careful inquiry of the neighbors, that you could any way arrive at an understanding of its purpose. [3] Such unaccountable masses of shades and shadows, that at first you almost thought some ambitious young artist, in the time of the New England hags, had endeavored to delineate chaos bewitched. [4] But by dint of much and earnest contemplation, and oft repeated ponderings, and especially by throwing open the little window towards the back of the entry, you at last came to the conclusion that such an idea, however wild, might not be altogether unwarranted.

[5] But what most puzzled and confounded you was a long, limber, portentous, black mass of something hovering in the centre of the picture over

three blue, dim, perpendicular lines floating in a nameless yeast. [6] A boggy, soggy, squitchy picture truly, enough to drive a nervous man distracted. [7] Yet was there a sort of indefinite, half-attained, unimaginable sublimity about it that fairly froze you to it, till you involuntarily took an oath with yourself to find out what that marvelous painting meant. [8] Ever and anon a bright, but, alas, deceptive idea would dart you through. [9] —It's the Black Sea in a midnight gale. [10] —It's the unnatural combat of the four primal elements. [11] —It's a blasted heath. [12] —It's a Hyperborean winter scene. [13] —It's the breaking-up of the icebound stream of Time. [14] But at last all these fancies yielded to that one portentous something in the picture's midst. [15] *That* once found out, and all the rest were plain. [16] But stop; does it not bear a faint resemblance to a gigantic fish? even the great leviathan himself?

[17] In fact, the artist's design seemed this: a final theory of my own, partly based upon the aggregated opinions of many aged persons with whom I conversed upon the subject. [18] The picture represents a Cape-Horner in a great hurricane; the half-foundered ship weltering there with its three dismantled masts alone visible; and an exasperated whale, purposing to spring clean over the craft, is in the enormous act of impaling himself upon the three mast-head. (1851/2002, pp. 13–14)

The prose here captures Ishmael's mental landscape, which is as fluid as the painting itself. As we listen to the passage we hear how sentences such as the second and fourth go on past the point when our syntactical ears expect them to stop, just as those in "Circles." Instead of mitigating this sense of thought spilling beyond grammatical boundaries, Ishmael increases it by adding an extra "and" between the first and second items in a series as well as between the second and last, which seems part of a general strategy of redundancy in constructions such as "shades and shadows," "puzzled and confounded," "chaos bewitched," and "at last came to the conclusion" and the piling up of adjectives, especially in sentences 5 and 6 and 7.

We might be tempted to call such writing wordy, but if we remember that Ishmael is rendering a series of mental processes rather than giving us only a result, we can witness a mind throwing up excess verbiage and elaborate syntax to grapple with an unknown, dimly perceived, threatening reality. It is a mind that seeks some kind of ordered, rational naming but that also has the intellectual honesty not to settle for glib answers. The syntax is almost consistently involuted, complex, and hypotactic, except for the run of five simple, paratactic, anaphoric sentences, 9 through 13, the ideas in which, we are told beforehand, are "bright, but, alas, deceptive." It is as if anything clear and distinct must necessarily be erroneously oversimplified in Melville's world, where bright ideas cancel one another out after suggesting a feeling tone of foreboding, conflict, and chaos. The "but, alas" could be a signature phrase for this entire passage, in which four of the sentences begin with "But" and another with "Yet."

What we are witnessing is a mind always turning back on itself, a mind to which flight and flux is more important than rest and stasis, the unknown as important as the known. This disposition is registered further in a series of indefinites and negatives rather than positive identifications, words that have the grammatical form of substantives but function as transitives: "unaccountable," "nameless," "indefinite, half-attained, unimaginable," "mass of something," "that one portentous something." These last two phrases indicate a related strategy, that of anticlimax, of tantalizing the reader with some kind of closure but never fully delivering, a pattern shaping each paragraph as well as movement of the entire passage. Our normal reading expectations lead us to look for some resolution in the last sentence of a paragraph, but these expectations are comically frustrated, for example, by sentence 4, in which we are redundantly led to "at last come to the conclusion" (drumroll) only to learn that the hypothesis offered "might not be altogether unwarranted," where the tentative double negative undermines any sense of an ending. Similarly, the second paragraph "at last" builds to "that one portentous something," the italicized "*That*," which once discovered, reveals all. But the last sentence of this second paragraph turns out to be another question, indeed a double question, addressed to a reader who has even less chance than Ishmael of supplying an answer. And even in this interrogative form, the possible "resemblance" to the whale is only "faint."

To our incipient relief, the last sentence of the passage does seem straightforward, specific, indicative; perhaps *that* finally finds its referent. But as we reread, the clarity of the syntax is counterpointed by the semantic context. In the previous paragraph, Ishmael could barely tell if *that* was a whale at all. Now it can be seen as "exasperated," and even assigned intentionality: "purposing to spring clean over the craft." This tone of certainty is further qualified, put under erasure, by the first sentence of the paragraph: "In *fact*, the artist's design *seemed* this," the oxymoron of "*a* final *theory*," which is also at once "my own" yet "partly based on the aggregated opinions of many aged persons." Indeed, the final phrase particularly suggests an alternate reading where these sodden old salts are trying to terrify the green Ishmael even more with a "fish story" that has little basis either in physical possibility or in the Rorschach blot of the painting.

𐆐 3 𐆑

Suppose Melville had Ishmael say only that he saw a picture of a whale jumping over a ship with three dismantled masts in a hurricane. Would that statement be as true as the entire three paragraphs that actually appear in the novel? What would be lost if Ishmael had given us only his conclusion, his bottom line? To get more accurately at the differences between the two versions, we can borrow a distinction made by William James in his 1909 *The Meaning of Truth* (1987) between *ambulatory* and *saltatory: Ambulatory* describes "knowing as it exists concretely, while the other view only describes its results abstractly taken" (p. 898). *Ambulatory*, as the word implies, gives all the intermediate steps from not knowing to knowing, including missteps and detours, and includes any particulars from which generalizations are made; *saltatory* versions give us only answers and certainties, a leaping or jumping to conclusions, as the word suggests. Ideally, the two should not be opposed as either/or binaries, but should describe poles of a single continuum. But in practice, philosophers often discard the particulars and processes and pretend that the generalization is separable and truer. For James, however, the ambulation is an indispensable part of knowing, and the generalization becomes meaningless without it: "My thesis is that knowing here is *made* by the ambulation through the intervening experiences. . . . Intervening experiences are thus as indispensable foundations for a concrete relation of cognition as intervening space is for a relation of distance" (1987, p. 122). As James said of Louis Agassiz, "No one sees further into a generalization than his own knowledge of details extends" (1995, p. 122). This preference for ambulation was anticipated by one of Samuel Taylor Coleridge's notebook entries, suggesting continuities from him through Marsh and Emerson to James: "In all the processes of the Understanding the shortest way will be discovered the last. . . . The longest way is more near to the existing state of the mind, nearer to what, if left to myself on starting the thought, I should have thought next. The shortest way gives me the knowledge best; the longest way makes me more knowing" (1962, vol. 3, p. 3023)

We can now see that Melville gives us not only Ishmael's conclusion, his "final theory," but also the processes through which he ambulated to get to that point. We can weigh how much warrant and certainty are behind the statement, whether it is one of a number of possibilities or the indisputable answer to the confusion. And we see not only what sense Ishmael made of an apparent chaos but also a sense of that chaos itself. What we witness as readers is not simply the painted object but a mind in the process of seeing, imagining, reconstructing that object. As we read Ishmael's ponderings on the threshold of his adventure, we can begin to see parallels with our own reading of this elusive, seemingly amorphous text created by "some ambitious young artist"—Melville was only 31 when he wrote *Moby-Dick*. The passage becomes self-reflexive in that Ishmael's problems in reading the painting become ours in reading him and the entire book.

To make more concrete William James's argument, I can describe a difference in learning between my children and myself. I was taught the multiplication tables in a thoroughly saltatory way many years ago in an authoritarian urban school system. The tables were given to us on a piece of cardboard, and as we memorized each table and recited them in front of the teacher, we were given a gold star at the top of that table. My children, by contrast, went to a Montessori school where they worked on several different math manipulatives to help them understand the concept of multiplication. One was a bead chain that had a separation between the number of beads for each table. For, say, the sevens table they would count out the first grouping of beads and write down *7* on a tag they placed at this point, then *14* after the next grouping, and so on. In a saltatory way, both they and I could write down the answer *49* on a paper-and-pencil test that asked, "7 x 7 = ?" But our actual knowing—both the process and the extent—was quite different. If someone asked them, "Now, can you tell me how many 7s there are in 49?" they could answer, while I, if I were able to come up with anything, could say only that division would not be taught until the following grade. Similarly, my children could visualize that 7 beads times 7 beads can easily be arranged as a square, and that a cube is formed by 7 times 7 times 7, so the concept of a number squared and cubed had an immediacy and use for them that it did not for me.

William James's analysis provides a philosophical underpinning for the two main stylistic strategies we have just chartered: the urge to restore the concrete, physical dimension to language, to reembody it, and the desire to make language both register and represent the shifts and turnings of the active mind. William James's work in psychology, which generally preceded his philosophical work, can help us understand this latter desire through another distinction he makes, that between "substantive" and "transitive" states of mind and their parallels in grammar. In *The Principles of Psychology*, published in 1890 (1992), James depicts the mind as a "stream of consciousness," containing both flux and discrete images:

> When we take a general view of the wonderful stream of our consciousness, what strikes us first is the different pace of its parts. Like a bird's life, it seems to be an alternation of flights and perchings. The rhythm of language expresses this, where every thought is expressed in a sentence, and every sentence closed by a period. The resting-places are usually occupied by sensorial imaginations of some sort, whose peculiarity is that they can be held before the mind for an indefinite time, and contemplated without changing; the places of flight are filled with thoughts of relations, static or dynamic, that for the most part obtain between the matters contemplated in the periods of comparative rest.
>   *Let us call the resting-places the 'substantive parts,' and the places of flight the 'transitive parts,' of the stream of thought.* It then appears that our thinking tends at all times towards some other substantive part than the one from which it has been dislodged. And we may say that the main use of the transitive parts is to lead us from one substantive conclusion to another. (pp. 159–160)

Just as with *saltatory* and *ambulatory*, the terms "substantive" and "transitive" should not be taken as excluding opposites but as poles of a continuum, where each passes into the other. For James, the mind is primarily a whole, a unity that can be segmented into pieces only through introspective analysis and the razor of language. This view of the mind is radically different from that of Locke, in which the atoms of sensation are the primary building blocks in creating larger associations and ideas. Indeed, James and our entire tradition always remain skeptical about the adequacy of language to represent consciousness in all its wholistic flux. As Emerson wrote in *Nature*, "Words are finite organs of the infinite mind. They cannot cover the dimensions of what is in truth. They break, chop, and impoverish it" (1983, p. 30).

But some words are more adequate than others. A prose that emphasizes the relations between substantives as much as the substantive itself and that holds particulars and generalizations together in a dialectical tension, will best present and encourage the process of thinking. William James continues to suggest how such a language might work:

> There is not a conjunction or a preposition, and hardly an adverbial phrase, syntactic form, or inflection of voice, in human speech, that does not express some shading or other of relation which we at some moment actually feel to exist between the larger objects of our thought. If we speak objectively, it is the real relations that appear revealed; if we speak subjectively, it is the stream of consciousness that matches each of them by an inward coloring of its own. In either case the relations are numberless, and no existing language is capable of doing justice to all their shades.
>
> We ought to say a feeling of *and*, a feeling of *if*, a feeling of *but*, and a feeling of *by*, quite as readily as we say a feeling of *blue* or a feeling of *cold*. Yet we do not: so inveterate has our habit become of recognizing the existence of the substantive parts alone, that our language almost refuses to lend itself to any other use. (1992, p. 162)

The "almost" is well taken, since we have seen such a use of language by Emerson, Thoreau, and Melville, a style that emphasizes relations rather than substantives—that explodes substantives such as the form of the circle or descriptions of a painting to foreground the movement of thought in words such as *yet* and *however*. Indeed, as we look at Ishmael's language, a sense of *but* comes through more clearly than any particular content. Similarly, Emerson's prose enacts more the motion of his thought than any single, static "truth." In "Self-Reliance," Emerson suggests that such a stasis would be death: "Life only avails, not the having lived. Power ceases in the instant of repose; it resides in the moment of transition from a past to a new state, in the shooting of the gulf, in the darting to an aim" (1983, p. 271). What helps create the sense of movement here, aside from the present participles "shooting," and "darting" is the rapid succession and clustering of prepositions as the sentence moves on—"in," "of," "from," "to," "in," "of," "in," "to"—as we begin to feel that the functional words are taking over from the lexical words. Emerson returns to this theme in "Plato": "Every great artist has been such by synthesis. Our strength is transitional, alternating; or, shall I say, a thread of two strands. The sea-shore, sea seen from shore, shore seen from sea; the taste of two metals in contact; and our enlarged powers at the approach and departure of a friend" (p. 641). The first laconic and abstract statement is explained by the second, the latter part of which is a concrete image that restores a tactile quality to the earlier word "strength." The rest of the passage is a series of correspondences, moving from the concrete to the abstract, from the grammatically simple to the complex, without itself completing a syntactical sentence. The alliterative and onomatopoeic chiasmus—"sea seen from shore, shore seen from sea"—makes us aware that the word describes not so much a thing in itself as a set of relations, at once a boundary and a meeting place. The echoing *t* sounds both between "taste" and "two" and within "taste" and "contact" reinforce the sense of joining in the gustatory metaphor; and again we see a preponderance of prepositions as we move toward the end of the passage.

As expected for one who values the ambulatory over the saltatory, relations over entities, transitives over substantives, James elaborates further on this Emersonian vision, with his own vivid images and turns of phrase: "Life is in the transitions as much as in the terms connected; often, indeed, it seems to be there more emphatically, as if our spurts and sallies forward were the real firing-line of the battle, were like the thin line of flame advancing across the dry autumnal field which the farmer proceeds to burn" (1987, p. 1181).

What we have been trying to trace in earlier chapters as an American paideia is also and inextricably a linguistic philosophy and practice, in which a sense of reality as wholistic, fluid, always novel, and always under construction, implies and is implied by a related set of styles. No one has reconstructed this stylistic literary dimension better than Richard Poirier, most notably in *The Renewal of Literature: Emersonian Reflections* (1987) and *Poetry and Pragmatism* (1992a). Poirier writes in the latter: "Emerson never asks us to reclaim some heritage of civic virtue or rational virtues as these have been embedded, so it is assumed, in works of the past; he wants us instead to discover traces of productive energy that pass through a text or a composition or an author, pointing always beyond any one of them" (pp. 37–38). Poirier's recuperation of what he calls a tradition of linguistic skepticism includes virtually all the writers we have been discussing. He sees the lines of influence moving from Emerson through William James to modernist writers who were at Harvard during James's tenure there. The most succinct summary of his position can be found in Ross Posnock's review (1992) of *Poetry and Pragmatism*:

> Emerson both inspires the kind of criticism Poirier practices and initiates his book's principal concern—the experiments in language conducted by the "extended tribe of Waldo" (principally those mentioned above, but also Thoreau, Dickinson, Dewey, Whitman, and Williams). Poirier describes its members as "Emersonian pragmatists" who share a "liberating and creative suspicion as to the dependability of words and syntax," a skepticism premised on the fact that language is a cultural, historical inheritance that at once entraps us and incites our evasive action. This action manifests itself in the act of troping, whereby the human will turns language from predetermined meanings and fashions and refashions new figures to live by. To retain energy, troping can only be a "momentary stay against confusion" (to borrow Frost's famous phrase), a stay that functions as "less a solution," in James's words, than as a "program for more work." Poirier shows the incessant, antagonistic, and exhilarating effort of Emerson and the "line of force" he engenders to keep words in motion and thereby escape (or at least loosen) the gravitational pull of the conventions and conformity that make language possible in the first place. (pp. 157–158)

As noted, these literary artists handle the tensions between form and openness, between society and the self, between what T. S. Eliot calls tradition and the individual talent, much more successfully than have American educators. American literature has become world literature, best known for its tradition of breaking with tradition, for its exuberant and perpetual incorporating of innovation. Meanwhile, American education is as inert and lifeless as a glacier. The contest between fluidity and stasis, between thinking and habit, has been repeatedly decided in favor of the latter.

There is a certain urgency, then, in seeing whether American teachers can learn something from American writers. Indeed, Poirier himself seemed to have envisioned such a possibility when he wrote:

> The greatest cultural accomplishment of pragmatism remains the least noticed, and one which it never clearly enunciates as a primary motive even to itself. It managed to transfer from literature a kind of linguistic activity essential to literature's continuing life but which it now wants effectively to direct at the discourses of social, cultural, and other public formations, always with an eye to their change or renewal. (1992b, p. 86)

A curious thing about this passage is that it is in the past tense. Yet it is difficult to find examples of this kind of conscious reshaping of our public formations, especially education, through the kinds of consciousness encouraged by philosophical pragmatism. Except for some of the small-scale experiments examined in this book, American education has stood in antithetical relation to such a vision. Further, Poirier and other academics leading the current revival of pragmatism have shown little interest in using their ideas to restructure even their own classrooms, let alone their own institutions. Only when we ourselves eliminate this gap between what we say and what we do can we move these insights about language into the social realm.

🐦 **4** 🐦

The question remains: how to use these insights about language and thought as a force for educational reform. We can begin with how we educate our educators. Reading some of the textbooks prepared for courses such as the History and/or Philosophy of Education or Social Foundations of American Education, I found that the complex thinkers we have been dealing with were reduced to the print equivalent of sound bites. The very turns of language, the protean play of thought that characterize and even constitute the active mind become homogenized into a single bland pudding. Take the following example from a typical text, *America's Teachers* (1998), by Joseph W. Newman:

> Wedded as they are to change and adaptation, pragmatists do not believe in absolute and unchanging truth. For pragmatists, truth is what works. Truth is relative because what works for one person may not for another, just as what works at one time or in one place or in one society may not work in another. Pragmatists admit the concept of relative truth, applied to morality, could lead to chaos. (p. 206)

And so on. While it is hard to disagree with any of the precedng quote, it is also hard to extract from it any sense of the nature and quality of pragmatist thinking. Although intended for university students, the prose rates a grade level of 7.7 on the Flesch-Kincaid scale. But despite this syntactic simplicity, it is not particularly clear how we move from one sentence to the next. Complex ideas are reduced to self-contained bumper sticker mottoes such as "Truth is what works," or banalities such as "What works for one person may not for another," and there are no concrete examples to anchor these vapidities. Ironically for a paragraph about pragmatism, there are no feelings of *if* or *but*.

One of the reasons this prose fails is that "ideas" are perhaps the least important part of a piece of writing by Emerson or Melville or James. To simply summarize and paraphrase is to create a collection of perches or resting places without the crucial flights and transitions; it is more like taxidermy than bird-watching. These Cliff's Notes of the Mind parallel the "cultural literacy" movement at the K–12 level. For example, the appendix to E. D. Hirsch Jr.'s *Cultural Literacy: What Every American Needs to Know* (1987), lists "Emerson, Ralph Waldo," as well as "James, Henry," and "James, William," with Jesse between the two of them, as though he were yet another family member (p. 181). One wonders how the students in the Core Knowledge schools that Hirsch's work has inspired come to "know" these figures. Cultural conservatives such as Hirsch and Allan Bloom offer us not so much a defense of reading as a defense of someone else having once read. As Saul Bellow has his character Herzog say, "We mustn't forget how quickly the visions of genius become the canned goods of the intellectuals" (1964, pp. 74–75).

The language of textbooks, unfortunately, is only a special case of a problem that pervades the academic discipline of education, which has difficulty finding a language to talk about the classroom that is neither trivial and anecdotal nor pretentiously abstract. Most often the general bias of schools and departments of education is toward active, humane, student-centered methods, but this impulse is thwarted by a soporific style constantly at odds with the dynamics of reform. Here is an example from what otherwise could have been a valuable book edited by Nadine Lambert and Barbara McCombs, *How Students Learn: Reforming Schools Through Learner-Centered Education* (1998), published by the American Psychological Association to inform laypersons about empirical studies of learning. While I was pleased to learn that these studies support the same views of learning as those in the present book, my mind numbed at the language, as in this example by Barbara McCombs:

> *Empowerment* in this model is reciprocal and is embodied in training for parents, teachers, administrators, and students. As parents, teachers, and administrators develop positive belief systems in themselves and their students, and as they acquire a higher level understanding of student's inherent mental health and how to uncover it through enhanced communication and interactions (will component), they are empowered to create a positive emotional climate and to develop enhanced interpersonal relationships with their students that embody qualities of mutual trust, respect, caring, and concern (social support component). As students display enhanced will and skill, teachers, parents, and administrators are empowered by seeing and realizing how they can nurture children's inner potential to learn and develop in positive ways. In addition, administrators are empowered by seeing and realizing how they can nurture teachers' inner potential for creative and wise educational practices that lead to enhanced student outcomes. (p. 393)

The diction is Latinate, polysyllabic, and repetitive, clogged by near-meaningless three-word noun phrases such as "positive emotional climate" and "enhanced personal relationships." If there are realities to which these composite abstractions relate, they have long since evaporated from the text. The problem underlying these difficulties is the lack of steady thinking in the process of writing. Does the writer stop to consider whether "mutual trust, respect, caring, and concern" are different elements or repetitive ways of talking about the same thing? Is "inner potential"—used twice—different from some kind of outer potential? And do administrators need to both "see" and "realize" this "inner potential"?

Another, more recent style of thoughtless educational writing has been influenced by the jargon of postmodernism, especially as it appears in much current literary criticism. Here is a sentence written by Peter Trifonas, the editor of *Revolutionary Pedagogies: Cultural Politics, Instituting Education, and the Discourse of Theory* (2000):

> Although this characterization of the chapters presented in this volume is self-consciously forefronted by the title of the anthology (and any title worthy of the appellation "title" should surely thematize the heterogeneity of a body of work so as to do just that!), the text does not speak only to those who have embraced the ethical value of opening the empirico-conceptual and epistemic limits of one's work and oneself to the risk of less than canonical modes of thinking. (p. xi)

Verbose, abstract, polysyllabic, this text was produced by a writer who is deaf to the sound of his own words. All three passages keep the reader at bay, the first two through a patronizing scorn of his or her intelligence, the third through an involuted and exclusionary language that makes sense, if at all, only to other initiates—making for a discourse that undercuts in its very utterance its political pretenses to help build a democratic community. If the language in which we write about education is to actually improve it, we need to create a continuity between it and the ways in which we speak to our colleagues and students at our best, a language imbued with an empathic desire to communicate, a self-awareness, and a responsiveness to ideas that arise through the act of writing itself.

In his chapter on the language of education in *Actual Minds, Possible Worlds* (1986), Jerome Bruner seeks such continuities. For Bruner, "a culture is constantly in process of being recreated as it is interpreted and negotiated by its members" (p. 123). There are certain institutions such as storytelling, science, and law that particularly serve the role of what Bruner calls a "forum" for these kinds of negotiations and explorings, and education should be one of the most central forums, giving "its participants a role in constantly making and remaking the culture—an *active* role as participants rather than as performing spectators who play out their canonical roles according to rule when the appropriate cues occur" (p. 123).

Bruner then gives an example from his own experience as a student of how the language of education can facilitate this process:

> I recall a teacher, her name was Miss Orcutt, who made a statement in class, "It is a very puzzling thing not that water turns to ice at 32 degrees Fahrenheit, but that it should change from a liquid into a solid." She then went on to give us an intuitive account of Brownian movement and of molecules, expressing a sense of wonder that matched, indeed bettered, the sense of wonder I felt at that age (around 10) about everything I turned my mind to. . . . In effect, she was inviting me to extend *my* world of wonder to encompass *hers*. She was not just *informing* me. She was, rather, negotiating the world of wonder and possibility. Molecules, solids, liquids, movement were not facts; they were to be used in pondering and imagining. Miss Orcutt was the rarity. She was a human event, not a transmission device. (p. 126)

Unlike his fellow psychologist Barbara McCombs, Bruner speaks not as a detached clinician but in an immediately personal, concrete, and ambulatory way. His language suggests the world we live in is extraordinary to the point of the miraculous, and that not the least miracle is the ability of the human mind to make some sense of it.

Miss Orcutt's language "invites"—to use Bruner's apt verb—her students to participate in the act of discovery in ways similar to how literary writers invite the reader to engage in the process of discovery. While as teachers we may not be able to speak in Emersonian or Melvillean prose, we can use a language that is more affective (hence effective) and engaging, more responsive to alternative possibilities. But we too use a classroom language that is less personal, less inquisitive, and less qualified than what we use in other situations. Bruner cites a study by his wife, Carol Feldman, who was

> interested in the extent to which teacher's stances toward their subject indicate some sense of the hypothetical nature of knowledge, its uncertainty, its invitation to further thought. She chose as an index the use of modal auxiliary markers in teachers' talk to students and in their talk to each other in the staff room, distinguishing between expressions that contained modals of uncertainty and probability (like *might, could,* and so on) and expressions not so marked. Modals expressing a stance of uncertainty or doubt in teacher talk to teachers far outnumbered their occurrence in teacher talk to students. The world that the teachers were presenting to their students was a far more settled, far less hypothetical, far less negotiatory world than the one they were offering to their colleagues. (p. 126)

Neither Bruner nor Feldman (C. F. Feldman & J. V. Wertsch, 1976) speculate in depth on the reasons for this situation, but it has a great deal to do with a teacher's sense of role and authority in the classroom. The impulse behind many teaching behaviors, especially those of beginners, is to convince the students and themselves that they really deserve to be where they are, that they know what they are talking about. On their side, students often display the speech characteristics that are the opposite of their seemingly self-assured teachers for a complementary reason—the fear of being "wrong." They will often hedge their bets by prefacing their remarks with "This may be beside the point but . . ." or "I don't know if this is what you're looking for, but . . ."

An essential aspect of active learning for both teachers and students, then, is the ability to monitor, reflect upon, and analyze one's own language. Every utterance we make has not only content, but also a stance toward that content and toward reality in general; each word if heard or read rightly is a witness to the absence or presence of mind behind it.

CHAPTER 6

Uniting the Child and the Curriculum:
John Dewey

It is not propositions, not new dogmas and the logical exposition of the world that are our first need, but to watch and tenderly cherish the intellectual and moral sensibilities and woo them to stay and make their home with us.

        —Ralph Waldo Emerson, quoted by John Dewey

The business of education is rather to liberate the young from reviving and retraversing the past than to lead them to a recapitulation of it.

        —John Dewey

PERHAPS THE SINGLE most harmful misconception in the history of American education is that John Dewey's ideas have already been tried on a widespread scale and found wanting. Dewey's name has sometimes been co-opted by advocates of narrowly vocational education, of life-adjustment curricula, and of permissiveness, all of which are contrary to the spirit of his work. It is ironic that perhaps the greatest proponent of the steady, unflinching application of mind in education has been so often misappropriated by movements encouraging mindlessness. Because of this misappropriation, even well-informed conservative critics of education tend to blame Dewey himself and react against his work by falling back on a traditionalism that is just as one-sided as these misappropriations, thus continuing the vicious cycle of setting progressives against conservatives and social against cognitive development. The most important aspect of Dewey's thought is that it is wholistic, that it seeks to join the act of mind to our daily actions, the accumulated wisdom of the culture to the immediate situation of the student. Dewey himself integrated his theory with his practice in his laboratory school at the University of Chicago (1896–1904), and what he discovered and enacted there has crucial lessons for us. And yet we continue to ride the pendulum between progressivism and traditionalism as each extreme by itself proves inadequate. We are still retreating from the challenge of constant mindfulness and radical democracy that Dewey poses to our practice.

The relation between conceptual thought and immediate experience was not abstract or external for Dewey, but the central issue in his own intellectual history. This personal development recapitulates a larger arc in the history of philosophy, from system to experience, from dualism to integration, or, as Dewey puts it in a brief memoir we will draw upon, "from absolutism to experimentalism." When Dewey left his position as a high school teacher to study philosophy at Johns Hopkins, he found himself particularly attracted to Hegelianism. As Dewey recounts, the sources of his attraction to Hegel were deeply personal, as we have seen:

> There were . . . also "subjective" reasons for the appeal that Hegel's thought made to me; it supplied a demand for unification that was doubtless an intense emotional craving, and yet was a hunger that only an intellectualized subject-matter could satisfy. . . . But the sense of divisions and separations that were, I suppose, borne in upon me as a consequence of a heritage of New England culture, divisions by way of isolation of self from the world, of soul from body, of nature from God, brought a painful oppression. . . . an inward laceration. . . . Hegel's synthesis of subject and object, matter and spirit, the divine and the human, was, however, no mere intellectual formula; it operated as an immense release, a liberation. (1930, p. 19)

Some of these separations, as we have seen, are important to form an ego, an identity of our own, separate from family, society, and our own unconscious; but for Dewey, as for Fuller and Adams, the process can be exacerbated beyond the necessary by certain cultural conditions—a religious orientation that too starkly opposes soul to body and divides people into saved and damned, a too rigid separation of gendered characteristics, a too impermeable barrier between the contemplative and the active.

But Hegel did not hold a permanent solution either intellectual or psychological, for Dewey then talks about "drifting away" (p. 20) from the German philosopher in the following 15 years: "The form, the schematism of his system now seems to me artificial to the last degree" (p. 21). Dewey scholars disagree on when he finally broke with Hegel, but certainly by the time he arrived as a professor at the new University of Chicago in 1894, he had left the Absolute behind him, increasingly convinced that there was no need to posit any entity beyond experience itself to create meaning and value. While Hegel's dialectic made logic a much more supple instrument than it had been, it was still ultimately only logic, and thus had a problematic relationship to any kind of integration between conscious and unconscious. For

Dewey, all logic is necessarily abstract, so to use it as the basis of a total system of the world is to take "only one moment of spirit" to "determine the nature of the whole" (1886/1969, pp. 164–165). Although in this sketch Dewey cites William James as his major outside influence, Emerson's vision of synthesis stands behind both these Pragmatists.

Dewey's 1903 tribute to Emerson is his most detailed elaboration of the viewpoint that all three came to share. Dewey reconceives the notion of logic by pointing to a more "finely wrought" sense of the term; he quotes Emerson as saying, "Logic is the procession or proportionate unfolding of the intuition" (Dewey, 1929, p. 69). This would seem to stand the traditional definition of logic on its head, but more accurately it posits a kind of logic intimately related to the processes of its own discovery, ambulatory as opposed to saltatory. For Emerson, Dewey says, "perception was more potent than reasoning; the deliverances of intercourse more to be desired than the chains of discourse; the surprise of reception more demonstrative than the conclusions of intentional proof" (p. 70). At this point, Dewey notices himself arguing that Emerson is more like a poet or artist than a philosopher.

Dewey then suggests that Emerson is the kind of philosopher who brings philosophy down to the quotidian, because he "takes the distinctions and classifications which to most philosophers are true in and of and because of their systems, and makes them true of life, of the common experience of the everyday man" (p. 73). Dewey sees in Emerson one who holds all philosophers "to the test of trial by the service rendered the present and immediate experience" (p. 74). In a most powerful passage, the voices of Emerson and Dewey fuse in an attack on the excluding elitism of most philosophy:

> Against creed and system, convention and institution, Emerson stands for restoring to the common man that which in the name of religion, of philosophy, of art and of morality, has been embezzled from the common store and appropriated to sectarian and class use. Beyond any one we know of, Emerson has comprehended and declared how such malversation makes truth decline from its simplicity, and in becoming partial and owned, becomes a puzzle and trick for theologian, metaphysician and litterateur. (p. 75)

In the process of praising Emerson, Dewey himself reprises "The American Scholar" by delineating a native tradition in philosophy qualitatively different from that of Europe. Dewey did not simply move from one "ism" to another but to a new conception of the philosophical enterprise common to all the figures we have already examined but never set forth in as much sweep and detail. As Louis Menand (2001) points out, this conception is not so much about ideas as how we hold ideas. Dewey's move away from a German idealism was just as liberating as James Marsh's move toward it, because each process liberated the thinking of its time from the prison-house of the conventional, suggesting that any paradigm can restrict the mind when it becomes an implicit worldview instead of a provisional tool consciously constructed by the individual.

We can further understand Dewey's shift by noting what he says about the difference in his writing. He recounts that his early articles, the first two of which were accepted by William Torrey Harris for the *Journal of Speculative Philosophy,* were highly schematic and formal, written with an ease and clarity that even Dewey admits is lacking in his later writing:

> I imagine that my development has been controlled largely by a struggle between a native inclination toward the schematic and formally logical, and those incidents of personal experience that compelled me to take account of actual material. . . . During the time when the schematic interest predominated, writing was comparatively easy; there were even compliments upon the clearness of my style. Since then thinking and writing have been hard work. It is easy to give way to the dialectic development of a theme; the pressure of concrete experiences was, however, sufficiently heavy, so that a sense of intellectual honesty prevented a surrender to that course. . . . On the other hand, the formal interest persisted, so that there was an inner demand for an intellectual technique that would be consistent and yet capable of flexible adaptation to the concrete diversity of experienced things. For that very reason I have been acutely aware . . . of a tendency of other thinkers and writers to achieve a specious lucidity and simplicity by the mere process of ignoring considerations which a greater respect for concrete materials of experience would have forced upon them. (1930, pp. 16–17)

On one level, this is an apologia for a writing style that no one would judge dazzling. Oliver Wendell Holmes's comment on it has become famous: "So methought God would have spoken had He been inarticulate but keenly desirous to tell how it was" (1941, vol. 2, p. 287). But this remark implicitly acknowledges Dewey's own analysis of a struggle between final, formulated wisdom and the particulars that fly in the face of any general truth. It would be letting Dewey off too easily to agree that intellectual honesty is incompatible with good writing; after all, we have seen how writers such as Emerson and Thoreau were able to exploit this tension to give their writing a sinewy strength, coloring philosophical ideas with the heft and texture of the daily. Still, there is a certain fresh if awkward quality in Dewey's best writing that comes from a willingness to press thought beyond the point where it has become hardened, to confront it again with the fluid realities it has tried to escape.

In a larger sense, Dewey's comments here show how a central problem of both education and prose style, the tension between form and openness, was for him a personal conflict in each act of writing and thinking. His moves toward solutions, then, have a perspicacity and immediacy found in few other writers on education. Dewey is able to make the problems of education continuous with the philosophical struggles he tries to mediate in writing about them. So the problem with Dewey's partial followers is particularly tragic in that his process of struggling with thought was so often later reduced to the kind of textbook summaries lamented in the precedng chapter. But before that happened, there was a time when his laboratory school and his writing created a dialectic more productive than anything found within the limits of academic philosophy itself. No verbal formulation alone could have brought about the integration, the healing of those inward lacerations, that Dewey yearned for; this could be satisfied only by relating his ideas to minded action.

 2

Dewey says that to understand his work as a philosopher, it is crucial to see

> the importance that the practice and theory of education have had for me: especially the education of the young. . . . I can recall but one critic who has suggested that my thinking has been too much permeated by interest in education . . . philosophers in general, although they are themselves usually teachers, have not taken education with sufficient seriousness for it to occur to them that any rational person could actually think it possible that philosophizing should focus about education as the supreme human interest in which, moreover, other problems, cosmological, moral, logical, come to a head. (1930, pp. 22–23)

Dewey, then, found in education the possibilities for integration that he sought in Hegel, a deepening relation between thinking and action, a way to relate abstract thought to human endeavor, intellectual interest to social concern.

Dewey wrote this after his direct involvement with the education of children was long over, but he envisioned a unifying and vitalizing effect even before he began, as this letter to his wife on his arrival at the University of Chicago reveals: "I sometimes think I will drop teaching phil—directly, & teach it via *pedagogy*. When you think of the thousands & thousands of young 'uns who are practically being ruined negatively if not positively in the Chicago schools every year, it is enough to make you go out & howl on the street corners like the Salvation Army" (Menand, 2001, p. 319). Dewey accepted the Chicago position because it made him head of three departments whose work he wished to integrate—philosophy, psychology, and education.

> There is an image of a school growing up in my mind all the time; a school where some actual & literal constructive activity shall be the centre & source of the whole thing, & from which the work should always be growing out in two directions—one the social bearings of that constructive industry, the other the contact with nature which supplies it with its materials. I can see theoretically, how the carpentry involved in building a model house should be the centre of a social training on one side, & a scientific on the other, all held within the grasp of a positive concrete physical habit of eye & hand. . . . The school is the one form of social life which is abstracted & under control— which is directly experimental, and if philosophy is ever to be an experimental science, the construction of a school is its starting point. (pp. 319–320)

The result is the laboratory school: the use of common occupations to teach both social and cognitive skills, the relation between physical work and mental growth, the notion of school as a community within itself. The school was conceived as working for Dewey and his colleagues as it would for the children: one's own acts of doing were to be the primary educational medium. Ideas would take form and life from being put into practice, which in turn would refine those ideas and yield more. There would be what psychologists call parallel process: The philosophers and educators would learn in the same way as the students. And they would not spin their ideas out of only their reading or their isolate selves but develop them in a social context of mutual endeavor.

So for Dewey the school was not associated with that bland category "community service," but was at the heart of a new conception of philosophy. In his preface to the most important source book on the school, he writes: "Ideas, even as ideas, are incomplete and tentative until they are employed in application to objects in action and are thus developed, corrected, and tested" (Mayhew & Edwards, 1936, p. 3). Dewey saw the rigidities of school as an institution analogous to the formal structures of logic and system-building; both resist the immediacies of experienced life: "The concrete circumstances of school life introduce many factors that are not foreseen and taken account of in theory. This is as formal and static as the life of teachers and children in school is moving and vital" (p. 11). Dewey, then, saw an experimental school not simply as a laboratory for ways to improve education but as one for the study and advance of philosophy and psychology. Teaching seemed to him the ideal arena to both test and discover ideas about how people learn (psychology), how the individual mind relates to group effort (social and moral philosophy), and how the mind relates to the world (epistemology).

The central problem for Dewey was how to reconcile the needs of the individual child with the larger arena of human culture. Arthur Wirth (1966) puts it this way:

While concentrating on how to organize, divide, and cover the content of knowledge, one may make the mistaken assumption that this, of itself, will ensure that learning will automatically be absorbed by the student. This leads to the other side of the educational problem. Experience is existentially real only in the lives of specific human beings. *The* problem for education is how to organize the meanings, the insights, the habits of mind into a functional pattern that will eventually become a part of the life and character of each student. Dewey wrestled constantly with the question of how to relate the logical *and* the psychological. (pp. 89–90)

In his summa on the subject, *Democracy and Education*, Dewey reformulates the problem as follows: "There is the standing danger that the material of formal instruction will be merely the subject matter of the schools isolated from the subject matter of life-experience. The permanent social interests are likely to be lost from view" (1916/1980, p. 11).

In "My Pedagogic Creed," written as the laboratory school was first taking shape, Dewey gives us an impassioned statement of the problem along with some solutions. The piece begins by Dewey's discussing "What Education Is"; education "proceeds by the participation of the individual in the social consciousness of the race" (1887/1972, p. 84). Dewey uses the example of language learning to suggest how education is constructive and transactive between the individual and the social environment: "Through the response to the child's instinctive babblings the child comes to know what those babblings mean; they are transformed into articulate language and thus the child is introduced into the consolidated wealth of ideas and emotions which are now summed up in language" (p. 84). Dewey sees the first steps in learning as initiated through the direct action of the child himself or herself. But children can make their needs and feelings known only through the social medium of language, which existed before them and which necessarily shapes and channels these personal needs, which indeed begins to structure the incipient consciousness. What happens in healthy development within the family is that there is a dynamic dialectic between the child adopting social modes and of thinking and doing and the family through empathy and interpretation understanding the uniqueness of the child.

What schools should do is continue this kind of dynamic interaction, which Dewey makes explicit in the second section, "What the School Is":

Education being a social process, the school is simply that form of community life in which all the agencies are concentrated that will be most effective in bringing the child to share in the inherited resources of the race, and to use his own powers for social ends. I believe that education, therefore, is a process of living and not a preparation for future living. (pp. 86–87)

Dewey posits that the knowledge needed to help the child function in society cannot effectively be taught by extracting and abstracting what we think that knowledge will be in the future and somehow infusing it in the student through textbooks; rather, it can be developed only in an environment where it is determined at least in part by the children themselves in performing social and physical tasks. As he writes in *The School and Society,* "The school itself shall be made a genuine form of active community life, instead of a place set apart in which to learn lessons" (1899/1976a, p. 10).

The main concept through which these ideals were embodied in the Laboratory School was that of the "occupations" of humanity, having children actively engage in practical necessities of feeding, sheltering, and clothing. In "My Pedagogic Creed" Dewey alludes to these:

> I believe accordingly that the primary basis of education is in the child's powers at work along the same general constructive lines as those which have brought civilization into being. I believe that the only way to make the child conscious of his social heritage is to enable him to perform those fundamental types of activity which make civilization what it is. (1887/1972, pp. 89–90)

This notion of occupations can easily be misinterpreted and it has been, as merely practical or anti-intellectual. But Dewey sees intelligence developing from physical understanding to more conceptual thinking: "I believe that the active side precedes the passive in the development of the child nature; that expression comes before conscious impression; that the muscular development precedes the sensory; that movements come before conscious sensations" (p. 91). Dewey does not want to train children to become simply cooks or carpenters. Just as he believes that in history, intelligence arises in relation to the need for action, so this kind of action—social at least as much as physical—serves as the basis for later processes of thinking.

 3

The laboratory school provides a context for Dewey's essay "The Child and the Curriculum," which I view as second only to "The American Scholar" as a central manifesto for active learning. Like the entire tradition, it shows us ways out of the stalemate between student-centered and traditional approaches. Dewey begins with the issue of conflict and contradiction in educational policy:

> Any significant problem involves conditions that for the moment contradict each other. Solution comes only by getting away from the meaning of terms

that is already fixed upon and coming to see the conditions from another point of view, and hence in a fresh light. . . . Easier than thinking with surrender of already formed ideas and detachment from facts already learned, is to just stick by what is already said, looking about for something with which to buttress it against attack. (1902/1976c, p. 273)

Dewey here is following in the footsteps of Emerson, who said, "By going one step farther back in thought, discordant opinions are reconciled, by being seen to be two extremes of one principle" (1983, p. 407). It is Dewey's brilliance in the essay to show how convincingly the notion can be applied to the opposition set forth in the title and the parallel terms associated with each:

"Discipline" is the watchword of those who magnify the course of study; "interest" that of those who blazon "The Child" upon their banner. The standpoint of the former is logical; that of the latter psychological. The first emphasizes the necessity of adequate training and scholarship on the part of the teacher; the latter that of need of sympathy with the child, and knowledge of his natural instincts. "Guidance and control" are the catchwords of one school; "freedom and initiative" of the other. Law is asserted here; spontaneity proclaimed there. The old, the conservation of what has been achieved in the pain and toil of the ages, is dear to the one; the new, change, progress, wins the affection of the other. Inertness and routine, chaos and anarchism are accusations bandied back and forth. (1902/1976c, p. 277)

Before trying to reconcile them, Dewey goes even further to show the opposition between the children's ways of knowing and the kind that the curriculum would force on them. The child's world is narrow and personal; it is integral and unified as he or she passes from one activity to another without being aware of abrupt transitions. The universe is "fluid and fluent; its contents dissolve and re-form with amazing rapidity" (p. 274). In school, by contrast, the various studies "divide and fractionalize the world. . . . Facts are torn away from their original place in experience and rearranged with reference to some general principle" (p. 274). The world becomes vastly extended in time and space, but in doing so becomes abstract, compartmentalized, impersonal.

Dewey takes pains to extensively formulate each position. The adherents of the curriculum say:

Ignore and minimize the child's individual peculiarities, whims, and experiences. . . . As educators our work is precisely to substitute for these superficial and casual affairs stable and well-ordered realities; and these are found in studies and lessons. Subdivide each topic into studies; each study into lessons; each lesson into specific facts and formulae. Let the child proceed step by step to master each one of these separate parts, and at last he will have covered the entire ground. (p. 276)

The other group says, "The child is the center, and the end. His development, his growth, is the ideal. . . . Learning is active. It involves reaching out of the mind. It involves organic assimilation starting from within" (p. 276).

One of the reasons Dewey can so well ventriloquize both positions is that he had close ties to each. To fully appreciate the genius of Dewey's solution, we must recontextualize it, reinstate it in its historical moment. By the late 1890s, the curriculum as the shaping force in education had found an eloquent philosophical spokesman in the person of William Torrey Harris, whom we have already encountered. Harris, whom we first saw as a young enthusiast of Alcott, was a Hegelian, editor of the *Journal of Speculative Philosophy*, the first philosophical journal in America not affiliated with a religious group. He accepted Dewey's first three articles; his belated but commendatory acceptance of the first had encouraged the young man to pursue his inclination to enroll in graduate study in philosophy. Harris went on be become first superintendent of schools for St. Louis, and then U.S. commissioner of education. He viewed the elementary curriculum as the "five windows of the soul"—arithmetic, geography, history, grammar, and literature—that rescued the young mind from its immediate narrowness and made it a part of the collective development of the race. Through this process the child's will and impulse control were also strengthened.

Opposed to Harris's sense of education as bringing children as efficiently as possible into the adult world were advocates of "child-study," led by one of Dewey's teachers at Johns Hopkins, G. Stanley Hall, and supported by American followers of the German educational philosopher Johann Herbart, a group with which Dewey was for a time allied. These child-study adherents combined a Rousseau-like sentimentality about nature and children with a kind of anthropological Darwinism that saw every individual recapitulating in his or her development the cultural history of the race. Younger children should be engaged with "primitive" cultures, adolescents with feudalism, and so on, although as Dewey pointed out, in practice this engagement often took only the vitiated form of reading later literary imitations of these cultures, such as Longfellow's *Hiawatha*. The main problem for Dewey, though, was the way this group placed their own abstract and sweeping theory over direct observation of the children before them. Although Dewey felt a certain affinity for the notion of inner development, the imposition of this theory on the curriculum was no less arbitrary and a priori than that of the Hegelians. Further, Dewey was disturbed by the intrinsic anti-intellectualism of the movement, whereby the child's well-being was stressed over any directed development of the mind. For Dewey, health was only a precondition for real mental growth, not an end in itself.

It is not that both sides were completely wrong-headed, but more that each side had only part of the truth and that partiality created a distorted and stunted education. Dewey's solution combined a sense of bipolar unity like that of Coleridge and Marsh with an epistemological twist on the recapitulation theory:

> Abandon the notion of subject-matter as something fixed and ready-made in itself, outside the child's experience; cease thinking of the child's experience as also something hard and fast; see it as something fluent, embryonic, vital; and we realize that the child and the curriculum are simply two limits which define a single process. Just as two points define a straight line, so the present standpoint of the child and the facts and truths of studies define instruction. It is continuous reconstruction, moving from the child's present experience out into that represented by the organized bodies of truth that we call studies . . . the initial and final terms of one reality. (p. 278)

As the child engages in social and intellectual activities (the two, as we have seen, are nearly synonymous in Dewey's thought, since social effort requires linguistic formulation), his or her mind will of itself move in the direction of the symbolic and abstract. The need for communication and the urge toward mastery will generate the same processes by which the human race created and developed culture. Conversely, the curriculum itself is merely a cross-section or snapshot of a point in time of this cultural advancement. What traditional education does is simply to take this snapshot and present it to students as a finished product in the most formal and abstract way.

What happens, as Emerson earlier suggested in "The American Scholar," is that the abstractions mean nothing to students when they are divorced from the processes from which they arose. To make the point that both Dewey's critics and his progressive followers often miss, Dewey is not against teaching children the intellectual constructs they need, only against the divorce of these constructs from a comprehensible context, one that transforms them from isolated, reified givens into instruments with which to pursue further thought:

> There is a sense in which it is impossible to value too highly the formal and the symbolic. The genuine form, the real symbol, serve as methods in the holding and discovery of truth. They are tools by which the individual pushes out most surely and widely into unexplored areas. They are the means by which he brings to bear whatever of reality he has succeeded in gaining in past searching. But this happens only when the symbol really symbolizes—when it stands for and sums up in shorthand actual experiences which the individual has already gone through. (p. 286)

Dewey, like Emerson, has seemed anti-intellectual to some in stressing the concrete and experiential, but both do so only because formal schooling has overstressed the opposite qualities.

The central task of education, then, is to immerse the child in the total process of symbol construction, of reenacting the source of the symbol by restoring the conditions that led to its creation—much as in the experience of my children learning multiplication through manipulatives. Education becomes a two-way street: the culture in general and the particular adults involved refresh their thinking by engaging in its etymology, just as Emerson's poet restores to language its initial specificity and dynamism. At the same time as we introduce our concepts to children, our own sense of them becomes unstiffened. In *Democracy and Education*, Dewey writes: "With respect to the development of powers devoted to coping with specific scientific and economic problems we may say that the child should be growing in manhood. With respect to sympathetic curiosity, unbiased responsiveness, and openness of mind, we may say that the adult should be growing in childlikeness" (1916/1980, p. 55). A specific case of Dewey himself learning from the children is given in "The School and Society": "I did not know until the children told me, that the reason for the late development of the cotton industry as compared with the woolen is that cotton fibre is so very difficult to free by hand from the seeds" (1899/1976a, p. 14).

Dewey's school was structured on the notion of letting the students' minds follow this entire cycle from action to thought back to action and so on. Dewey mediated between the textbook-based instruction endorsed by Harris and the culture-epoch sequence of child study by organizing his activities around basic occupations of the human race. While the activities constantly move back and forth between the tangible and the conceptual, there is an overall movement both within the scope of the activity and in the larger arc of each student's education toward the larger societal and scientific implications.

❦   4   ❧

Since Dewey was committed to eradicating harmful dichotomies, he felt that not only the classroom but the entire school should be a democratic community. Indeed, one of Dewey's most crucial insights is that genuine learning can occur only in schools where continual thinking and social interaction also pervade relations between teachers, administrators, and parents:

> It is easy to fall into the habit of regarding the mechanics of school organiza-
> tion and administration as something comparatively external and indifferent
> to educational purposes and ideals. . . . We forget that it is precisely such things
> as these that really control the whole system, even on its distinctively educa-
> tional side. No matter what is the accepted precept and theory, no matter what
> legislation of the school board or the mandate of the school superintendent,
> the reality of education is found in the personal and face-to-face contact of

teacher and child. The conditions that underlie and regulate this contact domi-
nate the educational situation. (1901/1976b, pp. 267–268)

At the center of our tradition is the notion that the teacher has to be able to
respond to the moment with an empathic thoughtfulness, and this cannot
be done by going through a script written by someone else or using materials and methods rigidly determined from outside the classroom. This is not
to endorse a structureless classroom, but to insist that the structuring be more
organically related to the students and the moment.

Dewey soon apprehended that we could eliminate what we customar-
ily think of as supervision if we gave teachers and administrators the time,
opportunity, and structures to work and plan together:

> Association and exchange among teachers was our substitute for what is called
> supervision, critic teaching, and technical training. . . . the tendency to mag-
> nify the authority of the superintendent, principal, or director is both the cause
> and the effect of the failure of our schools to direct their work on the basis of
> cooperative social organization of teachers. (Mayhew & Edwards 1936, p. 371)

Dewey also saw that if teachers were left completely alone, the exigencies
of running a school and their understandable concern for specific students
and immediate problems might swallow up everything else: "Cooperation
must, however, have a marked intellectual quality in the exchange of experiences and ideas. Many of our early failures were due to the fact that it was
too 'practical,' too much given to matters of immediate import and not sufficiently intellectual in content" (p. 371).

One way that Dewey, the director, and Ella Flag Young, the supervisor
of instruction, increased the intellectual level was by having the individual
teachers write reports. As we have noted, the very act of writing is a reflective and clarifying act, a stimulus to thinking. The administrators of the laboratory school specifically asked their teachers not merely to describe what
they were doing in a particular class, but how this activity related to what
went before and after. Laurel Tanner (1997) reprints some instructions that
she surmises were Dewey's own words: "The reports should in all cases
indicate not merely the actual subject matter, but the reason for taking it up,
its antecedents, and the points which are being led up to. . . . [T]he further
work that is to grow out of what has been undertaken should be indicated"
(p. 73). Another guideline focused the teachers' attention on the cognitive
value of handwork, which too often in progressive schools can drift into a
relaxation of the mind instead of acting as an enhancement for it: "In all
hand work, whether carpentry, sewing, etc., or art work, the reason or motive
for the work should be definitely stated, its connection or lack of connection with the other work of the school" (p. 73).

Dewey underscored the importance of these reports by using them as the basis for teachers' meetings. As one reads the notes for some of these meetings, one is impressed by the high conceptual level Dewey was able to elicit. For example, he began one of them by asking general questions: "Is the intellectual aim single or multiple? Is there any end which is comprehensive enough and definite enough to mean anything?" (p. 368), and:

> Is there any normal process of the mind which corresponds to this end which we want to reach, and if so, what is it? If there is a normal process, if the mind actually works toward it, just as the body is working toward health, what is the use of a teacher anyway? Where does the teacher come in? If this is a natural process, why does it not take care of itself? What is the relation towards this movement in the child's mind and the responsibility of the teacher? (p. 368)

By asking these large framing questions, Dewey uses a strategy that contrasts with his insistence that in childhood education we begin with the concrete and immediate. Dewey rightly senses that the teachers are fully immersed and entangled in their immediate situation and can grow further only by conceptualizing their ongoing work. They will naturally talk about their daily victories and frustrations, but need some prodding to keep rethinking crucial questions such as whether they are providing too little or too much guidance for the optimal growth.

For Dewey, then, the task of administering the school was synonymous with there being ongoing teacher education, in-service learning in the deepest sense of the term. Working with his teachers was meant to be continuous with the kind of preparation he would hope they would ideally have, a kind he tried to foster in his own department of pedagogy and which he sets forth most fully in "The Relation of Theory to Practice in Education." In this piece, Dewey distinguished the apprentice model of teacher education from the laboratory model. The former aims to produce as efficiently as possible new teachers to fit the existing system. As its name implies, it consists of a beginner, an apprentice, who takes direction from a master teacher, watches what that teacher does, and tries to replicate it. If this approach sounds familiar, it is because it is the model most widely used in what has come to be known as "student teaching."

Opposed to this notion is the laboratory model, which asks beginners not to focus so much on the techniques of teaching but to concentrate on the entire process of learning. Children are to be observed at least as much as the teacher. In a rare burst of eloquence, Dewey argues: "The student should not be observing to find out how the good teacher does it in order to accumulate a store of methods by which he also may teach successfully. He should rather observe with reference to seeing the interaction of mind, to see how teacher and pupils react upon each other—how mind answers to mind" (1904/1977, p. 260). Dewey is really advocating a total shift in teacher education from instructor performance and methodology to how students actually learn. The apprentice model may turn out functioning teachers more quickly, but those teachers often lack the ability to keep learning. Their "immediate skill" is purchased at "the cost of power to go on growing": "Such persons seem to know how to teach, but they are not students of teaching" (p. 256).

The most troubling aspect of apprentice teaching is that it posits the classroom as a realm hermetically sealed from the ways we learn outside it, from what Dewey calls "the continuity of experience." The apprentice model does not ask the beginning teacher to draw on self-reflections on how he or she learns but stresses routine mechanical methods:

> Unconsciously, but none the less surely, the student comes to believe in certain "methods" of learning, and hence of teaching which are somehow appropriate to the school—which somehow have their particular residence and application there. Hence he comes to believe in the potency for schoolroom purposes of materials, methods, and devices which it never occurs to him to trust to in his experience outside of school. (p. 259)

The laboratory method, by contrast, fosters not only self-reflection but also an independence of thought that asks the beginning teacher to understand as much as possible about the learning situation and to respond to the classroom situation primarily in light of this understanding. Dewey asks the beginning teachers to focus upon their own learning, even and especially in their learning how to teach. In short, Dewey asks us to put the process of thinking not only at the center of our children's education but of our teacher's as well.

Just as the Dewey School represents another road not taken in structuring learning for children, it also provides a brilliant but ignored model for the entire enterprise of educational research and development. Ellen Condliffe Lagemann makes this point effectively in *An Elusive Science: The Troubling History of Education Research* (2000): "Dewey became more and more convinced that educational scholarship and educational practice should be fused not merely in the same institution, but also in each and every person who worked in a school" (p. 50) and that his approach was far more cooperative, social, and thoughtful than that behind the more stratified systems of administration and schools of education coming into existence at the same time:

> At a time when the elaboration of administrative functions was generally seen as "progressive," Dewey's experience led him to oppose the growth of central supervisory personnel in the schools. Beyond that, in the face of arguments

concerning the greater need for training among high school teachers, he insisted that primary teachers need the same freedom and, presumably, therefore the same training. . . . His position was very much at odds with the hierarchy then developing among educational institutions. (p. 51)

In practice and in theory, then, Dewey had gone a long way toward a conception of education that was self-reflective, democratic, and participatory, that could learn from its daily workings. The administrative and teacher education aspects of his work are particularly relevant now because these are the points at which positive change, if it does happen, is most likely to occur. The school system has been so intransigent, so resilient in its very lack of flexibility, that to budge it even a little, many people will have to exert force on as many places as possible. But the best place to focus reform efforts, to try to break the vicious circle of mindless replication, is the classroom itself. Teachers will instruct their students only in ways in which they themselves have experienced genuine and gratifying learning, so it is essential that teacher education be proactive, uniting experiencing with thinking at every stage. The research of Paul Michalec (1998) suggests that teachers will teach in interactive, student-centered ways only if their own teacher education was conducted in this fashion. Michalec's findings confirm the hunch Dewey had as early as 1916 that active learning was not happening in the schools despite all the lip service to his ideas because of what we might call an enactment gap between what was being said and how it was taught:

> Why is it, in spite of the fact that teaching by pouring in, learning by passive absorption, are universally condemned, that they are still so entrenched in practice? That education is not an affair of "telling" and being told, but an active and constructive process, is a principle almost as generally violated in practice as conceded in theory. Is not this deplorable situation due to the fact that the doctrine itself is merely told? It is preached; it is lectured; it is written about. (1916/1980, pp. 43–44)

Dewey began to notice that his own ideas were falling victim to the kinds of methodization that both he and Emerson had identified as the main foes of thinking. At Teachers College, Columbia University, for example, Dewey's self-styled follower William Heard Kilpatrick popularized the "project method" that trivialized and narrowed the thrust of Dewey's ideas; our landfills are still clogged with the construction paper and papier-mâché artifacts that students have been asked to create about a book instead of, say, writing about it. Dewey's last public statement on education is painfully accurate. After citing Emerson to the effect that "the attained good tends to become the enemy of the better," he says:

The drive of established institutions is to assimilate and distort the new into conformity with themselves. . . . In teachers colleges and elsewhere the ideas and principles have been converted into a fixed subject matter of ready-made rules, to be taught and memorized according to certain standardized procedures and, when occasion arises, to be applied to educational problems externally, the way mustard plasters, for example, are applied. (1952, pp. ix, x)

In schools of education, then, Dewey's work has suffered the same fate as Bronson Alcott's work in the hands of Hiram Fuller, but on a much larger scale. There was a fatal disconnect between medium and message; schools of education most often adopt constructivist, student-centered approaches as their explicit orthodoxy, but present these ideas primarily through frontal lecturing by the instructor, along with the usual apparatus of textbooks, paper-and-pencil exams, and letter grades. One of the most deadening aspects here is the element of prefabrication; syllabi are constructed prescribing daily readings before a student even enters the door. And that reading is prefabricated in textbooks such as those examined in the preceding chapter, those weighty tombstones that more often mark the death of thought than provoke its extension. Their model of classroom training still follows the lines of what we have seen Dewey describe as the apprentice method, stressing teaching techniques and management as opposed to analyzing student learning or nonlearning.

We must follow Dewey in giving more freedom and responsibility to those who are in the process of learning to teach. If we are to trust them very soon with our children, we should ask them from the beginning to reflect on their own learning processes and to structure their own education as teachers accordingly. Of course, it is true, as Robert Frost once said, that there is a book side to everything and that many of us elders know books and concepts that will help beginners. We need not throw student teachers into the pool without any flotation, but we should be responsive and learned enough to suggest readings that speak to genuine problems and concerns arising from their classrooms at appropriate times. This kind of individualized and small-group guidance is, of course, labor intensive, but perhaps we can borrow the time from what we would have spent standing and delivering conventional lectures. Instead of trying to convince these students that we have already solved the problems of education and that all they have to do is learn the solutions, we can model a more open-ended and collaborative approach.

To help revitalize teacher education, we might reconsider and widen the conception of laboratory schools in colleges and universities. Where they still do exist, they almost always are within the self-contained worlds of departments or schools of education, much to the detriment of other departments. In *American Psychology and Schools: A Critique* (2001), for example,

Seymour Sarason shows how the abandonment of education by mainstream clinical psychology has injured this field as well as the children themselves. Similarly, consider the opportunities missed by other fields such as philosophy, sociology, literary studies, and political science to at once create and refine concepts while making a difference in the lives of children. One of the deleterious effects is that when the university researchers study how children learn, they most often confine themselves to our existing public schools. Biologists have long discovered a similar fallacy in trying to describe the behavior of animals only by watching them in a zoo. One of the opportunities of the Dewey School was to initially relax some of the confines to see how both children learned and teachers taught in a more natural, less institutionally constrained situation.

∾ 5 ∾

Dewey's direct involvement with the Laboratory School and with education on a daily basis ended in 1904 when he left Chicago for Columbia University, but he continued to write on education, most notably in the book we have seen him name as most central to his thought, *Democracy and Education* (1980/1916). He seemed well positioned to create change, since, like Emerson, he was a widely respected cultural spokesman and, unlike Emerson, he had a reputation as a successful educator. Two books that pick up where Barbara Finkelstein's study of schools leaves off, Larry Cuban's *How Teachers Taught: Constancy and Change in American Classrooms, 1890–1980* (1984/1993) and Arthur Zilversmit's *Changing Schools: Progressive Education Theory and Practice, 1930–1960* (1993), come to the depressingly similar conclusions that classroom practices remained virtually unchanged despite minor shifts in the rhetoric that schools used to describe what they do.

We have already seen how teacher education institutions blunted and thwarted Dewey's ideas. A related reason for his lack of impact is that his notion of education has rarely been grasped as a whole by practitioners, but rather various elements have been adopted piecemeal in ways that actually work against the larger conception. I remember that when I was a fourth-grader in the Boston public schools our usual drills were interrupted once a week for 75 minutes when the girls went to sewing and the boys did "manual training," making items such as cardboard cookbook covers for girls in another part of the system. This gesture toward Dewey's wish to unite the head and the hand actually increased this separation by relegating handwork to its own compartmentalized, diminished place—and added a further invidious distinction between the sexes that was never part of Dewey's original theory or practice. At the original laboratory school, boys cooked and girls worked in wood all together. One can see here evidence of Herbert Kliebard's contention in *The Struggle for the American Curriculum, 1893–1958* (1986) that the curriculum is not so much the result of a coherent philosophy as a set of compromises and equivocations between competing ideologies.

A similar but more insidious example of apparently Deweyan innovations that divide rather than unite is the use of vocational education as a tracking device to create an academic underclass. Dewey advocated involvement in work activities, especially industrial ones, as part of a general education for all students and warned against a more narrowly practical and stratifying approach:

> The ideal is not to use the schools as tools of existing industrial systems, but to use industry for the reorganization of the schools. There is a danger that the concentrated interests of businessmen and their influential activity in public matters will segregate training for industry to the damage of both democracy and education. . . . It is fatal for a democracy to permit the formation of fixed classes. (Dewey & Dewey, 1915, pp. 311, 313)

Ironically, another reason that Dewey's ideas have never been fully adopted is that they may be too democratic and egalitarian for American society. Dewey's emphasis, for example, on cooperative learning and measuring knowledge through action rather than through paper-and-pencil tests is of little use in a system whose main social function is to sift students. As David Labaree (1991) has said:

> Students are encouraged to focus more on winning than on learning, and schools more on sorting than on teaching. Under these circumstances, the current form of curriculum makes good sense. Students do not need to be engaged in a process of active inquiry in school; they merely need to learn as much as is necessary to acquired the desired grades and credits and degrees. Therefore, a teacher-centered form of instruction and a fractioned and fact-oriented form of curriculum are quite acceptable. (p. 518)

One of Dewey's most important contributions to the tradition of active learning is his insistence on the relation of learning how to think to creating a true democracy. As he wrote in *Schools of To-Morrow*: "The democracy which proclaims equality of opportunity as its ideal requires an education in which learning and social application, ideas and practice, work and recognition of the meaning of what is done, are unified from the beginning and for all" (Dewey & Dewey, 1915, p. 315).

CHAPTER 7

Education by Poetry:
Pedagogy and the Arts
in Early Modernism

John Dewey and others appear to look for a solution to the problem of education in psychology and sociology—in philosophy then. They might do worse than to seek it in poetry.

—William Carlos Williams

Thomas thinks he will write a book on what my definition of the sentence means for literary criticism. If I didn't drop into poetry every time I sat down to write I should be tempted to do a book on what it means for education.

—Robert Frost

I am for an art that is political-erotical-mystical, that does something other than sit on its ass in a museum. I am for an art that embroils itself with the everyday crap and comes out on top. I am for an art that tells you the time of day, or where such and such a street is. I am for an art that helps old ladies across the street.

—Claes Oldenburg

F ROM AROUND 1910 to the mid 1930s, innovative educators focused on the relevance to their work of poetry and the arts while poets and artists became especially involved in education. This was not a peripheral interest on the part of either, but the sharing of a deep root metaphor: the making of poetry and art became a paradigm for learning and teaching, as conversely did the activity of children for artistic creation. In *Were You Ever a Child?* (1919), Floyd Dell, a representative literary figure, juxtaposes two consecutive chapters to illustrate this complementarity: "The Child as Artist" and "The Artist as Child." At its best this convergence "had nothing to do with that flabby impressionality which is dignified under the name of the 'creative temperament,'" (Fitzgerald, 1925/1992, p. 6) to quote *The Great Gatsby,* the central novel of the period, but involved basic issues of knowledge and language. More specifically, artists and educators shared assumptions about the use of metaphor to bridge the abstract and the concrete, about the making of forms as crucial to the act of knowing, and about the need to deconstruct and reconstruct these forms.

After discussing the general matrix of ideas in modernism, we will look at the work of two poets particularly important in this cross-fertilization, Robert Frost and William Carlos Williams. Frost, a teacher himself for much of his career, wrote, "It slowly dawned on me that my poetry and my teaching were one, and if you knew my poetry at all well, you'd see that: that every little while there was the gleam of the teacher, that the two things were working" (1964a, p. 176). Williams argued, "From the particular and sensitive field of the artist—certain ways may be found for the elucidation of knowledge in the general field—especially in the art of poetry, since education is accomplished almost entirely by the use of words, and words have all their contours best defined in poetry" (1974a, p. 6). The work of these two poets will then be related to two innovative educators, Caroline Pratt and Margaret Naumburg. We will use Dewey's late work, *Art as Experience* (1934/1987) to conceptually integrate these strands.

To give us some guidance through such an artistically varied era, we begin with Sanford Schwartz's framework in *The Matrix of Modernism* (1985), in which he argues that beyond their obvious differences, the modern poets shared a coherent paradigm. Schwartz begins constructing this matrix by discussing four philosophers who were influential at the turn of the twentieth century: Friedrich Nietzsche, Henri Bergson, William James, and F. H. Bradley. Central to their thought is "an opposition between conceptual abstraction and immediate experience, or, more generally, between the instrumental conventions that shape ordinary life and the original flux of concrete sensations" (p. 5). Beginning with the ancient Greeks, abstractions have been the crucial tools of Western thought, but they can also constrain and buffer our experience of the world, as William James wrote:

> The universe has always appeared to the natural mind as a kind of enigma, of which the key must be sought in word or name. That word names the universe's *principle*, and to possess it is after a fashion to possess the universe itself. 'God,' 'Matter,' 'Reason,' 'the Absolute,' 'Energy,' are so many solving names. You can rest when you have them. You are at the end of your metaphysical quest. (1987, p. 509)

Modern philosophers and poets want to reverse this process and put these names back into observable relation with the particulars. While Plato wished to rescue permanent forms from the ongoing rush of experience, these modernists reverse Plato by retrieving what was left behind in the process. The answer for most of us is not to aim for a Zen-like denial of language, but to reinstate the immediate within the conceptual through an inventive and continuing use of new forms. As Schwartz says, "Like philosophers, the architects of the Modernist tradition explored the dialectic of form and flux, and were attracted to constructs that unify concrete particulars without suppressing the differences between them" (1985, p. 7).

The primary tool for doing so is metaphor, and to understand its power in modern thought we need to trace back with Nietzsche its basis of all thought:

> What . . . is truth? A mobile army of metaphors, metonyms, anthropomorphisms—in short, a sum of human relations which have been enhanced, transposed, and embellished poetically and rhetorically, and which after long use seem firm, canonical, and obligatory to a people: truths are illusions about which one has forgotten that this is what they are; metaphors which are worn out and without sensuous power; coins which have lost their pictures and now matter only as metal, no longer as coins. (1954, pp. 46–47)

While the process of making metaphors is liberating, their endings can too quickly forget their beginnings, and they become the "solving words," of which William James warned. We forget their metaphorical and linguistic nature and come to reify them as the structure of reality itself. Nietzsche suggests that we perform a kind of etymological archaeology on old metaphors while self-consciously fashioning new ones. The making of new metaphors, then, releases us from what Nietzsche sees as the prison-house of language by foregrounding the concrete, reversing the process of linguistic entropy. We can take as one example Ezra Pound's interest in the Chinese ideogram, the interpretation of which he bases on that of Ernest Fenellosa, who wrote in *The Chinese Written Character as a Medium for Poetry* (1936):

> Let us consider a row of cherry trees. From each of these in turn we proceed to take an 'abstract,' as the phrase is, a certain common lump of qualities which we may express together by the name cherry or cherry-ness. Next we place in a second table several such characteristic concepts: cherry, rose, sunset, iron-rust, flamingo. From these we abstract some further common quality . . . and label it 'red' or 'redness.' It is evident that this process of abstraction may be carried on indefinitely with all sorts of material. We may go on forever building pyramids of attenuated concept until we reach the apex 'being.' (p. 26)

The Chinese ideogram retains the concreteness that "being" jettisons; it is made up of superimposed, stylized images of the things from which "redness" is abstracted: rose, rust, cherry, flamingo. These particulars are not swallowed up by the more general concept, but remain as a kind of open and explicit etymology. Fenollosa says the ideogram "retains the creative impulse and process, visible and at work. Poetic language is always vibrant with fold on fold of overtones and natural affinities, but in Chinese the visibility of the metaphor tends to raise this quality to its intensest power" (p. 25). Pound and other modernist poets try to transpose this quality into their own work through a succession of clear yet diverse images from which one must construct the generalities and emotional attitudes that link them together. *The Cantos* or *The Wasteland* are not collections of static bits and pieces, but signs and stimulants for a unifying dynamism that only the reader can complete, a connecting of the dots through the process of imaginative reading.

The one serious omission in Schwartz's narrative is that he locates these views on metaphor in modernism without acknowledging the work we have already noted by 19th century Americans such as Emerson and Thoreau. Ernest Fenollosa, for example, born in Salem, Massachussetts, was deeply influenced by New England Transcendentalism, which shaped his interpretation—some sinologists would say misinterpretation—of how the Chinese written character works. The modernists' interest in rejoining the abstract and the concrete is directly continuous with the spirit of "The American Scholar" and "The Child and the Curriculum."

As an undergraduate at Amherst College, I remember driving across Massachusetts on a bright autumn afternoon with two poets. One of them looked at the brilliant fall leaves, the pastoral farms, the dilapidated stone fences, and said, "The New England countryside was really beautiful before Robert Frost gave it all a moral." We enjoyed a laugh at the time, but now I imagine Frost's ghost as having the last laugh, for I have come to appreciate how subtle, elusive, and complex his poetry is, how it actually works against the easy making of morals, against any certainty that can lapse into smugness. Frost wrote with his typical fondness for wordplay: "People are always asking what I stand for. I never hold tenets on anything—just tentatives. . . . I may sound like a man who never changes his mind. Maybe I'm one who never makes it up, but never the other" (Mertins, 1965, p. 378).

An earlier memory of mine is being assigned a high school essay on the tag line of Frost's "Mending Wall"—"Good fences make good neighbors"— presented to us without the rest of the poem, as if it were a truth for which we need only give five paragraphs of examples. Only later did I realize that this line, repeated in the poem, is countered and undercut by another twice-told line, "Something there is that doesn't love a wall," with its deliberate evasiveness and playful inversion. While the poem entertains the notion that the activity of fence building brings the two neighbors into community for a while, the speaker questions the rationale:

> "*Why* do they make good neighbors? Isn't it
> Where there are cows? But here there are no cows.
> Before I built a wall I'd ask to know
> What I was walling in or walling out,
> And to whom I was like to give offense.
> Something there is that doesn't love a wall,
> That wants it down." (Frost, 1972, p. 17)

Here, as often with Frost, the making of structures is positive but the finished structures themselves are not. Praise be, then, to the frost that topples the boulders and disrupts old saws.

What some of Frost's poems register is a certain relief bordering on delight, when these structures are relaxed or even destroyed, as in an early, breezy poem, "To the Thawing Wind":

> Come with rain, O loud Southwester!
> Bring the singer, bring the nester;
> Give the buried flower a dream;
> Make the settled snowbank steam;
> Find the brown beneath the white;
> But whate'er you do tonight,
> Bathe my window, make it flow,
> Melt it as the ice will go;
> Melt the glass and leave the sticks
> Like a hermit's crucifix;
> Burst into my narrow stall;
> Swing the picture on the wall;
> Scatter poems on the floor;
> Turn the poet out of door. (p. 7)

Traditionally, the wind and the coming of spring are associated with inspiration (literally, from its Latin etymology, a "breathing in"), but here their particular power is to release us from the confines of both a physical dwelling and a dwelling in old artworks. The thawing wind turns the "settled" snowbank into moving, ethereal steam, melts the solid ice into a fluid stream, and even dissolves the glass fixed in the window, removing any physical barrier between the poet and the world, subject and object. Most crucially it flutters and dispatches with the poet's previous work, which always threatens to restrain and repeat itself. Outdoors the poet is freer to find material for new letters instead of dwelling among old litter.

Frost's sense of accepting or creating structures only to playfully subvert them, his taking of the notion of "conventional wisdom" as an oxymoron, pervades his teaching as much as his poetry. In a sentence linking the two, he says, "I accept school just as I accept the sonnet form or any other social convention: only it seems to be in me to want to make school as un-schoolike as possible." (1963, p. 277). A look at Frost's educational career, from his reluctant studenthood to his becoming a teacher of considerable originality, suggests continuities with his vision of poetry.

One of the reasons Frost wanted to make schools as unschoolike as possible was that they made him sick. On his first day of kindergarten, he got lost before he reached the school, and when someone pushed him too high on a swing he got a stomachache. The following day, when it was time to return, the pain also returned, so his indulgent mother allowed him to skip not only the day but also the year. He was largely homeschooled for the first three grades, until his mother moved to Massachusetts after his father's death. Frost graduated valedictorian from high school, but these early feelings about formal schooling, compounded probably with homesickness, resurfaced at both Dartmouth and Harvard, where his aversion to formal learning again was marked with physical symptoms—fatigue, insomnia, and chest pains.

Unlike many teachers who themselves had bad experiences in school, Frost seemed to have remembered his own difficulties, when in 1906, more out of necessity than desire, he became a high school teacher himself at Pinkerton Academy near his New Hampshire farm. Unable to support himself as either a farmer or a poet, he accepted what was at first a part-time position teaching English. One of his goals was to have his students associate reading with pleasure; a frequent instruction accompanying assignments was

> *To be read—to be enjoyed*
> *Not studied—not skimmed* (Thompson, 1966, p. 333)

He emphasized not so much lectures as oral interpretation and close listening. Later he described his teaching at Pinkerton:

> I never kept on reading a book that made the class listless. If I saw the class uninterested I always closed the book and passed the rest of the hour some other way. I learned to watch for the "fidgets" on the part of the students, and when I saw them in evidence I recognized them as a danger signal. They were given the children to protect themselves with. (Lathem, 1966, p. 23)

One would expect a poet of Frost's talent to have a special sensitivity to literature, but what stands out in this passage is his sensitivity to students, his realization of how adults might end up boring students with the very things we are most enthusiastic about.

In 1911, Frost followed the principal of Pinkerton to New Hampshire State Normal School at Plymouth, where he taught one course in the psychology of education and one in the history of education. In the former he used two books by William James, *Talks to Teachers on Psychology* and *Psychology: The Briefer Course*. Frost had wanted to study with James, but in his one year at Harvard, James was on leave. But Frost did absorb James on his own, and found confirmations of his own disposition to think through and from experience instead of from a priori concepts. Frost discussed these readings informally; if he had any agenda, it was that psychology has no definitive answers, no solving words that can dictate success in the classroom. One day, Frost read his class Mark Twain's "The Celebrated Jumping Frog of Calaveras County" and drew the following moral: "Some teachers always load their students so full of facts that the students can't jump; other teachers know better and they tickle the students into having imaginative ideas of their own just by saying in effect, 'Flies, Dan'l'" (Thompson, 1966, pp. 372–373). In the first class of his other course, Frost found that the janitor had already piled on his desk stacks of the customary textbook on the history of education. Frost's first request was for volunteers to carry them back down to the stockroom; he assigned instead readings from Jean-Jacques Rousseau and Johann Heinrich Pestalozzi.

After receiving a small inheritance, Frost took his family to England, where he published his first two books. When he returned, the innovative president of Amherst College, Alexander Meiklejohn, hired him to teach, beginning in 1917. The students in one of his first classes suggested that the classroom itself did not fit Frost's relaxed approach, and soon the venue was shifted to evening meetings at a fraternity house. Frost pursued this direction to teach out of the box, feeling he could do more on the outskirts of the educational system than in its conventional settings. He was particularly interested in stimulating and encouraging original thought, and he would sometimes scatter slips of paper on which students could jot down their ideas during class. He would often leave the class with from 10 to 30 slips, some of which he felt were utterly disposable, but others so good he wished he could steal the ideas on them. Frost's sense that he could learn from his students as well as vice versa, is suggested in a later comment: "Long ago I gave up the idea of asking my students to tell me what they knew just that I might discover if they knew as much as I did. Now in classes I ask questions in the correct sense of the word, for I want them to tell me something new, something I did not know." (Abbot, 1925, p. 209). Frost sensed what

all good teachers discover, that just as in making love one has to give pleasure to get it, so in teaching one has to learn oneself in the process for the
students to do so.

Frost explicitly connected his teaching to his poetry in three related areas:
(*a*) the centrality of metaphor, (*b*) the value of making form as "a momen-
tary stay against confusion" (1972, p. 394), and (*c*) the pressures put on poetic
form by the urgencies of the immediate. In "Education by Poetry," Frost gave
his famous formulation of poetry as "saying one thing and meaning another"
(p. 33). Frost agrees with Nietzsche that no language apprehends reality
"directly," but that explicitly metaphorical language has the advantage of
being explicitly figurative and performative. This leads Frost to equate metaphor making with thinking itself. To use metaphor as a tool instead of being
used by it, one has to create the metaphor oneself, to be "at home" in it; otherwise, "you don't know how far you may expect to ride it and when it may
break down with you" (p. 334). Metaphor is useful not only when it works
but also when it does not, when we become aware of its limits, its tran-
sient temporality: "All metaphor breaks down somewhere. That is the beauty
of it. It is touch and go with metaphor, and until you have lived with it
long enough you don't know when it is going. You don't know how much
you can get out of it and when it will cease to yield. It is a very living
thing" (p. 335).

Frost's sense of the need to make metaphor and then the need to go
beyond any single metaphor can be seen as a special case of our second
category, his attitude toward form in general:

> There is at least as much good in the world that it admits of form and the
> making of form. And not only admits of it, but calls for it. . . . Anyone who has
> achieved the least form to be sure of it, is lost to the larger excruciations. I
> think it must stroke faith the right way. The artist[,] the poet[,] might be ex-
> pected to be the most aware of such assurance. But it is really everybody's
> sanity to feel it and live by it. Fortunately, too, no forms are more engross-
> ing[,] gratifying, comforting, staying than those lesser ones we throw off, like
> vortex rings of smoke, all our individual enterprise and needing nobody's co-
> operation; a basket, a letter, a garden, a room, an idea, a picture, a poem. For
> these we haven't to get a team together before we can play. (p. 344)

"Vortex rings of smoke" suggests an evanescent shape that dissolves as soon
as it is made, briefer even than a poem, also formed out of breath. Larger
forms threaten to substitute themselves for the novelty and chaos of the
universe, and thus reduce the need for making more forms. Of our background in confusion and darkness, Frost says, "To me any little form I assert
upon it is velvet, as the saying is, and to be considered for how much more
it is than nothing. If I were a Platonist I should have to consider, I suppose,

for how much less it is than everything" (p. 345). Frost even gave a specific time for how long the satisfaction and clarification of life through form could last: "I don't try to make any permanent clarifications for myself but only shape some things together—for betting purposes. . . . I'm such a lover of form that getting the better of one little poem makes me comfortable for a whole week" (MacCann, 1939, p. 1).

The existing forms that loomed largest for him were the conventions of prosody, especially the iambic pentameter line and the sonnet, which he accepted just as school, as a structure to be altered around the contours of one's individuality. Similarly, he accepts the regularity of the pentameter line only to run across it the immediacy of the rhythms of the speaking voice, what he called "getting the sound of sense" (1972, p. 261). The conventional practice of verse takes these rhythms and overregularizes them to the point of creating too extreme a difference between poetry and the spoken language, just as school has removed the process of learning so far from what happens outside that any resemblance becomes coincidental. What Frost says about poetry has equal relevance to education: "Poetry has seized on this sound of speech and carried it to artificial and meaningless lengths. We have it exemplified in Sidney Lanier's musical notation of verse, where all the tones of the human voice in natural speech are entirely eliminated, leaving the sound of sense without root in experience" (p. 263). For Frost, the ideal poetic line would fuse an existing form with an utterance made in a specific human context. As he wrote in a letter, "You get more credit for thinking if you restate formulae or cite cases that fall in easily under formulae, but all the fun is outside saying things that suggest formulae that won't formulate— that almost but don't quite formulate" (1963, p. 47). This strategy foreshadows the late poem "Directive," spoken by a guide "who only has at heart your getting lost," so that eventually you will become "lost enough to find yourself" (1972, p. 156).

It is in this sense particularly of losing and finding and losing again that Frost's sense of poetry and teaching most powerfully fuse, as George Whicher suggests:

> As he talked, he seemed to be constantly inviting his audience to help him find just the right form of words. He spoke slowly, often rolling up a phrase with many heaves as though it were a stone to be placed in a wall that needed mending. We felt that we were watching an arduous creative triumph, the shaping into form of ideas drawn from the dark abyss of the unconscious mind. (1950, pp. 34–35)

Significantly, Whicher says nothing about the content but speaks of the process in which Frost involved himself and his audience, and he relies on our knowledge of the poetry to imply that the stone wall of thought is not a permanent structure. This intersection of poetry and teaching has been well summarized by Pamela Davis (1994): "Frost saw reality as formless and chaotic, and in order to handle that, one had to participate in constant ordering and reordering of this reality. . . . Both thoughts and poems involved an act of making, active shaping of the raw material of ideas. Teaching for Frost was in essence a public performance of such activity" (p. 38). Although neither Frost's poetry nor his teaching was didactic, both were pedagogical in process, stimulating the mind through playful perplexity. In one of his last poems, he says: "It takes all sorts of in-and outdoor schooling / To get adapted to my kind of fooling" (1972, p. 174).

⁄ 3 ⁄

We have seen Frost say that the fun is in saying things that suggest formulae but just won't formulate. Williams Carlos Williams took this further by completely discarding old forms—the iambic line, sonnets, schoolrooms: "But my failure to work inside a pattern—a positive sin—is the cause of my virtues. I cannot work inside a pattern because I can't find a pattern that will have me. My whole effort . . . is to find a pattern large enough, modern enough, flexible enough to include my desires. And if I should find it I'd wither and die" (Tashjian, 1978, p. 10). But this difference in degree should not obscure the fact that he and Frost share a convergent vision, viewing the problems of creating an American poetry and education as parallel.

To the casual reader, Williams is often no more than the poet of concrete images such as red wheelbarrows and broken glass. His tag line "No ideas but in things" has often been misread as an example of a kind of homespun primitivism, but only because the first two words are overemphasized at the expense of the last three. Indeed, his ideas about language and education form a seamless continuity with those of the Transcendentalists. A useful way to appreciate these ideas is through reading Williams's writings on history, especially his volume of prose meditations, *In the American Grain* (1925), and his 1934 essay "The American Background," the latter beginning with the following preface:

> They saw birds with rusty breasts and called them robins. Thus, from the start, an America of which they could have had no inkling drove the first settlers upon their past. They retreated for warmth and reassurance to something previously familiar. But at a cost. For what they saw were not robins. They were thrushes only vaguely resembling the rosy, daintier English bird. Larger, stronger, and in the evening of a wilder, lovelier song, actually here was something the newcomers had never in their lives before encountered. Blur. Confusion. A bird that beats with his wings and slows himself with his tail in landing. (p. 9)

From this moment, at once origin and fall, Williams sees American culture as the battleground between two vectors, the new versus the old, the "related" versus the "unrelated," the "primary" versus the "secondary" (p. 10). The old language is needed for security and orientation, but can block out what is unique in the present. Williams does not see this situation as restricted to America, but rather the conditions of American history make more acute something that happens in every moment of our lives. For Williams, the discovery of America is only a metaphor for the discovery of the new: "Not that this direct drive toward the new is a phenomenon distinctively confined to America: it is the growing edge in every culture. . . . Thus the new and the real, hard to come at, are synonymous" (p. 17).

This moment of robins versus thrushes is not something that happened once in American history but is a pivot point in every instance of our daily lives. The conflict defines the cutting edge at which Williams's own writing will play itself out, as he suggests in his preface to *In the American Grain* (1925): "In these studies I have sought to rename the things seen, now lost in chaos of borrowed titles, many of them inappropriate, under which the true character lies hidden. . . . It has been my wish to draw from every source one thing, the strange phosphorus of life, nameless under an old misappellation" (p. v). Williams puts language itself at the center of his investigation of American culture and becomes its archaeologist. Although our language has been distorted from the beginning, if we go back and examine it closely, we trace those distortions and detect something of the "thrush" before it is "lost," obliterated by "robin," to ferret out "the strange phosphorus of life," still present ready to be struck into flame. Williams's work is one of recuperation, sifting through the mistakes of the past to find what is still quickening and enabling.

For example, Williams sees Columbus as mistaken in trying to impose his will on this novel landscape. But he also sees in Columbus sensitivity to the freshness of the New World. Unlike the English settlers, Columbus relished the differences between the old and new and registers them in the language of his journals:

> Branches growing in different ways and all from one trunk; one twig is one form and another is a different shape and so unlike that it is the greatest wonder in the world to see the diversity; thus one branch has leaves like those of a cane, and others like those of a mastic tree; and on a single tree there are five different kinds. The fish so unlike ours that it is wonderful. Some are the shape of dories and of finest colors, so bright that there is not a man who would not be astounded, and would not take great delight in seeing them. (p. 26)

Columbus's connoisseurship of the new becomes the central virtue of a long line of linguistic and epistemological heroes, such as the Jesuit priest Père

Sebastian Raslès: "Contrary to the English, Raslès recognized the New World. . . . It is a living flame compared to their dead ash" (p. 120). Raslès responded to America with senses that were both receptive and actively assimilating, as this series of participles and then infinitives suggests: "For everything his fine sense, blossoming, thriving, opening, reviving—not shutting out—was tuned . . . to create, to hybridize, to crosspollenize—not to sterilize, to draw back, to fear, to dry up, to rot. It is the sun" (p. 121).

Williams's villains are those who merely want to harness this newness for their own utilitarian ends, figures such as Benjamin Franklin, who appropriated even lightning: "He didn't dare let it go in at the top of his head and out at his toes, that's it: he had to fool with it. He sensed the power and knew only enough to want to run an engine with it" (p. 155).

Williams's sense of redemption for America includes surrender, but that is only part of an entire paradigm that he sets out most explicitly in the chapter on Sam Huston called "Descent." At 15 Huston ran away from home to live with the Cherokees and then "reascended to the settlements for school" (1925, p. 212). When Huston later ran into problems with his marriage, he resigned the governorship "and took the descent once more, to the ground. He rejoined the Cherokees. . . . But his primitive ordeal, created by a peculiar condition of destiny (the implantation of an already partly cultured race on a wild continent) has a plant in its purpose, in its lusts' eye, as gorgeous as Montezuma's garden of birds. . . . But he who will grow from that basis must sink first" (p. 213). To make this "descent" requires a special range of capabilities—a willful courage yet also a willingness to abandon the structures that create not only culture but also the self. At a basic level, this movement of descent and ascent, of a journey to the frontier and back, corresponds to certain rhythms of consciousness that lie at the heart of the creative process and of learning. First, we must go into the world around us and into our own minds in all their naked confusion, leaving behind language and other cultural symbols. Then we must name what we have found, giving it a structure that in turn shapes and intensifies the experience itself.

Williams's poetry frequently extols the qualities needed for the descent, as in "Smell":

> Oh strong-ridged and deeply hollowed
> nose of mine! what will you not be smelling?
> What tactless asses we are, you and I, boney nose
> always indiscriminate, always unashamed . . . (1951, p. 153)

Williams plays havoc with the conventional, restricted notion of the self by the ludicrousness that results from addressing those "nosey" narcissistically exuberant aspects of himself as a separate entity. The fun is not at the expense of the nose but of the fellow trying to curb this stinker who persists in his less-than-gentlemanly activities. Similarly, he addresses "K. McB." as "you exquisite chunk of mud": "Do they expect the ground to be / always solid? / Give them the slip then; / let them sit in you; / soil their pants; / teach them a dignity / that is dignity, the dignity / of mud!" (p. 157) just as he praises Thomas Jefferson for walking to his inauguration in the mud "out of principle" (1934, p. 15). The poem uses what Henri Bergson views as the basic stuff of laughter, the confrontation of the stiff, the formal, with a protean, intrusive reality, always curling up around it: "when they try to step on you, / spoil the polish" (1951, p. 157). By contrast, the ascent is embodied in every poem by its shape as language, as poetic form; it is not as compelling as the descent, but it too requires its heroisms: "She loves you / She says. Believe it / —tomorrow. / But today / the particulars / of poetry / that difficult art / require / your whole attention" (1963, p. 46).

As a doctor Williams was able to alternate a daily emergence into the world and its people and capture some of this descent in the words he formed on his prescription pads between patients and at night. Aside from his poems he wrote novels, short stories, plays, and essays, but of most relevance to our own exploration is a book of essays centered on education, written between 1928 and 1930 but published only after his death, with the title he chose, *The Embodiment of Knowledge* (1974a). The book, appropriately enough, is dedicated to his two sons, schoolboys at the time, and one of its keynotes is contained in what he wrote on the first page: "I'd like this to be printed as it is, faults and all. But don't waste too much time on it, if you feel inclined to spend any time on it at all. It is intended to go along *with a life* and to be in no sense its objective" (p. 2). Williams makes Emerson's skeptical qualifying of books immediate by reflectively pointing out that he himself is now speaking from a book, one that should have only a limited value to his sons' present lives. Indeed, few writers have so forcefully articulated the dangers of misusing writing of the past as has Williams, particularly in an essay at the center of the book beginning "Afraid lest he be caught in a net of words, tripped up, bewildered and so defeated—thrown aside—a man hesitates to write down his innermost convictions" (p. 104). Williams describes the classics in vivid terms:

> The classics, the sayings, the elucidations, are dead as shells, as fossils of plants . . . prehistoric plant cells still visible so that species can be determined and varieties named. These things represent men who . . . wrote fresh from the whole body and who went on living after. . . . To live cannot be learned from the writings of others. It is the life of writing that comes from inside. (p. 105)

Or, as he writes in his long poem *Paterson*: "We read: not the flames / but the ruin left / by the conflagration" (1992, p. 123). We cannot, though, simply turn away from the books of the past. They have too great a hold on our minds already and must be actively questioned, probed, and deconstructed: "Language is the key to the mind's escape from bondage to the past. There are no 'truths' that can be fixed in language. It is by the breakup of the language that the truth can be seen to exist and thus it becomes operative again" (1974a, p. 19). Williams creates smaller, more temporary, more flagrantly fictive forms to replace and subvert the larger, totalizing forms constructed by philosophers, economists, and other big thinkers. For Williams, to write creatively is to use language in a defiantly revolutionary way: "Now life is above all things else at any moment subversive of life as it was the moment before—always new, always irregular. Verse to be alive must have infused into it something of the same order, some tincture of disestablishment, something in the nature of an impalpable revolution, an ethereal reversal" (1957, pp. 23–24).

The antidote to reading, both for creative artists and for students, is to write, and particularly to write poetry. One can demystify the words, the sentences, the structures, on the page only by writing one's own, by realizing where they come from, how long they are good for (not long at all), and when, to use Frost's notion, a metaphor works and when it breaks down. Williams says, "To say what must be said; to say it once that it may blossom once like a holly-hock or a bird—then let it begin to die—even while he himself is alive he will see his own writing grow older and die" (1974a, p. 105). Writing poetry, then, becomes both a central method for the educator and a metaphor for every other kind of learning: "Data should be present in activities which, in particular, have newly organized their material, such as, let us say, in poetry. How better than in poetry, that has undergone a revolution in its conception within twenty-five years. . . . To words and their significance—which is the special field of the poet—the educationalist must turn willy-nilly in the end" (p. 6). As with Dewey, Williams feels we must start with the immediate, with things, which in turn we build into larger structures, but only and always realizing how selective and fictive these are. As Williams begins his own epic, "To make a start, / out of particulars / and make them general, rolling / up the sum, by defective means. . . . In ignorance / a certain knowledge and knowledge, / undispersed, its own undoing" (1992, pp. 3–4).

※ 4 ※

The Country and City School and the Walden School, the two schools I have chosen as embodiments of this modernist vision, were both begun in 1914 in Greenwich Village and challenged some of the conventional wisdom about the larger movement in which they were a part. This conventional wisdom is that they overemphasized individual expression over a sense of community and that they signaled a retreat from larger social concerns. More recent scholarship, however, has suggested that such divisions are not that clear-cut and that the radicals of Greenwich Village saw art itself as the way to change society. For example, Edward Abrahams (1986) has described what he calls the Lyrical Left in this time and place:

> A loose coalition of cultural radicals living in New York City, dreamed of changing the world with pens, paint, brushes, and new publications. They thought they could liberate society by combining radical politics and modern culture. . . . In a burst of creative excitement they founded experimental magazines, clubs, theaters, art galleries, and schools. (p. ix)

This confluence of art, personal development, and community building is suggested by a statement by Margaret Naumburg:

> These early artistic enterprises serve to bring into conscious life the buried material of the child's emotional problems. Gradually his energies are transformed from unconscious, ego-centric attachments, to the wider intercourse of social life. This, indeed, is the function of all art; self-expression in forms that are of social and communicable value. The individual's unconscious energy creates material with meaning to the group. (1917/1973, p. 45)

Of course, the exact shape this dialectic took varied between schools and individuals, but all the important experiments recognized this reciprocal relation, especially our two exemplary schools, the Country and City School, founded by Caroline Pratt, and the Walden School, run by Margaret Naumburg with the help of her sister, Florence Cane. Each represents the confluence of artistic and educational revolutions in different ways. Pratt moved into Greenwich Village because of the low rents and working-class clientele and only later made the acquaintance of artists and rebels, who sent their children to her and supported her work. Naumburg and Cane were part of this community already, partly through their marriages to the literary figures Waldo Frank and Melville Cane and partly through their own talents and interests.

Caroline Pratt began her teaching at the age of 16 in a one-room school in Fayetteville, New York, the rural community in which she was born. A neighbor who found her promising secured for her a scholarship to Teachers College, Columbia University. As she recounts in her autobiography, *I Learn from Children* (1948), she became disillusioned with traditional methods in her kindergarten course when her plump instructor insisted that the students all dance like butterflies. At a deeper level, she was troubled by the emphasis on quiet docility and mystic symbolism. After concluding that kindergarten was designed "to prepare the children for the long years of discipline ahead" and "got them ready to be bamboozled by the first grade" (p. 11), she was advised to switch to manual training, with which she was no less satisfied: "Your pupils had to master one skill after another—and all in the abstract, all carefully skirting around any practical application, all strictly in accord with the idea that education was practice, but never by the slightest taint practical" (p. 12).

She was teaching in small schools in New York settlement houses when she had something of an epiphany watching a friend's 6-year-old son making a miniature railroad system from blocks, odd paper boxes, and material salvaged from the trash:

> I thought that this was one little boy's way of learning about the world he lived in; he had observed for himself, had gathered his facts, and was here, before my eyes, writing the perfect child's textbook of what he had seen. Here, in a combination of map, model, and working drawing with sound track—such a combination as had never existed in any classroom, more's the pity—he was setting down his understanding of the way things worked, the relationships of facts to each other, the causes and effects, the purposes and functions. This was thinking, this was learning. This was the way a young child, if freed to do so, would go about educating himself on the subject which was of most immediate, intense interest to him—the world in which he lived. (p. 19)

What Pratt grasped early in her career is that such activities are not simply artistic or creative but also cognitive. Pratt discovered well before Piaget that we come to know the world not simply by imbibing it through senses but by making representations, models of it; she says of this boy: "He was reconstructing a part of his world in which he was most interested. . . . He was learning about the world, thinking about it, reasoning about it, accepting this, rejecting that, putting it together and making it work" (p. 28). Younger children tend make their representations more physically through their own bodies and through what they fashion with their hands than more symbolically through words and abstract schema. The boy in the example combines a mimetic modeling of the trains themselves with a schematic map of the entire system, and one of the tasks of education is to help facilitate this kind of cognitive growth by structuring tasks that move children toward more abstract and symbolic modalities. The process cannot be forced or rushed, but the fuller the opportunities to work at one level, the richer and faster will be movement to the next level.

In the autumn of 1914 Pratt began her own school, soon to be known as the Play School in a three-room apartment in Greenwich Village, but she took the entire city as her classroom. For example, she and the children spent a good deal of time at the docks, watching the river traffic, speaking to the tugboat men and bargemen. They then went back to the school to process and assimilate these experiences through representational play: "Here the children put to use the facts they had acquired, some by asking questions, but most through their own eyes and ears. Young children are readier to put their thoughts into action than into words. It is a truer exercise for them to push an imaginary barge down a river and unload it into an imaginary wagon than to tell you how it is done" (p. 43).

As the beginning children got older and the school expanded, activities became more long-term and cumulative. The 7-year-olds constructed a model city focusing on the theme of the social interdependence of its inhabitants. The 8-year-olds ran the school post office, the 9-year-olds managed the school store, the 10-year-olds made all the school signs and helped administer the lunchroom. The 11-year-olds operated two full-size printing presses on which they produced not only their own illustrated magazine, but also school forms, library cards, and other items. The standard curricular subjects such as math, reading, and writing were taught as far as possible through these community activities, as were most artistic modes. But to show the emphasis the school put on the latter, it employed a separate art teacher, the first of which was William Zorach, the expressionist sculptor, who had displayed at the avant-garde Armory Art Show of 1913.

Indeed, it is in this link between education and artistic process that Pratt's practice and theory is most compelling. In "Pedagogy as a Creative Art" (1926), Pratt begins with an account of how creative artists use the process of turning material into forms as a way of understanding both the world and the self:

> Creative artists are quite as much interested in what their materials do to them as in what they do to or with their materials. Each time they produce they study the product in relation to themselves and not as a thing in itself. The study of himself in relation to his product is what seems to keep the creative artist true to his purpose. He becomes his own critic. He keeps himself aloof from his forms and undominated by them. His forms are in constant flux. (p. 1)

Again the educative activity is in the making of the forms and not in the forms themselves. Frost outlined a similar sense of creation in "The Figure a Poem Makes": "It begins in delight and ends in wisdom. . . . It has an outcome that though unforeseen was predestined from the first image of the original mood. . . . It finds its own name as it goes" (1972, p. 394). Pratt says that the creative artist starts out with "an idea to be sure but it is an idea which he needs to clarify though his method of dealing with it. He is dominated by a desire to clarify this idea for *himself*" (1926, p. 3).

Pratt felicitously applies this conception of an artist to what the student does in using forms in play and work and what the teacher does in forming the classroom. In traditional schooling, children are given forms of mathematical computation divorced from any immediate use, so that they "may have the mechanical forms clearly in mind but cannot apply the right form to the problem to be solved. Working the forms while using the materials, having a hand in the formulations clears the atmosphere in a surprising way" (p. 8). Similarly, the principal or educational psychologist cannot simply give forms of teaching, as in lesson plans, methods, and curricula, to the teacher, "the person who learns about his materials from working with them just as the plastic artist does. The person who actually sets up and helps to destroy the forms through which he works" (p. 10). Both the student and the teacher learn and grow from the forms they make, which paradoxically make these very forms no longer relevant, because the making of them has already changed the maker. The teacher needs to notice carefully when forms become repeated because "opposed to the desire to explore and discover is the tendency to fall back on forms already established":

> Pedagogy seems to me to mean helping children to get what they intrinsically need as evidenced by their behavior in the growth process. It means setting up and discarding forms through which the children and teacher can realize together their fundamental needs. In this new pedagogy signs of stagnation are watched for with the greatest care. When a teacher finds herself closely repeating a form over a long period she learns to be suspicious and watches the children for such signs as diminishing interest. (p. 7)

Perhaps because of these attitudes, the City and Country School is still an ongoing enterprise.

Nearby, Margaret Naumburg started the Children's School, probably the first American school based explicitly on the principles of depth psychology. In an early statement (1917/1973) she says:

> The new psychology has uncovered the true nature of primitive thought and has shown that it still lives on in the unconscious mental being of the adult as well as of the child. Most of our thinking is in this primitive or "fantasy" form; and only a minor part of our mental life occurs as *directed* thought. Yet all our methods of education up to the present time have taken into account only this later type of mental process. (p. 41)

Although the Play School is sometimes seen as an instance of Freudianism (Beck, 1958–1959; Cremin, 1961), it was more accurately Jungian in its orientation. Both Naumburg and the art director, Florence Cane, were analyzed by the noted Jungian Dr. Beatrice Hinkle. More significantly, their school embraced a view of art as not simply a sublimation or rechanneling of unconscious energies but as a way of bringing these energies to consciousness to expand and integrate the psyche. This connection with Jung's thought aligns the school with the 19th-century tradition of Romanticism we have traced, a convergence underscored by Naumburg's renaming it the Walden School 3 years after its inception.

In the tradition of "The American Scholar" and anticipating Dewey's *Art as Experience*, Naumburg and Cane focused on the learning processes inherent in the making of art rather than in the finished products. As Cane writes in "Art in the Life of the Child" (1932): "The direction of my teaching has been towards the liberation and growth of the child's soul through play and work and self-discipline involved in painting" (p. 42). But Cane did not view making art solely as an expressivist activity revealing to the children their own psyches; it also taught lessons about the nature of perception, the physics of light, the structuring of the external world: "As [the child] makes these fantastic patterns and forms he gains empirical experience. In placing colors next to each other often enough he discovers harmony; in interlacing lines he finds rhythm; and in opposing masses he learns balance" (p. 43). Further, Naumburg tried to bring together the aesthetic and the practical by having the students decorate the school, even to the extent of working with a professional plasterer in creating frescoes. The children first created designs, and when they "were ready, they were submitted to both classes and some of the teachers for consideration and suggestion. These discussions brought out the necessity of relating the degree of room light to the intensity of color scheme chosen" (Naumburg, 1926, p. 163).

Besides these artistic activities, the Walden School engaged its students in work-play situations similar to those described in Caroline Pratt's school. And like Pratt, Naumburg had her own roster of illustrious guest teachers: Lewis Mumford in English, Hendrik Willem Van Loon in history, Alexander Goldweiser in anthropology, and Ernest Bloch in music. Paul Rosenfeld in *Port of New York* (1924) includes an essay on Naumburg and the school among 13 others on the boldest innovators in writing, painting, and photography. Both Naumburg and Cane went on to do pioneer work in the field that later became known as art therapy, but it was their belief in the cognitive value of art and the artistic aspects of cognition that one hopes will be the most widespread.

ℂ 5 ℂ

Dewey's own laboratory school has been justifiably criticized for not giving the children enough time and encouragement for individual artistic expression. While there was a great deal of handwork, most of this was directed toward group projects of a utilitarian nature. Fortunately, Dewey had a flexible, resilient mind and a long life, and after 2 decades of teaching at Columbia

University, he made the artistic process itself his paradigm for learning about the world. Some of this turnabout was due to his collaboration with Albert Barnes, the rich, eccentric inventor, who had assembled an impressive collection of modern and primitive art, but Dewey's interest was also redirected by living in the artistic ferment of Manhattan in the 1920s. *Art as Experience* (1934/1987) makes explicit many of the basic assumptions behind experimental education of the time.

Dewey dismantles what he calls the museum conception of art, in which works are regarded as isolated from their living contexts of both production and reception:

> The very perfection of some of these products, the prestige they possess because of a long history of unquestioned admiration, creates conventions that get in the way of fresh insight. When an art product once attains classic status, it somehow becomes isolated from the human condition under which it was brought into being and from the human consequences it engenders in actual life-experience. (p. 9)

This leads him to the paradox that "to understand the meaning of artistic products, we have to forget them for a time, to turn aside from them and have recourse to the ordinary forces and conditions of experience that we do not usually regard as esthetic" (p. 10). In other words, for Dewey, as for Emerson, the entire process of creation is privileged over the artifact itself, made a fetish by those who treasure the past over the continuing act of mental expansion.

Dewey then goes beyond Emerson in constructing a theory of specifically what happens in the artistic process. Dewey sees the human being, "the live creature" as he titles his first chapter, as constantly striving to create a harmony both between the self and its environment and within the self itself:

> Life itself consists of phases in which the organism falls out of step with the march of surrounding things and then recovers unison with it—either through effort or by some happy chance. And, in a growing life, the recovery is never mere return to a prior state, for it is enriched by the state of disparity and resistance through which it has successfully passed. . . . Life grows when a temporary falling out is a transition to a more extensive balance of the energies of the organism with those of the conditions under which it lives. (pp. 19–20)

That art could be a major instrument in creating this state of unity is a new development in Dewey's thought, but it was already an axiom of the thinkers and writers of the period. For example, in the first issue of *The Seven Arts* (1917), Waldo Frank, Naumburg's husband, wrote:

And all the elements of nature, all the materials of his own hand are hard things indeed to make his own. Intuitively, man has felt this issue and realized that he must be forever recreating life into a form that he can grasp if he would not be submerged. . . . By art he lifts up the more hidden bases of existence and makes them his experience; he achieves that sense of unity and *at-homeness* with an exterior world which saves him from becoming a mere pathetic feature of it. (pp. 295–296)

The state of unity itself, though, is less important in Dewey's mind than the movement or transition to such a state: "The moment of passage from disturbance into harmony is that of intensest life" (1934/1987, p. 22). Accordingly, the artist does not value the state of unity itself beyond the conditions of disparity and conflict it subsumes: "He does not shun moments of resistance and tension. He rather cultivates them, not for their own sake but because of their potentialities, bringing to living consciousness an experience that is unified and total" (p. 21).

So even the condition of unity, like the artwork itself, is not something to be dwelled in and upon; Dewey writes, "If a conclusion is reached, it is that of a movement of anticipation and culmination, one that finally comes to completion. A 'conclusion' is no separate and independent thing; it is the consummation of a movement" (p. 45). To try to stay with the conclusion itself is to be fixed in the static while the onrush of life passes us by, so we need to make every conclusion a new beginning: "Any attempt to perpetuate beyond its term the enjoyment attending the time of fulfillment and harmony constitutes withdrawal from the world. Hence it marks the lowering and loss of vitality" (p. 23). What we can take with us is only the memory and promise that such a unity can be attained, just as we are both haunted and energized by the myths of Eden and the Golden Age: "Through the phases of perturbation and conflict, there abides the deep-seated memory of an underlying harmony, the sense of which haunts life like the sense of being founded on a rock" (p. 23).

This constant process of creating a state of unity, falling away from it, and creating it anew is undergone not only by the artist but also by the audience. The viewer or reader must re-create the object, achieve a harmony with it that is not simply an instantaneous impression but the result of an analogous process of relating and synthesizing:

Without an act of recreation the object is not perceived as a work of art. The artist selected, simplified, clarified, abridged and condensed according to his interest. The beholder must go through these operations, according to his point of view and interest. In both, an act of abstraction, that is, of extraction of what is significant, takes place. In both, there is comprehension in its literal signification—that is, a gathering together of details and particulars physically scattered into an experienced whole. (p. 60)

What we see in Dewey's theory is a joining of the two major elements we have been tracing in the history of the active learning: the urge toward re-integration and the necessity of constantly creating new forms. If we attempt to hold on to the state of unity beyond its time, it becomes a habit that masks more authentic forms of unity, so there is no end to the creative process: "Art throws off the covers that hide the expressiveness of experienced things. It quickens us from the slackness of routine and enables us to forget our-selves by finding ourselves in the delight of experiencing the world about us in its varied qualities and forms" (p. 110).

CHAPTER 8

Opening Classrooms and Minds:
The 1960s and 1970s

We speak increasingly of control, as if we feared that everything would collapse into nothing if we let loose our (illusory) hold on things. And so I have been urging one simple truth through all these pages: that the educational function does not rest upon our ability to control, or our will to instruct, but upon our human nature and the nature of experience.

—George Dennison

THE DECADE FROM the mid-1960s to the mid-1970s was the best of times and the worst of times for proponents of active learning in American education. They were the best of times because efforts based on principles such as the "open classroom" became cultural phenomena, accompanied by handbooks, newsletters, networks, and the active support of the federal government. There were no longer only isolated schools conducted by particularly gifted experimenters such as Bronson Alcott or Caroline Pratt, but enough teachers, students, and momentum to reach the critical mass of a "movement." This time saw the greatest body—both in quantity and quality—of books about education in our country's history. Indeed, the period could claim the creation of an entire nonfiction genre that combined personal narrative, cultural analysis, and radical social prophecy in books of often extraordinary literary merit, such as John Holt's *How Children Fail* (1964/1982), Herbert Kohl's *36 Children* (1967), James Herndon's *The Way It Spozed to Be* (1968), and George Dennison's *The Lives of Children* (1969). Borrowing both visionary energy and organizational techniques from the civil rights and antiwar movements, large numbers of committed young people turned to education as a way to transform and liberate the entire society.

But they were the worst of times in the rapidity with which these promises faded. When the chalk dust cleared, the final score was Establishment 1, Movement 0. The open classroom changed from a pedagogical concept to an architectural one, and dividing walls, literally and figuratively, went back up in thousands of schools. The conditions of poor schools and the oppression of racial minorities that Jonathan Kozol described in *Death at an Early Age* (1967) have not improved but have persisted long enough to furnish material for his later book *Savage Inequalities* (1991). Many of the teacher-writers that that my own generation read for inspiration and strategy left the classroom themselves, burned-out and discouraged. The good news was that my 1969 class at the Harvard Graduate School of Education enrolled more members of Phi Beta Kappa than either the medical school or the law school; the bad news was that we averaged less than 3 years in the field before leaving it.

In both respects, the first exuberant burst of hope and activity and the sudden fizzle, this generation of educators resembled the Transcendentalists. The deeper connection is that both groups represented an ambivalent rejection of American society in the name of America itself. Both had an acute awareness of the gaps between what Allen Ginsberg has called "the lost America of love" (1956, p. 30), that ideal of harmony with nature, of democratic community, of psychic wholeness, and the social and political realities that undermine it at every turn. Like Simon and Garfunkel's cars on the New Jersey Turnpike, we've all come to look for America, an America that never really existed but that has persisted on the horizon of our imaginations despite centuries of brutal betrayal.

It is the persistence of this vision that should keep us from wallowing in nostalgia or becoming cynical and apathetic. Whatever opportunities were lost then can still be recuperated through the very awareness of past failures. The print record still remains as a guide and a goad for younger and better people. This chapter will begin with some general history and then we will focus on two representative texts by John Holt and George Dennison to ferret out the lessons that the period still has for us.

28° 2 *«8*

Paradoxically, many of the writers and teachers who embodied the tradition of active learning were unaware of it as a historical phenomenon and would have been surprised to find themselves in a book like this. In a typical retrospective comment, Herbert Kohl says that although he felt he was exploring new territory at the time, he has "since learned that we were reinventing a tradition that reaches back to American progressive-education movements that developed as early as the 1840s" (1998, p. 14). And in a synoptic article on the education books of this period, Kohl reflects:

These days, I see my work in the context of the progressive education movement of the late 19th and early 20th centuries. Like John Dewey in his earlier years, Francis Parker, Lucy Sprague Mitchell, and Jane Addams, I strove for the full development of every child's capacities as well as for the democratic transformation of society, in the hope that a wonderful education would lead to a decent adult life. At the time, however, I made no connection between the practices of these progressive pioneers and what was going on in the schools. In fact, I had not read much of their work. (1991, p. 69)

There were exceptions to this amnesia, as we shall see in George Dennison's extensive use of Dewey's thought, but generally Kohl's comments are characteristic of most of his contemporaries. From one perspective, this is not very surprising, since reformers are always advocates of the now and the new, and like Stephen Dedalus view the past as a nightmare from which they are trying to awake (Joyce, 1922/1986, p. 28). As Lawrence Cremin (1961) observes: "Reform movements are notoriously ahistorical in outlook. They look forward rather than back" (p. 8). It is my hope that conceptualizing a tradition will help us see an essential coherence that is sometimes obscured by a proliferation of techniques, catchphrases, and classroom strategies. I argue that beneath a diversity of practices and settings, from public schools to urban storefronts to rural retreats, is a core of ideas that gives to students and teachers more conscious choice in shaping the educational situation and an urge to integrate symbols and experience.

But if direct and conscious continuities between the historical tradition and the events of the 1960s and 1970s are difficult to find, from where did the immediate impetus come? The background is complex and tangled, but a few major threads can be traced. Virtually all histories of this period in education begin with the 1957 Soviet launch of the unmanned space satellite Sputnik. The immediate effect on American education was to accelerate trends and programs that had already been initiated. For example, a year before Sputnik, Jerrold Zacharias of the Massachusetts Institute of Technology initiated the Physical Sciences Study Committee, financed by the National Science Foundation (NSF). In 1958, the group, under the rubric Elementary Science Study (ESS), became affiliated with the Education Development Center (EDC) in Newton, Massachusetts, to which belonged also teachers such as William Hull and Madison Judson who were involved in bringing to American attention the innovations of the British infant schools, especially those in Leicestershire. These schools adopted what they called "the integrated day" or "the developmental classroom" in which children moved at liberty between various activity centers and worked on long-term projects that combined manual and cognitive skills. If this sounds like the laboratory school at the University of Chicago, it was in part because Dewey's work

was one of the main inspirations, along with that of the cognitive psychologist Jean Piaget and British writers such as Susan and Nathan Isaacs and
Basil Bernstein. William Hull brought back news from these schools in 1961,
anticipating the work of Joseph Featherstone (1971) and of Lillian Weber,
who through her Open Corridor program in the New York City schools
and her book *The English Infant School and Informal Education* (1971),
re-Americanized this approach.

From this convergence of scientists and open education activists, what
began as the development of better educational materials turned into an
initiative for more experiential, connected learning. Diane Ravitch comments,
"Ironically, while NSF curriculum development had begun in the strongly
cognitive, antiprogressive spirit of the late 1950s, the curriculum developers
at ESS followed the concepts of 'inquiry' and 'discovery' full circle back to
the progressive tradition" (1983, p. 224). As perceptive as this statement is,
I find that "ironically" misses the mark and would chose another adverb—
perhaps *significantly*, or even *predictably*. For these scientists and educators, genuinely interested in getting children to think scientifically themselves,
discovered the power of giving them the opportunity to explore, generate
their own hypotheses, and spend as much time as they need on the process
itself, rather than try to "cover" a great deal of material. Indeed, one of their
leaders, the philosopher David Hawkins, has said the task of education is to
uncover a subject rather than cover it. Hawkins's ideas are put forth elo-
quently in an article first published in 1966, "Messing About in Science," a
result of his own experience with pendulums in a fifth-grade classroom.

Hawkins discusses three phases in the learning of science, but since he
does not want us to view or use them in any given order, he distinguishes
them by geometrical shapes rather than by numbers or letters. One of these
phases gives the article its title, "messing about," which consists of letting
students play on their own with relevant materials—in this case weights,
brackets, and various lengths of string. Hawkins notes that there is a tendency to view this phase as merely preliminary, a teaser to real learning,
but it is one of the strengths of his vision to see it as the phase that most
profoundly engages children in doing science: "When learning is at the most
fundamental level, as it is here, with all the abstractions of Newtonian me-
chanics just around the corner, don't rush! When the mind is evolving the
abstractions which will lead to physical comprehension, all of us must cross
the line between ignorance and insight many times before we truly understand" (1974, p. 68). Another phase is to make available to the child what
Hawkins calls "multiply programmed" material that will help the child further along the path he or she is moving on already. A third phase is simply
presenting the children relevant outside material in the forms of print and
informal lectures, such as a short talk on Galileo's observations and gener-

alizations on pendulums. As Hawkins says, "Theorizing in a creative sense needs the content of experience and the logic of experimentation to support it. But these do not automatically lead to conscious abstract thought"; and then, punning on the shape he assigns this phase, he adds "Theory is square!" (p. 74). Hawkins points out that all three phases are necessary for good science teaching. Although his article is most remembered for its "messing around" stage, he emphasizes this only in reaction to traditional methods that use almost exclusively the square phase. For Hawkins, free play and open exploration need to be supplemented and complemented with book learning and disciplined observation in a series of back-and-forth movements that constantly illuminate and qualify each other.

This is important to remember because there were also groups who took their lead from a more one-sided theorist, A. S. Neill, the founder of Summerhill, a private English boarding school, and author of a 1960 book of the same name. Summerhill was probably the most extreme application of libertarian principles to education: The students were not required or even advised to go to class or to do anything in particular. While Neill would claim there was no imposition of outside values, his own inclinations, conveyed to the students in subtle ways, were more toward shopworking and relaxing in nature than toward reading, writing, or math. Since he felt that students would grow naturally toward health and competence when they were free of coercion and repression, there was little if anything that adults could or should do. *Summerhill: A Radical Approach to Child Rearing* received little attention when it was published at the beginning of the decade, in the antiprogressive atmosphere of this period but by 1969 the book was selling at the rate of more than 200,000 copies a year. Neill was an engaging writer, and when the times became more conducive, his work was one of the few specific accounts of an alternative approach to the boredom of conventional schooling.

It should be clear from my summary that I do not see a place for Summerhill in the tradition of active learning. Probably the major effect of Summerhillian adaptations in this country was to evoke the term *Romantic* to characterize the entire movement, a term suggesting sentimentality, nostalgia, primitivism, and permissiveness. The adjective was given currency by Peter Schrag in a 1967 *Saturday Review* article, "Education's 'Romantic' Critics," in which the use of quotation marks suggests his own uneasiness with the label. Shrag was generally sympathetic to the critics he discusses, mainly Edgar Z. Friedenberg, Paul Goodman, Jules Henry, and John Holt. But for others who considered themselves Realistic or Practical, the very use of *Romantic* was all they needed to indict anyone associated with the movement.

I have tried in this book to rescue Romanticism from these negative connotations on the grounds that it is a vision of integration, not of one-sided emphasis on the emotions or individual subjectivity. From this perspective, if we differentiate Summerhill and the extreme American "free schools" that followed in its wake, we can see the term more as an honorific pointing toward an important historical continuity. Edgar Friedenberg makes the crucial point that engagement with specifics and greater freedom to learn are actually more thought provoking and sustaining than are traditional methods: "Our insistence that concrete experience form the basis for education opened Romantic critics to the charge of being anti-intellectual, which was frequently and vituperatively made. Conventional schooling, I would argue, is far more weakly rooted in the intellect than alternative schooling, since it depends so heavily on conventional wisdom and officially certified facts" (1990, p. 181). As we will see, John Holt and George Dennison launch their critiques from precisely this viewpoint: The act of thinking is actually retarded and discouraged by the current structures of schooling. Charles Silberman in his 1970 bestseller, *Crisis in the Classroom,* extends this diagnosis to the way the system itself functions, stifling any reflections about its own workings and refusing to apply intelligence to itself: "It simply never occurs to more than a handful to ask *why* they are doing what they are doing— to think seriously or deeply about the purposes or consequences of education" (p. 11). Later in the book, he elaborates on the results of what he identifies as "mindlessness"; after quoting Alexis de Tocqueville that "what we call necessary institutions are often not more than institutions to which we have grown accustomed," Silberman writes:

> So it is with schools in their traditional form. The "necessity" that makes schooling so uniform over time and across cultures is simply the "necessity" that stems from unexamined assumptions and unquestioned behavior. The preoccupation with order and control, the slavish adherence to the timetable and the lesson plan, the obsession with routine qua routine, the absence of noise and movement, the joylessness and repression, the universality of the formal lecture or teacher-dominated "discussion" in which the teacher instructs an entire class as a unit, the emphasis on the verbal and the de-emphasis of the concrete, the inability of students to work on their own, the dichotomy between work and play—none of these are necessary; all can be eliminated. (pp. 207–208)

As this suggests, to place thinking at the center of our teaching in terms of what we ask of both our students and ourselves is a move that would seem radical or Romantic only in a system that had gone so far in the opposite direction.

Another important element of the 1960s and 1970s was the application of a particularly literary sensibility to writing about schooling. Herbert Kohl (1991) reflects that he and his Harvard roommate, Jonathan Kozol, wanted

to be both teachers and writers but had not thought of putting the two together until they underwent the intense school experiences that resulted in
their first books. Before he began teaching, Kozol spent a year on a Fulbright
trying to write a great novel. On the West Coast, James Herndon was deeply
interested in poetry and was friends with several of the experimental writers
in the Bay Area. For years George Dennison was an unsuccessful novelist and
playwright; his literary talent was fulfilled only in his book on education.

By combining their literary talents with fierce social commitments, the
writers of this period were able to find forms that effectively combined the
personal and the political. The very titles of the books convey a deep concern with the actual students they came to love: *36 Children, The Lives of
Children, How Children Fail.* But the books focused on the teachers as well
as the students, each becoming a kind of bildungsroman, tracing the drama
of the author's growth into fuller understanding of self, schools, and learning. Often the school year itself afforded the temporal structure for the narrative, in which the teachers and students became familiar characters with
whose conflicts, alliances, and destinies the reader can become as deeply
involved as in any novel.

Most significantly, these books were written in a style that complemented
and reflected the educational tradition of active learning, a style that engaged
the play and interaction of the concrete world, that was ambulatory rather
saltatory, that was simple and graceful in diction and syntax but resonantly
nuanced and complex. One particularly effective device was the use of the
telling detail, as in this example from Miriam Wasserman's *The School Fix,
NYC, USA* (1970):

> Mrs. White introduces me to the children. "This is Mrs. Wasserman, children,
> a very distinguished writer. Say 'Good morning, Mrs. Wasserman.'" "Good
> morning, children." "This is a very s-l-o-w class, h-o-l-d-o-v-e-r-s," she spells,
> trying to enlist my gaze in an understanding complicity. I look away, ashamed.
> The well-trained children stand neatly behind their chairs. At a signal, first the
> girls sit, then the boys. Miss White says, "Feet flat on the floor, heads up, sit
> straight, hands clasped on desk." I think that some kind of posture exercise is
> about to begin, but it turns out to be the required position of the morning. . . .
> During the hours of tutelage, the children must give over to her keeping their
> bodies as well as their souls. One ingenious boy, held immobile, has learned
> to ripple his abdominal muscles behind the desk. He does this on and off
> throughout the morning, looking down surreptitiously at his jiggling belt buckle.
> (pp. 88–89)

The passage economically suggests the teacher's condescending attitude
toward her students, the valuing of stiff and artificial forms of external behavior over genuine thought and feeling, the obsessive but ultimately futile

quest for control. The jiggling belt buckle here becomes an image of a secret sense of joy and selfhood just as the style itself stands as a counterforce to the imposed leveling and monotonous uniformity of the school culture it describes. It is no accident that James Herndon affixes as his epigram to *Notes from a Schoolteacher* the following from Edgar Friedenberg: "Experience is never categorical; what matters about it is always detailed and personal" (Herndon, 1985, p. 11). The books not only describe pedagogy consistent with active learning, but also enact its values in their telling, in their balance between concrete narrative and larger social and educational issues.

➤ 3 ⛆

John Holt, in *How Children Fail*, first published in 1964, uses all these techniques to show in precise detail how the structures of schooling block the act of thinking. At first it seems to be a running diary of Holt's classroom observations over a period of 4 years. But as he observes his students' behavior, he begins to form hypotheses about why they are acting in such irrational and self-defeating ways, and creates activities to test these hypotheses further. The interest of the book, then, becomes not only its insights but also the ambulatory journey of discovery, embodying its faith in the mind's ability to make sense out of the world. Indeed, this faith is a key value in both education and literary technique, as Herbert Kohl suggests when he says Holt "never derived theory from theory, but stayed as close as possible to experience itself, this *making sense of experience*" (1998, p. 4). The revised edition of 1982 contains later sections of commentary inserted into these entries in which Holt further reflects on incidents and issues from the perspective of 2 decades later. The book, then, is a particularly fortuitous convergence of subject matter and form, modeling a mind learning about learning.

Holt's background was similarly fortuitous in that it was free of the truisms and preconceptions created by formal course work in education. After serving on a submarine in World War II, he drifted into a position, team teaching with William Hull, at the Colorado Rocky Mountain School, where he had not only daily exposure to an innovative teacher but also the opportunity to sometimes observe the classroom as neither a teacher nor student. As Holt points out, it is extremely difficult for a single teacher to see the students accurately, for as soon as he or she looks at any one of them, the look itself alters behavior as surely as if they were electrons: "A teacher in class is like a man in the woods at night with a powerful flashlight in his hand. Wherever he turns his light, the creatures on whom it shines are aware of it, and do not behave as they do in the dark" (1964/1982, pp. 33–34). Even when student teachers have similar opportunities, they spend too much time watching the teacher, not the students: "Their concern is with manipulating and controlling children rather than understanding them" (p. 34).

As Holt begins to observe, he finds himself puzzled by children who seem to have a vested interest in failure, who would rather say immediately that they don't know instead of trying to think a problem through. What he comes to see is that a quick admission of failure is less anxiety provoking. Early in the book he formulates this hypothesis: "I find myself coming to realize that what hampers their thinking, what drives them into these narrow and defensive strategies, is a feeling that they must please the grownups at all costs" (p. 29). That this might be crucial comes home to him in the game of 20 questions he plays with the children. The children have 20 questions through which to discover a certain number between 1 and 1,000. After fairly quickly learning that guessing individual numbers from the beginning is not going to work, they soon ask questions such as "Is it between 1 and 500?" But having the intelligence to devise this question, they then sabotage themselves. If the answer is yes, they cheer; if not, they are disappointed, without realizing that either answer gives them the same amount of information. This kind of thinking leads to what he calls "producer" strategies as opposed to "thinker" strategies, in which the producing of the right answer becomes the primary goal.

Holt shows a remarkable ability to empathize with children based on their verbal and nonverbal behavior:

> The valiant and resolute band of travelers I thought I was leading toward a much-hoped-for destination turned out instead to be more like convicts in a chain gang, forced under threat of punishment to move along a rough path leading nobody knew where and down which they could see hardly more than a few steps ahead. School feels like this to children: it is a place where *they* make you go and where *they* tell you to do things and where *they* try to make your life unpleasant if you don't do them or don't do them right. . . . Each task is an end in itself. The children don't care how they dispose of it. If they can get it out of the way by doing it, they will do it; if experience has taught them that this does not work very well, they will turn to other means, illegitimate means, that wholly defeat whatever purpose the task giver may have had in mind. (pp. 38–39)

Since for most schoolchildren getting the right answer is more important than learning anything, they put most of their mental energies into strategies for doing so, and Holt describes these in detail. There is, for example, the mumble strategy, in which students deliberately try to be inaudible, realizing that the teacher is listening for the right answer and is likely to read it in an ambiguous signal. This has its written equivalent in the sloppy-handwriting strategy, in which the student will create on a spelling test a hieroglyphic that can be interpreted as several different letters. Another strategy is to just wait it out, to look blank as the teacher breaks down the question into more elementary parts and finally ends up giving the answer away.

In delineating these strategies, Holt does not try to blame the victims by implying that the strategies are a sign of moral failure on the part of students but suggests that they are often a rational response to the irrational situations we often put them in. For example, he recounts one classroom where the teacher went through a list of words, having the children classify them as a group under the headings of Noun, Adjective, and Verb. Instead of trying to figure this out grammatically, the students would carefully watch the subtle changes in the teacher's body position as she was poised to write the next answer on the board in the correct column. But as Holt points out, the task itself was meaningless and even puzzling, because many words can fit in two or more categories depending on how they are used in sentences. The teacher was confusing the way our syntax divides the world on the basis of the structure of reality itself, and thus was confusing her students, as suggested in the following interchange, in which she asks the children about the word *dream*:

> She was thinking of the noun, and apparently did not remember that "dream" can as easily be a verb. One little boy, making a pure guess, said it was a verb. Here the teacher, to be helpful, contributed one of those "explanations" that are so much more hindrance than help. She said, "But a verb has to have action; can you give me a sentence, using 'dream,' that has action?" The child thought a bit, and said, "I had a dream about the Trojan War." Now it's pretty had to get much more action than that. But the teacher told him he was wrong, and he sat silent, with an utterly baffled and frightened expression on his face. (p. 27)

By multiplying examples of both the absurd things we ask children to do and their strategies for doing them, Holt earns his conclusion, which parallels the critique of traditional education made by Dewey:

> In many ways, we break down children's convictions that things make sense, or their hope that things may prove to make sense. We do it, first of all, by breaking life up into arbitrary and disconnected hunks of subject matter, which we then try to "integrate" by such artificial and irrelevant devices as having children sing Swiss songs while they are studying the geography of Switzerland, or do arithmetic problems about rail-splitting while they are studying the boyhood of Lincoln. Furthermore, we continually confront them with what is senseless, ambiguous, and contradictory; worse, we do it without knowing that we are doing it, so that hearing nonsense shoved at them as if it were sense, they come to feel that the source of their confusion lies not in the material but in their own stupidity. Still further, we cut children off from their own commonsense and the world of reality by requiring them to play and shove around words and symbols that have little or no meaning to them. (p. 275)

Holt wrote the most effective critique of the ways our schools do business not through sweeping indictments of capitalist society and the "system," but by describing in detail self-defeating actions of both teachers and students in the classroom. No one at the time—or since, for that matter—has successfully refuted his data and analysis, so there was every reason to believe that in a rational world his critique would be heeded. That his book had no permanent effect on education in the way that, say, Rachel Carson's *Silent Spring* affected agriculture or Ralph Nader's *Unsafe at Any Speed* affected auto safety suggests the extent to which education has become a system that cannot learn about itself.

☞ 4 ☜

John Holt's favorite book on education was George Dennison's *The Lives of Children: The Story of the First Street School* (1969) and their admiration for each other's work turned into a close personal friendship. As with *How Children Fail*, Dennison's *Lives of Children* seems to be informally structured, but this structure comes out of Dennison's skills as a literary artist as well as his sense of how we all learn. Chapters of direct narration and exposition about the nature of this small school are interspersed with daily journal entries and with a few theoretical and historical chapters, such as that containing a discussion of Tolstoy's schooling of peasant children. These are related and further conceptualized in the last chapter, which has as one of its primary concerns the theories of John Dewey.

This methodological self-consciousness is evident in the first few pages, as when Dennison notes that *freedom* is too abstract and elusive a word and that its meaning becomes clear only through context and examples:

> It is another name for the continuity of the fullness and final shape of activities. We experience the activities, not the freedom. The mother of a child in a public school told me that he kept complaining, "They never let me *finish* anything!" We might say of the child that he lacked important freedoms, but his own expression is closer to the experience: activities important to him remained unfulfilled. (1969, p. 4)

Dennison respects both the experience of the child and the ability of language to capture the situation most accurately when it stays close to that experience through concrete narrative. By contrast, Dennison later dismantles the prose of a writer in *The Urban Review* as the "quintessence of the self-absorption of bureaucratic research" (p. 251). Dennison fully grasps how writing and teaching are related, that if we write about education in constructs that have little relation to the realities of schooling, no matter how good our intentions, we are perpetuating a system that stops thought.

Dennison also sets out the three primary points that he wishes "to bring out in detail" (p. 8). This may seem incongruous in the light of the generally ambulatory mode that these books adopt, but Dennison's book is such a montage of apparently contrasting styles and genres that such initial bearings are called for. Further, his three points can serve as an epitome of our entire tradition. The first is "a point made repeatedly by John Dewey and very poorly understood by many of his followers, that the proper concern of schools is less a preparation for adult life than the widening and enriching of the present lives of children" (p. 9). The second point deserves quoting in full:

> When the conventional routines of a school are abolished (the military discipline, the schedules, the punishments and rewards, the standardization), what arises is neither a vacuum nor chaos, but rather a new order, based first on relationships between adults and children, and children and their peers, but based ultimately on such truths of the human condition as these: that the mind does not function separately from the emotions, but thought partakes of feeling and feeling of thought; that there is no such thing as knowledge *per se*, knowledge in a vacuum, but rather all knowledge is possessed and must be expressed by individuals; that the human voices preserved in books belong to the real features of the world, and that children are so powerfully attracted to this world that the very motion of their curiosity comes through to us as a form of love; that an active moral life cannot be evolved except where people are free to express their feelings and act upon the insights of conscience. (p. 9)

We see here the Romantic (in its positive sense) emphasis on giving feeling and relation its due and reuniting them with thought as well as the continuing emphasis on embodied knowledge. Books, when read rightly, are not antithetical to this immediately human world, but offer additional human voices entering into dialogue with our own. Dennison's third point is that the present school system is the antithesis of this conception: "The present quagmire of public education is entirely the result of unworkable centralization and the lust for control that permeates every bureaucratic institution" (p. 9).

Dennison immediately plunges into a description of the First Street School, its teachers and students. Four teachers, three full time and one half time (Dennison himself), and twenty-three students ranging in age from 5 to 13, occupied a third of a midtown Young Men's Hebrew Association building. Dennison sees the small size of the school not as an accidental dimension but as crucial for the intimate contact that needs to be established as a base for learning. Removing restraints can be only a first step: "These two things taken together—the natural authority of adults and the needs of children—are the great reservoir of organic structuring that comes into being when arbitrary rules of order are dispensed with" (p. 25). Dennison describes this process of organic structuring in the detailed narratives of several students: Maxine, a sexually curious and confused 9-year-old who was allowed to drift into the youngest group for a while as a way of getting the nurturing and regressive release she needed; Vincente, who changed from a screamer to a talker, as he played with all three groups; and José, whose narrative weaves through the entire book.

After the general argument of the first chapter, the reader encounters in the second chapter a series of daily journal entries spanning 2 months in the middle of the school year, followed by a third chapter in the style of the first that begins with this general reflection:

> Perhaps after these excerpts from the journal, something of our intimate, informal style may be apparent. What may not be so obvious is that there was any connection between this style and the advances in learning made by the children. And here we come to one of the really damaging myths of education, namely, that learning is a result of teaching; that the progress of the child bears a direct relation to the methods of instruction. Nothing could be farther from the truth. . . . The causes are in the child. When we consider the powers of mind of a healthy eight-year-old—the avidity of the senses, the finesse and energy of observation, the effortless concentration, the vivacious memory— we realize immediately that these powers possess true magnitude in the general scale of things. (p. 73)

The rest of the chapter extends the story of José, who came to this country at the age of 7 from Puerto Rico, knowing how to read Spanish, and after 5 years of public education in New York could read neither this language nor English. Chapter 4 is a general reflection on how infants learn language, a process that happens with almost no direct instruction through natural, daily interactions with family: "Knowledge is gained in immediately instrumental forms. The gain is accompanied by use and pleasure. The parents do not pose as models, but are living their lives" (p. 94). By contrast, if we wished to interfere with the infant's learning and his growth, Dennison suggests the following:

> 1) turn his attention back upon himself by letting him know that he is being observed, measured, and compared with others; 2) destroy his innate sense of his own peerage among sensible forms by insisting that they are to be apprehended in standardized ways and that their uses are effectively controlled by others; 3) make his passage among persons dependent upon the measurements to which he has been subjected; 4) apply physical coercion to his freedom to move, to express his feelings, to act upon his doubts, to give or refuse his attention—all of which will convince him that learning is an act of disembodied will or of passive attention, neither of which he can find within him-

self; 5) present him with new forms in a rigidly preordained order and quantity, so that he will give up utterly the hope of the organic structure which
proceeds outward from his own great attraction to the world. (pp. 95–96)

It is only after this general discussion that Dennison returns to José so that
we can now see how his school not only failed to teach him to read English
but also erased his literacy in Spanish and reconsider the radical assertion
that his reading problem "is not a fact of life but a fact of school administration. It does not describe José but describes the action performed by the
school" (p. 77).

The book proceeds in this manner, seeming to tack but actually reaching its goals in an ambulatory and effective way. Of particular intensity are
Dennison's observations of how his students play and fight with minimum
adult interference. Although he clearly loves his students, he does not sen-
timentalize them; he shares with the reader his frequent anger and frustra-
tion with them, so that one empathizes with the teacher as well as the students.
Dennison does not portray himself as the Hollywood version of an inner-
city teacher who miraculously gets through to the tough cases through his
or her charisma and toughness, but shows instead how a genuine community works: "When adults stand out of the way so children can develop among
themselves the full riches of their natural relationships, their effect on one
another is positively curative" (p. 82). Dennison does recount, though, some
brief glimpses of his own unorthodox, risk-taking teaching ploys, as when
he tells José that he was going to punch him for every mistake in a reading
exercise: "This was such an accurate parody of the pressure he puts on himself that he burst out laughing and ventured to make a few mistakes" (p. 138).

This extensive discussion of children in the concrete lends texture and
credibility to the generalizations in the preceding chapter of this present
volume of how to implement Dewey's ideas in the 1960s. Dennison makes
one of the points of chapter 6 here, that against its own spirit Dewey's work
has been turned into "methods." Dennison argues, using a metaphor we have
seen common in the 1920s, that method and technique really cannot be taught,
only learned, because "the work of the teacher is like that of the artist; it is
a shaping of something given" (p. 257). We can move from mechanical
conceptions of method to the living situation only by "passing through ourselves" (p. 257).

Dennison moves deeper into the reasons why it is difficult to enact
Dewey's conception of education. To put these ideas into action

requires, first, that the educator be modest toward experience, modest toward
the endless opening-outward and going-onward of life, for this going-onward
is the experience of the young. Precisely this fact of life, however, evokes
anxiety, sorrow, regret, and envy in the hearts of adults. It is not easy to give

oneself wholeheartedly to the flow of life that leaves one, literally, in the dust. If we often scant the differences between the young and ourselves, and prefer the old way, the old prerogatives, the old necessities, it is because at bottom, we are turning at all times from the fact of death. Yet just this is what modesty toward experience means: a reconciled awareness of death. It is a difficult spiritual task; and it lies right at the heart of the educational function. (pp. 257–258)

One of the mysteries this book has wrestled with is the persistence of old forms in the midst of young people. As a fact it is undeniable, but it is difficult to explain. Silberman's "mindlessness" is circular, not really a definition. Dennison's explanation borrows elements from the gurus of the time, Norman O. Brown and Herbert Marcuse, who maintain that it is our refusal to accept the reality of death and its complement, the living flow of life, that leads us to build monuments we think will last forever, such as pyramids, skyscrapers, and systems of schooling. But Dennison avoids the shrillness and self-righteousness of much 1960s radical rhetoric by showing it as an inner struggle, by using *oneself* and *we*.

After suggesting this conflict at the heart of teaching, Dennison, in the following paragraph, describes how "organization" can become a psychological defense and a counterproductive strategy:

> To be open to experience means, too, that we cannot repeat past successes with past techniques. We cannot organize the educational event in advance. Certainly we can plan and prepare, but we cannot organize it until we are in it and the students themselves have brought their unique contributions. And so there is a point beyond which our tendency to organize becomes inimical to experience, inimical to teaching. Yet just this tendency to organize and to elevate the gratifications of the profession—the status of expertise, the pleasures of jargon, the pride of method—is composed largely of two things, both inescapably human and hard to transcend: anxiety and vanity. (p. 258)

We have seen this tendency to overorganize since Horace Mann, but rarely have its causes and negative effects been expressed so succinctly and well. That the work of Holt, Dennison, and other authors of the time was little heeded should not prevent us from enacting their insights now.

Both men have since died of cancer, and one of Dennison's recollections of the last stages of Holt's illness is particularly poignant:

> I took him driving to see the views from certain hills—long views of wooded slopes, fields, streams, our large river, and several ponds. Again and again he said, "How beautiful it is!" He was sitting beside me in the front seat. We drove on and he began to talk about his work. "It could be such a wonderful world," he said, "such a wonderful place." His body began to shake and he dropped

his head, crying uncontrollably—but he kept talking through the sobs, his voice strained and thin. "It's not as if we don't know what to do," he said. "We know *exactly* what to do, and it would work, it would work. They're going to wreck it." We do all have feelings of this kind, but not many people, at the end of life, would feel this heartbroken passion for the world itself. (Holt, 1990, p. 276)

The natural background is more than just a setting here, for it suggests the American version of pastoral, where the flaws of societal life are underscored by their contrast to a pristine and nurturing landscape. The passage is a particularly apt epitaph for the work of both men. The final verdict on the 1960s and 1970s is still not in; it will depend on whether we decide to treat these years as a quaint and curious chapter in history or as a living and usable legacy.

CHAPTER 9

Enacting the Active Mind:
Teaching English, Teaching Teaching

Despite his insistence that we make students aware of the principle
scribo, ego sum—I produce texts, therefore I am—Professor Scholes
and all the rest of us have stopped short of the next step: a recognition that the *classroom* is also a text, produced by teacher and student in collaboration. There is a semiotics of *that* text, too, and it is
time we studied it. . . . Why do we talk about what texts we should
teach, ignoring the one text we must *all* teach: our own action in the
classroom.

—Susan R. Horton

THIS CHAPTER WILL bring the tradition of active learning up to the
current moment in two complementary ways. I will discuss how I have
tried to embody its ideas in my own teaching and at the same time
relate these ideas to recent thinking in literary, philosophical, and psychological theory. One of the main arguments of this book has been that ideas
about education have to be put into practice if they are to be made viable
and complete. Only by enacting them can we see their full implications and
begin to further clarify them. Otherwise they are only shadows on the walls
of our cave, solipsistic soliloquies.

The ideas that have more fully shaped my own discipline of literary
studies in the past 30 years are sometimes grouped under the umbrella of
poststructuralism, which takes aim at the very notion of interpreting. To offer
an interpretation of a text is to inflict violence upon it, to impose one's own
will, to project a coherence that the text could not possibly have. This
polysemous quality is caused not by the particularly ambiguous and emotive nature of literary language as earlier critics had posited, but by the nature
of language itself, more accurately viewed as a field of competing meanings
with nodes that tend to untie themselves on closer inspection. I felt that as
a set of ideas, these had great potential to open up the classroom in more
student-centered, democratic, negotiatory ways.

It was naive of me to think that a new set of ideas about texts would of itself lead to new ways of teaching. Even before these ideas appeared, there was already widespread assent that literature is emotional as well as cognitive, but we rarely allow time and space for the expression of feelings. We acknowledge that literature generates a number of divergent responses, but in the classroom we usually work to get to some kind of convergence or closure before the period ends. We sense the complexities of how reading and writing have individual and creative dimensions, yet insist on ranking students through single numerical grades.

The situation crystallized for me when during a series of job interviews I asked the candidates, most of whom were still in graduate school, if their more theoretically advanced teachers ran their classrooms any differently from their more traditional teachers. It seemed that at what are considered the more prestigious graduate schools, the structures of authority in the classroom itself, the ways in which students and teachers interacted—or did not interact— remained untouched. Despite poststructural skepticism about the validity of any single interpretation, despite insights about the transactional and subjective aspects of the reading process, teachers of graduate students more often than not droned on themselves—often about these very ideas—without enacting any of them. While a rhetoric that was more politically radical entered our professional discourse, it seemed that we were merely trying to outflank each other on the left by articulating the most knowing and antiauthoritarian ideas in print while ignoring the very actualities of our lives as teachers.

If there was one aspect of the new developments that I felt had the most potential for uniting practice and pronouncements, it was reader response theory. This theory, which shared the poststructuralist sense that there is no univocal meaning embedded in the text, looked to two Americans for its base, Louise Rosenblatt and Stanley Fish. I remember having been encouraged to think along these lines in 1970 by a British critic usually not associated with the approach. I had heard a provocative lecture by Frank Kermode comparing Henry James's "The Turn of the Screw" to an "impossible object," one of those optical illusions that can be "read" in two contradictory ways, as, say a cube with either its rear or its front side protruding, or a fork with either two or three prongs. The illusion works because our eye and mind transform what is on one level a two-dimensional object into a three-dimensional construct, and there are at least two different ways to do this. Analogously, we do not merely absorb a similarly flat literary text but actively imagine it, creating a construct that is based on our previous experiences, satisfying in some ways, and internally coherent. No side in "The Turn of the Screw" debate, Kermode suggested, neither those who see the ghosts as the governess's hallucination nor those who see them as real within the frame of the story, has been able to defeat the other because James seems to have deliberately constructed the story as a platform for both possibilities. Although this story may seem a special case—James himself called it "a piece of ingenuity pure and simple . . . an *amusette* to catch those not easily caught" (1984, pp. 1184–1185)—I felt similar processes happening with every work I taught. Students were selectively perceiving different parts of the same text. I began to ask myself questions such as: Were all these responses equally valid? As a teacher should one try to bring them to a sense of closure or let them all stand in their unresolved multiplicity and individuality? How much does the text itself control responses as opposed to how much each reader "pops out" or constructs that text as an imaginative unity?

When reader response criticism broke most noticeably on the scene with the appearance in 1980 of two well-conceived anthologies, *Reader-Response Criticism: From Formalism to Post-Structuralism*, edited by Jane Tompkins, and *The Reader in the Text: Essays in Audience and Interpretation*, edited by Susan Suleiman and Inge Crosman, I read them avidly for answers. There was considerable intellectual excitement in the way theorists such as Wolfgang Iser, Stanley Fish, and Norman Holland were able to reconceptualize the reading process, but I still felt a lack of concrete texture, of specific analyses. What these writers gave with one hand, the idea that meaning is created in the interaction of reader and text, they took away with the other, as it remained only an idea. Instead of actual readers, we encountered "the implied reader," "the ideal reader," "the narratee,"—arguably as much constructs of the isolated critic as any single interpretation of the text itself. At this point I began to wonder if the best laboratory, the most dependable source of data, might not be the classroom itself.

With these questions in mind, and with the hope of bringing into graduate education a course that would relate theory to classroom practice, I began teaching Theory and the Teaching of Literature. This course was built around a beginning undergraduate course that we all taught together. We met for the hour immediately after each undergraduate class to share our perceptions and analyses of it, to relate it to theories we had read or formulated ourselves, to plan the upcoming class in the light of all this, and to form new hypotheses that would be confirmed, denied, or qualified by what we were to see in that upcoming class. We also read carefully and often as a group the undergraduates' papers and other written responses, so in effect the undergraduate class, both in its oral and written dimensions, became the main "text" for the graduate course. I hoped to get both the graduate students and myself to read that text with the same kinds of passionate attention and theoretical conceptualizing that we expect for the best readings of literary texts.

The first time I taught the course, I made the mistake of running the undergraduate course myself for the first couple of weeks, to try to do some modeling and initiate the graduate students gradually. But I soon realized that with teaching, as with most things, the only way to really learn is to do it oneself, and that the graduate students should jump in the water the very first day. One ability I hoped to teach the graduate students was to learn from mistakes. What I learned from this false start was the huge gap between my perceptions of my own lecturing and what was really going on, an immediate example of how important it is to have classroom observers not confined to the roles of teacher or student. As I lectured, I consistently saw upturned, interested faces. But I did not realize how much my looking affected the very behavior I was trying to see, how I was enacting the kind of distorted perception that John Holt described. It was primarily the graduate students who were really absorbed in the lectures, not the undergraduates, who were often more interested in doodling and writing letters.

It was not simply this perceptual difficulty that created the gap between my sense of the classes and the graduate students' collective account of them. The difference also has to do with the inherent distance between talking and listening, between being able to move about and being confined to a seat, between being a lecturer and being a lecturee. I blush to say it, but I was never tired or bored by my own lectures. And yet I know I cannot keep my mind from wandering after about a half hour of someone else's lecture, no matter how good it is. As Clark Bouton and Russell Garth have pointed out, "The active role of the teacher in the traditional classroom contrasts sharply with the passive role of the students. It is not surprising that teaching is the best learning. The teacher's activity makes the traditional method a very effective method of learning—for the teacher" (1983, p. 78). This realization helped explain why often what I thought were the most brilliantly original parts of my lectures often lagged the most for the students. I was thinking things out for the first time, discovering what I had not fully seen before; but these ideas by their very nature were not yet in a form that was particularly clear or incisive to my listeners. These were also my most enthusiastic moments of lecturing, but clearly they were not the ones that created the most enthusiasm in the students. I mention this for those who think enthusiasm works like a virus: If the teacher is enthusiastic, those in proximity will catch the bug. Although I feel that short, well-prepared lectures can be useful, it is also important to be aware that we are always embodying our values in the classroom by what we choose to do, and that to lecture is to value having thought over thinking, the transmission of knowledge over its making. Another recovering lecturer, Stephen Monk, writes: "My TAs [teaching assistants] and I spent all the time telling students how we did mathematics. Their job was to imitate us when they did the homework. The message was that learning was to take place not on course time, but on their own time, away from teachers and away from one another" (1983, p. 8). The implication of all this—particularly as the graduate students began to do their own teaching—became evident. Why should we hoard all the wealth and shoulder all the responsibility? Why have just one person prepare to run a class when every student could benefit from such preparation?

When we turned to discussions with the entire group of 40 undergraduates with one or two of the graduate students moderating, however, the results were often disappointing. We ran into the common problems of only a few students dominating the discussion, of lack of focus and analysis, of participants more concerned with their own points than listening to one another. We had more success when we split the class of 40 into groups of 6 to 8; the 15 graduate students paired off, one running the discussion, the other taking notes on the process, with the pair switching roles in the following class. Still, something was missing in terms of undergraduate involvement and initiative. We eventually came to what we called the structured and prepared discussion. The crucial move here is to have the undergraduates themselves prepare in writing for each class session. That informal writing, then, became the ticket of admission to the class discussion. If a student showed up without having done it, we would sit him or her down in a corner of the classroom to complete it right there and then. While this might sound punitive, we did find that the rock on which so many discussions wrecked was lack of student preparation. Not only is one working at less than full strength, but even the prepared students start to sign off in resentment at having all the work put on them alone. All the discussion techniques and interpersonal skills we worked on were futile if the students had not read the text.

But the writing was much more than a check on the reading. It deepened, clarified, even created, the students' response. For writing is not merely the setting down of what we already know, but itself a method of discovery, a cognitive tool. As we push our vague, fuzzy thoughts to precision, we find the very act of writing makes us articulate things we didn't know we knew. Before it is written out, our knowledge remains locked in our own subjectivity, shadowy and inert. As we shape it into words and sentences, it becomes more objective, something external that we ourselves can scrutinize, analyze, reshape. As W. H. Auden (1948) has said, "How can I know what I think till I see what I say?" (p. 172).

In an even deeper sense, my own experiences as a teacher and my reading in the tradition of the active mind have convinced me that knowledge is not truly one's own unless it is articulated. It has been said that you really don't know something unless you can articulate it; I would go further to say you really don't know it *until* you articulate it. In the past few years, those who have wanted to reunite reading and writing in English studies have made the point often and convincingly that the act of reading and the act of writing are essentially both acts of interpretation; to construe is to construct, to understand is to invent. Writing about what one has read moves the whole process into a fuller dimension and make the act of reading more active, deliberate, intense, and closely related to one's immediate experience.

As a forum and format for both the undergraduates' and our daily writings, we adopted the notion of a dialectical journal from Ann Berthoff (1987), in which students leave substantial room, either 3-inch margins or on the back of each page, to reread and write back to what they had written previously, keeping a kind of reflective, running dialogue with themselves. To this structure we also offered them a list of questions, usually asking them to focus on specifics in the text itself. The care and imagination with which we structured the journal questions was crucial. As the semester went on, we increasingly tried to become the first Montessori teachers at the university level. We brought to bear on constructing the questions all the insight and learning that we might otherwise have tried to dispense during the class hour itself, our greatest challenge being to make them structured and specific as well as open ended. The problem with some "discovery" approaches is that what the students are supposed to discover is predetermined and carefully controlled; the fix is already in. To get around this problem, we as teachers tried to focus on the processes by which we as readers came to an understanding of the text—for example, what words and images are repeated, what more becomes revealed in the first paragraph after one has read through the entire text, what effects are created by the syntax and rhythms of sentences—rather than on final interpretations. We asked one another what came to be known as the epistemological question: not what we know, but how we came to know it.

As an example of the kinds of questions we asked, here is the sequence on Wallace Stevens's poem "Gubbinal" (1954)

> That strange flower, the sun,
> Is just what you say.
> Have it your way.
>
> The world is ugly
> And the people are sad.
>
> That tuft of jungle feathers,
> The animal eye,
> Is just what you say.
>
> That savage of fire,
> The seed,
> Have it your way.
>
> The world is ugly,
> And the people are sad. (p. 16)

Please consider the following questions, but don't just answer them in order; try to relate your answers to each other. When you're finished, read what you've written and see what other insights and connections you can make.

In what ways can the sun be said to be a "strange flower"? How does this metaphor work for you? Similarly, what about the other images for the sun— "that tuft of jungle feathers," "that animal eye," "that savage of fire," "that seed"? Are the images related? Is there a progression through the poem? Why does the speaker say, "the world is ugly and the people are sad"? Why is it repeated? Is there more than one speaker? In what ways is the sun "just what you say"? What questions do you have here that you'd like to raise with the class?

Earlier in my career I might have asked the class first what Stevens is suggesting here about the relation of language to perception. And I would have gotten the skimpy, vague generalities that the question deserved. To say that this poem is about the power of articulation would not be wrong; it would just be banal and superficial. The questions ask the students not simply to find out what the poem means, to get to some bottom line, but to immerse themselves in it imaginatively. Questions about individual words and images are intentionally meant to make the reading more deliberate, to slow it down enough to allow the poem to resonate through the imagination. While there are no right answers to such questions as "Are the images related? Is there a progression through the poem?" they are important in having the student see *how* one does or does not make meaning out of a poem. To ask, for example, how the sun is a strange flower, is to at once draw the students into the texture of the poem and to generate a series of disparate responses. Some students seize upon the visual qualities of an orb that appears to radiate lines, as in a child's drawing of the sun. Others are more emotive, talking about feelings of natural freshness they associate with both, others more conceptual and scientific as they talk about both participating in cycles or growing from small beginnings. Even students who see no resemblances can help to underscore how the sun can be described as a *strange* flower. The very act of producing and sharing responses gives the students an intrinsic, ambulatory knowledge of what it means to say the "sun / Is just what you say," a knowledge that they can then be asked to articulate.

As we have seen throughout this book, generalizations about how metaphor works or how language can alter our sense of the world are intelligible to the students only to the extent that these ideas emerge from and relate back to their own experiences of metaphor and language. Stevens's writing, like that of other participants in the tradition of active learning, is particularly helpful in easing students into the journaling situation for several reasons. As the preceding discussion suggests, his poetry tends toward self-reflection; in a playful way it examines its own workings. Although most poetry does this to some extent, Stevens's work is particularly aggressive in challenging and involving the reader as a participant in the making of meaning. As David Walker (1984) has noted, a Stevens poem often is "a poem whose rhetoric establishes its own incompleteness; it is presented not as completed discourse but as a structure that invites the reader to project himself or herself into its world, and thus to verify it as contiguous with reality" (p. 18). Further, Stevens writes at a level of difficulty that is just beyond the grasp of most students when they first read the poems, yet comes just within their reach as they begin writing about them; Stevens once wrote, "Poetry must resist the intelligence almost successfully" (1957/1989, p.197). In response to questions about Stevens's poems, many students begin with a statement to the effect that they have no idea what is going on and then proceed to write a couple of pages that contain some powerful insights. Indeed, it was exciting for us as teachers to see a student's mind unfold through the course of a journal entry and the course of a semester. One frequent movement is the students' increasing use of them to work out things for themselves—mnemonics such as diagrams, charts, and drawings appear more often. A related trend is that the individual entries get longer, far beyond what a student would have to write just to fulfill the assignment.

To say more about the relation of the journals to other kinds of course writing, I must recount one of our perennial surprises in the graduate class, the dullness of the students' first formal papers compared to their earlier journals. If we had only the formal papers to go on, as most teachers do, we would come to the same harsh judgment—that students cannot read, write, think critically, or whatever students are currently not supposed to be able to do. As in the classroom itself, to measure something is to change it. And whatever pleas and disclaimers we make before the papers are due, the situation itself activates the mindset with which students have approached the task in previous courses. Students who are lively and original in their journals—and most of them become so quickly—suddenly revert to a style that is stilted, tentative, wordy, and vacuous. We get introductions that begin with the nature of the universe and funnel down to some nearly tautological thesis statement, conclusions that merely reprint the topic sentence of each previous paragraph. The act of writing often becomes again for students an adversarial situation, in which the goal is to get as quickly as possible through the minefield with the minimum of red ink exploding in your face.

After our initial shock, we have found ways to ease our students into the formal writing situation more naturally, having them read their drafts out loud to one another and revise them in small groups. But the disparities between the journals and the essays are instructive, and the reasons for the differences go beyond the procrustean forms of organization that many students are taught and the error-centered approach by which they are graded.

More fundamental are the premature demands placed on student writing for something called "clarity." When I go over papers and point out to students some elements in the text that run counter to their thesis, a frequent response is, "Well, I saw that, but it would have wrecked my whole paper to put it in." In our demands that students be immediately intelligible at breakneck speed, we often encourage their own impatience with complexities and contradictions, with the hard work of thinking. The situation is exacerbated when writing becomes a separate course isolated from genuine academic inquiry and is narrowly focused on issues of form and rhetorical strategy. If the student is not actively engaged in learning something new but forced to write, say, a description of a dorm room or a comparison-contrast paper on "anything," the prose, however neat and correct, is going to be deadly. The views of David Bartholomae and Anthony Petrosky (1986) are a welcome alternative:

> It's this lesson that we want to teach students: that reading and writing begin in confusion, anxiety and uncertainty; that they are driven by chance and in-tuition as much as they are by deliberate strategy or conscious intent; and that certainty and authority are postures, features of performance that are achieved through an act of speaking or writing; they are not qualities of vision that precede such performance. (p. 105)

In helping students learn to write, then, we do not want them to excise their most problematical writing but instead to push even harder on those cruxes in which the deepest kinds of insights are likely to emerge.

Even when we began using student writing to structure the classes, we underestimated or overlooked some of the ways it intensified the classroom experience. At an early stage, for example, we wrote an assignment on Denise Levertov's "Stepping Westward," asking detailed questions only of the first half of the poem. We hypothesized that once the discussion pump was primed, it would keep flowing, and we could do the rest of the analysis right in class. The results were disastrously instructive. All the air hissed out of the discussion as soon as we came to the end of the questions; the sec-ond half of the class turned into one of those awkward tooth-pulling ses-sions we all dread. It seemed that the actual writing created a depth of response in the undergraduates that was difficult to replicate with a section of the text on which they had not written, no matter how well the discus-sion started. How, then, did the journals shape class discussions? We found that not only did the number of students who were participating increase, but also the conversation was particularly deepened by the additional voices. Normally, the students who talk in class are not necessarily the best think-ers, just the quickest or glibbest. Preparing the journal assignments gave the more deliberate thinkers a chance to articulate and rehearse their ideas, making them far more ready to speak on their own. Further, the act of writing gave them more of a stake in the discussion, increased their commitment to positions they had formed. And if, as often happens, some of the brightest students are also the shyest or least self-assured, the worksheets made it easier to call on them or draw them out in other ways with a minimum of embarrassment. We frequently began classes by going around the group having each student say in a couple of sentences—or read from their writing if they preferred—what they felt their most significant discovery was. In terms of process, this broke the ice—everyone had already spoken—and in terms of content, it put a number of fruitful, provoking, and conflicting positions on the table.

A question that came up frequently in the graduate class was whether it should be a primary goal to have every student speak. If the discussion among a portion of the students is animated and productive, why push to include everyone? Our eventual answer was analogous to the reasons for having everyone write: One learns more by articulating than by just absorbing. Even students who spoke only once or twice in a class seemed to be more engaged than those who tried to be just bystanders. Further, there are times in the rhythms of learning when one wants to generate as many and as widely divergent responses as possible, and what one gets from a handful of talkers cannot compare in richness to a symphony from the entire class.

Beyond written work, there were other techniques and strategies we found helpful for discussions. More often than not, it was a matter of giving up bad habits rather than of learning a new set of complex skills. One of these widespread habits is the hidden agenda, in which the teacher really has his or her own points to make, but tries to pull them out of student discussion instead of saying them directly. Although the agenda itself may be hidden, the fact that there is one soon becomes apparent as student comments are either reinforced or rejected in accordance with their proximity to the teacher's line of thought and not examined in the open marketplace of class reaction. Even when teachers renounce their own agendas, they often retain some vestigial habits that inhibit open discussion. The most common is having the feeling that they must make some kind of response to every student comment, to pass judgment or acknowledge in some other way— even with just an *uh-huh*—what every student says. This blocks the normal flow of discussion by making the teacher a kind of central switchboard to which all comments are addressed and only then sent back out to the rest of the class. We called this the Ping-Pong effect, in which the ball bounces monotonously back and forth from teacher to class to teacher again. What we were striving for was something more like volleyball. Having the students move their chairs into a circle does help somewhat, but will not entirely solve the problem. Just as we are used to speaking in response to each comment, students are used to speaking directly only to us as teachers. Sometimes we found it helpful to explicitly direct students during the first few discussions to speak to the entire class. If this seemed too awkward or blunt, we used the technique of not looking directly at the student speaking but instead at the other members of the class. While the undergraduates at first found this disconcerting, they soon got the message and began to search the room for eye contact with other students.

The habit of speaking after each student is a special case of our general tendency to talk too much, to not allow enough silence in the classroom and to not make the students themselves feel any responsibility for breaking the silence. One thing that helps is realizing that the silences are never as long to the students as they seem to the teacher, who usually feels too much responsibility for them. Further, we should remember that silence is not a mental vacuum. The mind does not switch off during them, and indeed sometimes they are necessary for genuine thinking to occur. Classes are rarely experienced as slow or boring because of too much silence, but more often because of too little depth, of discussants not really building on one anothers' comments.

Once we learned to let an open discussion happen, though, certain anxieties remained. What happens if it gets too open, if student comments become too diffuse, too anecdotal, too digressive? At one point we handled our feelings about this by agreeing to mentally allot each class what we called a 10-minute "bullshit quota" in the interests of keeping the discussions lively and unimpeded. But as we analyzed the classes, it became clear that one person's bullshit is another's insight. A more formal way of conceptualizing this is to use Lev Vygotsky's (1962) notion of a "Zone of Proximal Development," the distance between the actual developmental level as determined by individual problem solving and the level of potential development as determined through problem solving and guidance. A more advanced student may actually be able to teach a less advanced one more effectively than a professor or even a graduate student because the students speak the same language and are at a closer developmental level. What may seem banal or intuitively obvious for the professor who may have passed this way decades ago and forgotten his or her own learning processes may need to be stated, clarified, reiterated, explicated by undergraduates for one another. What we found to be increasingly important for good teaching—more so than eloquence or brilliance—is a kind of steady patience and confidence in the ability of the mind to construct its own orders and create its own patterns.

It is a patience, though, that should not be taken just on faith. Especially since this was an academic course and not merely a teacher "training" program—horrible phrase—I was careful not to let us get completely absorbed in the practical details of the classroom, but rather to have us continually conceptualize what we saw and did. As noted, I felt that postmodern thinking, especially reader response theory, was potentially relevant to creating and analyzing a more open classroom. Fortunately, the first year I taught the course there appeared a special issue of *College Literature* titled *The Newest Criticisms*, containing a full bibliography and articles that clearly explored the relevance of theory for pedagogy. The most powerful of these articles for our own work was Robert Crosman's "How Readers Make Meaning" (1982). In it he showed how his own reading of Faulkner's "A Rose for Emily" was expanded and reevaluated in the light of a student response that at first reading seemed "off the wall" or just plain "wrong," in which a student compares Emily to her own grandmother in a nostalgic reverie. This article confirmed our own growing realization that what students said should not so much be weighed in the scales of evaluation as carefully listened to for what was revealed about the interaction between text and the student. In other words, anything a student says is data, subject matter for our own analyses and interpretations. But, the question was soon raised, should we be completely accepting of all responses? Should we take them as they are or try to widen and deepen them? Our answers were similar to the ones David Bleich came to in *Subjective Criticism* (1978): that the very act of having students discuss, argue about, negotiate, their readings enriched their minds and their reading abilities. If they were just "popping out" the text from one perspective, or feeling just one part of the elephant, it was crucial to get them to see how others did it differently, to put their own hands on the parts of the elephant that their peers were feeling.

Once this process was begun, it was important for us to have the undergraduates become reflective about it. In other words, we found it valuable to have the undergraduates engage in the same kinds of observing and conceptualizing that we as a graduate class had been doing from the start—not to arrive at the single best reading but to catch red-handed the ways readings are made. We noticed, for example, that the primary way the students were making sense out of Nathaniel Hawthorne's "Rappaccini's Daughter" was through the convention of "character." That is, they constructed a unified psychological reality for each of the four main figures and then tried to work toward any larger meaning through their feelings and judgments about those psychological units. But in the actual give-and-take of the classroom, the undergraduates soon discovered that their psychological character readings conflicted with one another. Instead of trying to mediate these disagreements, we tried to point out, as does Kenneth Dauber in his *Rediscovering Hawthorne* (1977), that the author may have been providing fodder for all sides, something like what James did with "The Turn of the Screw," that the story's "meaning" may have less to do with the characters' personalities than with the stances it takes toward what Hawthorne foregrounds in his preface as "an inveterate love of allegory" (p. 975). That is, readers, like Giovanni in the story itself, may be too quick to allegorize other people, to extract from confusing and complex experiences some kind of simplified, polarized meaning. Indeed, although both students and teachers complain about the difficulties of making meaning of difficult works, we found that equal difficulties lay in the students' making meanings too rapidly and easily. In Norman Juster's children's book *The Phantom Toll Booth* (1961) there is an overcrowded Island of Conclusions, to which the inhabitants travel very quickly by jumping, but from which it is far less easy to escape (pp. 164–170).

As the semester went on, we began to notice and create all kinds of analogies and parallel processes between the undergraduates' readings of the texts and our readings of these readings. What became increasingly pressing in both classes was the constructed nature of all knowledge. This led neither the undergraduates nor us to an impairing skepticism or nihilism about everything being relative or fictive, but to a realization that our constructions were useful and powerful to the extent that we knew where they came from and how they were made. We discovered further that what we found out through scrutinizing the responses of readers to texts and measuring this against literary theories can be extended to a general critique of traditional education by linking it to concepts in cognitive science and philosophy. In some aspects, the students' reading of a text can serve as a synecdoche for their reading of the world. Particularly suggestive is a line of thought called constructivism, which, as Jerome Bruner explains in *Actual Minds, Possible Worlds* (1986, pp. 93–105) has powerful potential for reuniting philosophy and psychology. Indeed, constructivism in philosophy can be seen as a late development in the tradition of the active mind, with prominent constructors of this tradition such as Nelson Goodman clearly working in the line of American pragmatism.

The two most important tenets of constructivism for this work are that what we know depends on how we come to know it, and that the knowledge we construct does not so much match external reality as fit it. I will use an example first given by Paul Watzlawick (1984) to illustrate both these related ideas. It was a dark and stormy night. A sea captain without charts has managed to steer his ship through a long, narrow, dangerous channel. The very fact that he has survived proves that his course does not directly conflict with the actual shape of the strait, but the course also does not give us the best route or the exact topography; in other words, in a functional sense his course worked or fit an existing reality but did not necessarily map or match it. Most of our formulations have a similar status. We make them not in a vacuum of abstraction but with certain goals in specific contexts.

And only by making them ourselves can we be fully aware of their provisional nature, of the amount of hunch, serendipity, blind luck, and false starts involved. To return to Bruner's title, there is a range of possible "worlds" that "fit." Two common errors of traditional education are to make students think the world(s) we present them in our courses really "match,"—in other words, correlate directly with the structure of reality—and to simply give them our final formulations, saving them the effort of making their own knowledge. For to know has to be a set of active processes—perceiving, creating, inventing, formulating, and articulating, and not necessarily in this or any other linear order. Truman Capote once harshly said of Jack Kerouac's work that it's not writing, it's typing. Capote, I feel, was wrong, but I have to say just as harshly of most of our pedagogy at the university level that it's not teaching, it's talking.

Another attempt to enact the ideas delineated in this book was a course I was able to offer in our undergraduate honors program, which I co-taught with Dr. Mary Ann Shea, director of the Faculty Teaching Excellence Program, titled "The Experience of Education." In thinking about the first course, I realized that the experience was probably richer for the graduate students than for the undergraduates we taught, because the former could relate all their readings and writings to their ongoing teaching. We designed the honors course to provide an analogous experience for undergraduates, and we took their own current involvement in education, their lives as students, as the focus. We did not intend to produce future teachers as much as to help the students become more reflective about the learning they are immediately undergoing in the interest of enriching that learning. The primary text for this course was to be the students' own journals, in which they monitor and articulate this learning in the light of readings and discussions. We wanted these students also to experience writing as a way of thinking, of fixing their experience for a while so that it can be scrutinized. To this end, we used the dialectical notebook described earlier, which was reinforced by our reading of books such as those by Holt and Dennison, which also can be viewed as examples of this form. In the course, the students are asked to view the activities in their other courses through reflective lenses, to observe the structures and processes of their own education as well as the content. One assignment is to compare the syllabi from their various courses. Despite the varied subject matter, from music appreciation to organic chemistry, it was remarkable how similar they all looked, with requisite midterms and finals in the same places.

In addition to asking students to reflect on their experiences in other classes, we created shared learning situations within our own classroom and analyzed them. In one such case, we adopted an idea from Eleanor Duckworth (1987) and asked students to figure out why and how the moon has phases. But the equipment we brought in as manipulatives—flashlights, balls of various sizes—was not up to the task. With just a minute of class time left, we were all still puzzled and frustrated. Then one of the students suddenly exclaimed, "Just look at everybody's face!" We were sitting around a circular table with windows on only one wall, and according to our positions, the shadows on our faces corresponded to the different appearances of the moon, with the student directly facing the window as the full moon, the one facing away as the new moon, and the rest of us as all the gradations between. The student had created a wonderful analogy between faces and phases, and the analogy was enriched by the circumstance that as we looked at the physical light on one another, we could also see the figurative light of understanding break out as the idea dawned on each of us.

One conclusion that emerged from both these courses is the power for educational change of that vast, underused resource, the students' own minds. Students come to us generally unobservant and inarticulate about their own education, but they can soon easily be helped to learn how to be perceptive and reflective about their school experiences. This kind of metacognition can only help their own learning, even when it does not result in structural change. What if the students in a high school or college were given the time and assistance to take on the project of improving their own education—observing their own and other classrooms, making hypotheses, collecting data, interviewing themselves and their teachers, reading in cognitive psychology and in the history and philosophy of education, experimenting with different structures?

I can understand John Holt's heartbreak in the Maine woods, for not only has the history of American education been so dismal, but also the opportunities for it being otherwise have been so rich, plentiful, and philosophically fresh. Yet as I work with these young people I realize that these opportunities have not been permanently foreclosed. We have an indigenous tradition of active learning that has already been enacted sporadically. The rigor mortis of our current school system can be reversed through listening to these voices from the past and opening ourselves to those of the future. We need only trust more the mind's abilities and desires to make sense of the world by interacting with it, to not only master the old formulations but also go beyond them in the creation of new ones. The materials for a new American paideia lie before us all the time in the immediacies of our own lives seen fully in the light of the active mind.

References

Abrahams, E. (1986). *The lyrical Left: Randolph Bourne, Alfred Stieglitz, and the origins of cultural radicalism in America*. Charlottesville, VA: University Press of Virginia.

Abrams, M. H. (1971). *Natural supernaturalism: Tradition and revolution in Romantic literature*. New York: Norton.

Abbot, W. (1925). Robert Frost: Professor of English. *The Michigan Alumnus, 32*, 208–209.

Adams, H. (1983). *Novels; Mont Saint Michel; The education*. New York: Library of America.

Albee, J. (1901). *Remembrances of Emerson*. New York: R. G. Cooke.

Alcott, A. B. (1830). *Observations on the principles and methods of infant instruction*. Boston: Carter & Hendee.

Alcott, A. B. (1836 and 1837). *Conversations with children on the Gospels* (Vols. 1–2). Boston: James Munroe.

Alcott, A. B. (1861). *Superintendent's report of the Concord schools to the school committee for the year 1860–61*. Concord, MA: Town of Concord.

Alcott, A. B. (1866). The school-house and school of my youth—by a teacher. *American Journal of Education, 16*, 130–134.

Alcott, A. B. (1868). *Tablets*. Boston: Roberts Brothers.

Alcott, A. B. (1877). *Table-talk*. Boston: Roberts Brothers.

Alcott, A. B. (1938). *The journals of Bronson Alcott* (Vols. 1–2). O. Shepard (Ed.). Boston: Little, Brown.

Alcott, L. M. (1871). *Little men: Life at Plumfield with Jo's boys*. Boston: Roberts Brothers.

Auden, W. H. (1948). Squares and oblongs. In C. D. Abbott (Ed.), *Poets at work: Essays based on the modern poetry collection at the Lockwood Memorial Library, University of Buffalo* (pp. 170–175). New York: Harcourt Brace.

Bartholomae, D., & Petrosky, A. R. (1986). *Facts, artifacts, and counterfacts: Theory and method for a reading and writing course*. Upper Montclair, NJ: Boynton/Cook.

Beck, R. H. (1958–1959). Progressive education and American progressivism: Margaret Naumburg. *Teachers College Record, 60*, 198–208.

Beiser, F. C. (1998). A Romantic education: The concept of *Bildung* in early German Romanticism. In A. O. Rorty (Ed.), *Philosophers on education: New historical perspectives* (pp. 284–299). London: Routledge.

Bellow, S. (1964). *Herzog*. New York: Viking Press.

Berthoff, A. E. (1987). Dialectical notebooks and the audit of meaning. In T. Fulwiler (Ed.), *The journal book* (pp. 71–77). Portsmouth, NH: Boynton/Cook.

Bleich, D. (1978). *Subjective criticism*. Baltimore: Johns Hopkins University Press.

Bloom, A. (1987). *The closing of the American mind: How higher education has failed democracy and impoverished the souls of today's students*. New York: Simon & Schuster.

Bloom, H. (1982). *Agon: Towards a theory of revision*. New York: Oxford University Press.

Boorstin, D. J. (1958). *The Americans: The colonial experience*. New York: Random House.

Bouton, C., & Garth, R. Y. (1983). Students in learning groups: Active learning through conversation. *New Directions in Teaching and Learning, 14*, 73–82.

Bruner, J. (1986). *Actual minds, possible worlds*. Cambridge, MA: Harvard University Press.

Buell, L. (1973). *Literary transcendentalism: Style and vision in the American renaissance*. Ithaca, NY: Cornell University Press.

Cane, F. (1932). Art in the life of the child. In G. Hartman & A. Shumaker (Eds.), *Creative expression: The development of children in art, music, literature, and dramatics* (pp. 42–49). New York: John Day.

Capper, C. (1987). Margaret Fuller as cultural reformer: The conversations in Boston. *American Quarterly, 39*(4), 509–528.

Capper, C. (1992). *Margaret Fuller: An American Romantic life; the private years*. New York: Oxford University Press.

Carafiol, P. (1982). *Transcendent reason: James Marsh and the forms of Romantic thought*. Tallahassee, FL: University Presses of Florida.

Carlson, L. A. (1978). Bronson Alcott's "Journal for 1836." In J. Myerson, (Ed.), *Studies in the American Renaissance, 1978* (pp. 17–104). Charlottesville, VA: University Press of Virginia.

Carlson, L. A. (1981). Bronson Alcott's "Journal for 1837" (pt. 1). In J. Myerson, (Ed.), *Studies in the American Renaissance, 1981* (pp. 27–132). Charlottesville, VA: University Press of Virginia.

Carlson, L. A. (1988). "Those pure pages of yours": Bronson Alcott's *Conversations with children on the Gospels. American Literature, 60*(3), 451–460.

Carlson, L. A. (1993). Bronson Alcott's "Journal for 1838" (pt. 1). In J. Myerson, (Ed.), *Studies in the American Renaissance, 1993* (pp. 161–244). Charlottesville: University Press of Virginia.

Coleridge, S. T. (1829). *Aids to reflection*. J. Marsh (Ed.). Burlington, VT: Chauncey Goodrich.

Coleridge, S. T. (1962). *The notebooks of Samuel Taylor Coleridge* (Vols. 1–3). K. Coburn (Ed.). London: Routledge and Kegan Paul.

Coleridge, S. T. (1997). *Biographia literaria*. N. Leask (Ed.). London: Everyman. (Original work published 1817)

Cremin, L. A. (1961). *The transformation of the school: Progressivism in American education*. New York: Random House.

Crosman, R. (1982). How readers make meaning. *College Literature, 9*, 207–215.

Cuban, L. (1993). *How teachers taught: Constancy and change in American class-rooms, 1890–1990*. (2nd ed.). New York: Teachers College Press. (Original work published 1984)

Dahlstrand, F. C. (1982). *Amos Bronson Alcott: An intellectual biography*. East Brunswick, NJ: Associated University Presses.

Dauber, K. (1977). *Rediscovering Hawthorne*. Princeton, NJ: Princeton University Press.

Davis, P. (1994). Teacher-poets: Robert Frost's influence on Theodore Roethke. In E. J. Wilcox (Ed.), *His "incalculable influence on others": Essays on Robert Frost in our time* (pp. 37–45). Victoria, BC: University of Victoria English Literary Studies.

Dell, F. (1919). *Were you ever a child?* New York: Knopf.

Dennison, G. (1969). *The lives of children: The story of the First Street School*. New York: Random House.

Dewey, J. (1910). *How we think*. Boston: D.C. Heath.

Dewey, J. (1929). *Characters and events* (Vols. 1–2). New York: Holt, Rinehart & Winston.

Dewey, J. (1930). From absolutism to experimentalism. In G. P. Adams & W. P. Montague (Eds.), *Contemporary American philosophy: Personal statements* (pp. 13–26). New York: Macmillan.

Dewey, J. (1952). Introduction. In E. Clapp, *The use of resources in education* (pp. vii–xi). New York: Harper.

Dewey, J. (1969). Psychology as philosophic method. In *The Early Works: 1882–1898* (Vol. 1, pp. 144–167). Carbondale, IL: Southern Illinois University Press. (Original work published 1886)

Dewey, J. (1972). My pedagogic creed. In *The Early Works: 1882–1898* (Vol. 5, pp. 84–95). Carbondale, IL: Southern Illinois University Press. (Original work published in 1887)

Dewey, J. (1976a). The school and society. In J. A. Boydston (Ed.), *The Middle Works: 1899–1924* (Vol. 1, pp. 1–109). Carbondale, IL: Southern Illinois University Press. (Original work published in 1899)

Dewey, J. (1976b). The educational situation. In J. A. Boydston (Ed.), *The Middle Works: 1899–1924* (Vol. 1, pp. 257–313). Carbondale, IL: Southern Illinois University Press. (Original work published in 1901)

Dewey, J. (1976c). The child and the curriculum. In J. A. Boydston (Ed.), *The Middle Works: 1899–1924* (Vol. 2, pp. 271–291). Carbondale, IL: Southern Illinois University Press. (Original work published in 1902)

Dewey, J. (1977). The relation of theory to practice in education. In J. A. Boydston (Ed.), *The Middle Works: 1899–1924* (Vol. 3, pp. 249–272). Carbondale, IL: Southern Illinois University Press. (Original work published in 1904)

Dewey, J. (1980). Democracy and education. In J. A. Boydston (Ed.), *The Middle Works: 1899–1924* (Vol. 9). Carbondale, IL: Southern Illinois University Press. (Original work published in 1916)

Dewey, J. (1987). Art as experience. In J. A. Boydston (Ed.), *The Later Works: 1925–1953* (Vol. 10). Carbondale, IL: Southern Illinois University Press. (Original work published in 1934)

Dewey, J., & Dewey, E. (1915). *Schools of to-morrow*. New York: Dutton.

Duckworth, E. (1987). *The having of wonderful ideas and other essays on teaching and learning*. New York: Teachers College Press.

Eliade, M. (1965). *The two and the one*. J. M. Cohen (Trans.). New York: Harper & Row. (Original work published 1962)

Emerson, E. W. (1917). *Henry Thoreau as remembered by a young friend*. Boston: Houghton Mifflin.

Emerson, R. W. (1883). *Lectures and biographical sketches*. Boston: Houghton Mifflin.

Emerson, R. W. (1939). *The letters of Ralph Waldo Emerson* (Vols. 1–6). R. L. Rusk (Ed.). New York: Columbia University Press.

Emerson, R. W. (1959–1972). *The early lectures of Ralph Waldo Emerson* (Vols. 1–3). S. E. Whicher & R. E. Spiller (Eds.). Cambridge, MA: Harvard University Press.

Emerson, R. W. (1969). *The journals and miscellaneous notebooks of Ralph Waldo Emerson* (Vol. 7). A. W. Plumstead & H. Hayford (Eds.). Cambridge, MA: Harvard University Press.

Emerson, R. W. (1983). *Essays and lectures*. New York: Library of America.

Featherstone, J. (1971). *Schools where children learn*. New York: Liveright.

Feldman, C. F., & Wertsch, J. V. (1976). Context dependent properties of teacher's speech. *Youth and Society, 7*(3), 227–258.

Fenollosa, E. F. (1936). *The Chinese written character as a medium for poetry*. E. Pound (Ed.). San Francisco: City Lights.

Fergenson, L. R. (1991). Margaret Fuller as a teacher in Providence: The school journal of Ann Brown. In J. Myerson (Ed.), *Studies in the American Renaissance, 1991* (pp. 59–118). Charlottesville, VA: University Press of Virginia.

Finkelstein, B. (1989). *Governing the young: Teacher behavior in popular primary schools in 19th-century United States*. New York: Falmer Press.

Fitzgerald, F. S. (1992). *The great Gatsby*. New York: Scribners. (Original work published 1925)

Frank, W. (1917). Vicarious fiction. *The Seven Arts, 1*(2), 291–298.

Friedenberg, E. Z. (1990). Romanticism and alternatives in schooling. In J. Willinsky (Ed.), *The educational legacy of Romanticism* (pp. 157–187). Waterloo, Ont.: Wilfrid Laurier University Press.

Frost, R. (1963). *The letters of Robert Frost to Louis Untermeyer*. New York: Holt, Rinehart & Winston.

Frost, R. (1964a). Playing for mortal stakes. In H. W. Hewlett (Ed.), *In other words: Amherst in prose and verse* (pp. 170–184). Amherst, MA: Amherst College Press.

Frost, R. (1964b). *Selected letters*. L. Thompson (Ed.). New York: Holt, Rinehart & Winston.

Frost, R. (1972). *Poetry and prose*. E. C. Lathem & L. Thompson (Eds.). New York: Holt, Rinehart & Winston.

Frye, N. (1968). *A study of English Romanticism*. New York: Random House.

Fuller, M. (1852). *Memoirs of Margaret Fuller Ossoli*. W. H. Channing (Ed.) (Vols. 1–2). Boston: Phillips, Sampson.

Fuller, M. (1859). *Life without and life within; or reviews, narratives, essays, and poems*. A. B. Fuller (Ed.). Boston: Brown, Taggard, & Chase.

Fuller, M. (1983–1994). *The letters of Margaret Fuller.* R. N. Hudspeth (Ed.). (Vols. 1–6). Ithaca, NY: Cornell University Press.

Fuller, M. (1992). *The essential Margaret Fuller.* J. Steele (Ed.). New Brunswick, NJ: Rutgers University Press.

Ginsberg, A. (1956). *Howl and other poems.* San Francisco: City Lights.

Hawkins, D. (1974). Messing about in science. In D. Hawkins, *The informed vision: Essays on learning and human nature* (pp. 63–75). New York: Agathon Press.

Herndon, J. (1968). *The way it spozed to be.* New York: Simon & Schuster.

Herndon, J. (1985). *Notes from a schoolteacher.* New York: Simon & Schuster.

Higginson, T. W. (1884). *Margaret Fuller Ossoli.* Boston: Houghton Mifflin.

Hirsch, E. D., Jr. (1987). *Cultural literacy: What every American needs to know.* Boston: Houghton Mifflin.

Holmes, O. W. (1941). *Holmes-Pollock letters: The correspondence of Mr. Justice Holmes and Sir Frederick Pollock* (Vols. 1–2). M. D. Howe (Ed.). Cambridge, MA: Harvard University Press.

Holt, J. (1982). *How children fail.* Reading, MA: Addison Wesley. (Original work published 1964)

Holt, J. (1990). *A life worth living: Selected letters of John Holt.* S. Sheffer (Ed.). Columbus, OH: Ohio State University Press.

Hurston, Z. N. (1937). *Their eyes were watching God.* New York: J. B. Lippincott.

James, H. (1984). *Literary criticism.* New York: Library of America.

James, W. (1987). *Writings, 1902–1910.* New York: Library of America.

James, W. (1992). *Writings, 1878–1899.* New York: Library of America.

James, W. (1995). *The correspondence of William James: Vol. 4. 1856–1877.* I. K. Skrupskelis & E. M. Berkeley (Eds.) Charlottseville, VA: University Press of Virginia.

Jervis, K., & Montag, C. (Eds.). (1991). *Progressive education for the 1990s: Transforming practice.* New York: Teachers College Press.

Johnson, H. H. (1910, April 21). Margaret Fuller as known by her scholars. *Christian Register*, 426–429.

Joyce, J. (1986). *Ulysses.* New York: Vintage. (Original work published 1922)

Jung, C. (1969). *Psychology and religion: West and East.* (R. F. C. Hull, Trans.). Princeton, NJ: Princeton University Press.

Juster, N. (1961). *The phantom tollbooth.* New York: Knopf.

Katz, M. (2001). *The irony of early school reform: Educational innovation in mid-19th-century Massachusetts.* New York: Teachers College Press. (Original work published 1968)

Kliebard, H. M. (1986). *The struggle for the American curriculum, 1893–1958.* New York: Routledge.

Kliebard, H. M. (1992). *Forging the American curriculum: Essays in curriculum history and theory.* New York: Routledge.

Kohl, H. (1967). *36 children.* New York: New American Library.

Kohl, H. (1991). Reflections: Tales told in and about school; educational writing of the sixties and early seventies. *Mothering, 61,* 69–72.

Kohl, H. (1998). *The discipline of hope: Learning from a lifetime of teaching*. New York: Simon & Schuster.

Kornfeld, E. (1997). *Margaret Fuller: A brief biography with documents*. Boston: Bedford Books.

Kozol, J. (1967). *Death at an early age: The destruction of the hearts and minds of Negro children in the Boston public schools*. Boston: Houghton Mifflin.

Kozol, J. (1991). *Savage inequalities: Children in America's schools*. New York: Crown.

Labaree, D. F. (1991). Does the subject matter? Dewey, democracy, and the history of the curriculum. *History of Education Quarterly, 31*, 513–521.

Lagemann, E. C. (2000). *An elusive science: The troubling history of education research*. Chicago: University of Chicago Press.

Lambert, N. M., & McCombs, B. L. (Eds.). (1998). *How students learn: Reforming schools through learner-centered education*. Washington, DC: American Psychological Association.

Lathem, E. C. (1966). *Interviews with Robert Frost*. New York: Holt, Rinehart & Winston.

Lears, T. J. J. (1983). *No place of grace: Antimodernism and the transformation of American culture, 1880–1920*. Chicago: University of Chicago Press.

MacCann, R. (1939, May 2). Poet startles audience with sense of humor. *University Daily Kansan*, 1.

Marsh, J. (1829). Preliminary essay. In S. T. Coleridge, *Aids to reflections* (pp. vii–liv). Burlington, VT: Chauncy Goodrich.

Marsh, J. (1973). *Coleridge's American disciples: The selected correspondence of James Marsh*. J. J. Duffy (Ed.). Amherst, MA: University of Massachusetts Press.

Mayhew, K. C., & Edwards, A.C. (1936). *The Dewey School: The laboratory school of the University of Chicago, 1896–1903*. New York: Appleton-Century Crofts.

McCuskey, D. (1940). *Bronson Alcott, teacher*. New York: Macmillan.

McNiece, G. (1992). *The knowledge that endures: Coleridge, German philosophy, and the logic of Romantic thought*. New York: St. Martin's Press.

Melville, H. (2002). *Moby-Dick*. H. Parker & H. Hayford (Eds.). New York: Norton. (Original work published 1851)

Menand, L. (2001). *The metaphysical club*. New York: Farrar, Straus & Giroux.

Mertins, L. (1965). *Robert Frost: Life and talks-walking*. Norman, OK: University of Oklahoma Press.

Messerli, J. (1972). *Horace Mann: A biography*. New York: Knopf.

Michalec, P. (1998). *Constructivist and teacher-centered bridges over the theory/practice divide in teacher education*. Unpublished doctoral dissertation, University of Colorado, Boulder.

Miller, E. H. (Ed.). (1969). *A century of Whitman criticism*. Bloomington, IN: Indiana University Press.

Monk, S. (1983). Student engagement and teacher power in large classes. *New Directions for Teaching and Learning, 14*, pp. 7–12.

Myerson, J. (1978). Bronson Alcott's "Journal for 1836." In J. Myerson (Ed.), *Studies in the American Renaissance, 1978* (pp. 17–104). Boston: Twayne.

Myerson, J. (Ed.). (2000). *Transcendentalism: A reader.* New York: Oxford University Press.

Naumburg, M. (1926). How children decorate their own school. *Progressive Education: A Quarterly Review of the Newer Tendencies in Education, 3,* 163–167.

Naumburg, M. (1973). A direct method of education. In C. Winsor (Ed.), *Experimental schools revisited: Bulletins of the Bureau of Educational Experiments* (pp. 41–45). New York: Agathon Press. (Original work published 1917)

Neill, A. S. (1960). *Summerhill: A radical approach to child rearing.* New York: Hart.

Newman, J. W. (1998). *America's teachers: An introduction to education.* New York: Longman.

Nietzsche, F. (1954). *The portable Nietzsche.* Walter Kaufmann (Trans. & Ed.). New York: Viking.

O'Connor, D. (1996). Thoreau in the town school, 1837. *Concord Saunterer,* new series 4, 150–172.

Packer, B. L. (1995). The Transcendentalists. In S. Bercovitch & C. R. K. Patell (Eds.), *The Cambridge history of American literature: Vol. 2* (pp. 329–604). Cambridge, Eng.: Cambridge University Press.

Peabody, E. P. (1835). *Record of a school: Exemplifying the general principles of spiritual culture.* Boston: James Munroe.

Peabody, E. P. (1836). *Record of a school: Exemplifying the general principles of spiritual culture* (2nd ed.). Boston: Russell, Shattuck.

Poirier, R. (1987). *The renewal of literature: Emersonian reflections.* New York: Random House.

Poirier, R. (1992a). *Poetry and pragmatism.* Cambridge, MA: Harvard University Press.

Poirier, R. (1992b). Pragmatism and the sentence of death. *Yale Review, 80*(3), 74–100.

Posnock, R. (1992). Reading Poirier pragmatically. *Yale Review, 80,* 156–169.

Pound, E. (1934). *The ABC of reading.* New Haven, CT: Yale University Press.

Pratt, C. (1924). *Experimental practice in the City and Country School.* New York: E. P. Dutton.

Pratt, C. (1926). Pedagogy as a creative art. In C. Pratt and J. Stanton, *Before books: Experimental practice in the City and Country School* (pp. 1–26). New York: Adelphi.

Pratt, C. (1948). *I learn from children.* New York: Simon & Schuster.

Pratt, C., & Deming, L. C. (1973). The Play School. In C. Winsor (Ed.), *Experimental schools revisited: Bulletins of the Bureau of Educational Experiments* (pp. 21–34). New York: Agathon Press. (Original work published 1917)

Pynchon, T. (1997). *Mason and Dixon.* New York: Henry Holt.

Ravitch, D. (1983). *The troubled crusade: American education, 1945–1980.* New York: Basic Books.

Ravitch, D. (2000). *Left back: A century of failed school reforms.* New York: Simon & Schuster.

Reid, T. W. (1890). *The life, letters, and friendships of Richard Monckton Milnes* (Vols. 1–2). London: Cassell.

Richardson, R. D. (1995). *Emerson: The mind on fire*. Berkeley, and Los Angeles, CA: University of California Press.

Rosenfeld, P. (1924). *The Port of New York: Essays on fourteen American moderns*. New York: Harcourt, Brace.

Sanborn, F. B. (1884). *Henry D. Thoreau*. Boston: Houghton Mifflin.

Sanborn, F. B., & W. T. Harris. (1893). *A. Bronson Alcott: His life and philosophy*. Boston: Roberts Brothers.

Sarason, S. B. (2001). *American psychology and schools: A critique*. New York and Washington, DC: Teachers College Press and the American Psychological Association.

Schiller, F. (1965). *On the aesthetic education of man*. R. Snell (Trans.). New York: Frederick Ungar. (Original work published 1795)

Schneider, H. (1974). Review of George Dykhuizen, *John Dewey. The Journal of the History of Philosophy, 12,* 541–543.

Schrag, P. (1967, February 18). Education's "Romantic" critics. *Saturday Review, 50,* 80–82.

Schwartz, S. (1985). *The matrix of modernism: Pound, Eliot, and early 20th-century thought*. Princeton, NJ: Princeton University Press.

Shuffleton, F. (1985). Margaret Fuller at the Greene Street School: The journal of Evelina Metcalf. In J. Myerson, (Ed.), *Studies in the American Renaissance, 1985* (pp. 29–46). Charlottesville, VA: University Press of Virginia.

Silberman, C. E. (1970). *Crisis in the classroom: The remaking of American education*. New York: Random House.

Simmons, N. C. (1994). Margaret Fuller's Boston conversations: The 1839–1840 series. In J. Myerson, (Ed.), *Studies in the American Renaissance, 1994* (pp. 195–226). Charlottesville, VA: University Press of Virginia.

Smith, D. (1984). Emerson and deconstruction: The end(s) of scholarship. *Soundings, 67,* 379–398.

Snyder, A. D. (1929). *Coleridge on logic and learning, with selections from the unpublished manuscripts*. New Haven, CT: Yale University Press.

Steele, J. (2001). *Transfiguring America: Myth, ideology, and mourning in Margaret Fuller's writing*. Columbia, MO: University of Missouri Press.

Stevens, W. (1954). *The collected poems of Wallace Stevens*. New York: Knopf.

Stevens, W. (1989). *Opus posthumous* (New ed.). M. J. Bates (Ed.). New York: Knopf. (Original work published 1957).

Suleiman, S., & Crosman, I. (Eds.). (1980). *The reader in the text: Essays in audience and interpretation*. Princeton, NJ: Princeton University Press.

Tanner, L. (1997). *Dewey's laboratory school: Lessons for today*. New York: Teachers College Press.

Tanner, T. (1971). *City of words: American fiction, 1950–1970*. New York: Harper.

Tarnas, R. (1991). *The passion of the Western mind: Understanding the ideas that have shaped our world view*. New York: Harmony Books.

Tashjian, D. (1978). *William Carlos Williams and the American scene, 1920–1940*. New York: Whitney Museum of American Art.

Thompson, L. (1966). *Robert Frost: The early years, 1874–1915*. New York: Holt, Rinehart & Winston.

Thoreau, H. D. (1906). *The journal of Henry David Thoreau*. B. Torrey & F. H. Allen (Eds.) (Vols. 1–14). Boston: Houghton Mifflin.

Thoreau, H. D. (1958). *The correspondence of Henry David Thoreau*. W. Harding & C. Bode (Eds.). New York: New York University Press.

Thoreau, H. D. (1971). *Walden*. J. Lyndon Shanley (Ed.). Princeton, NJ: Princeton University Press. (Original work published 1854)

Thoreau, H. D. (1980). *The natural history essays*. Salt Lake City, UT: Peregrine Smith.

Thoreau, H. D. (1981–1997). *Journal*. R. Sattelmeyer (Ed.) (Vols. 1–5). Princeton, NJ: Princeton University Press.

Tompkins, J. (Ed.). (1980). *Reader-response criticism: From formalism to post-structuralism*. Baltimore: Johns Hopkins University Press.

Torrey, J. (1843). *The remains of the Rev. James Marsh, D.D., with a memoir of his life*. Burlington, VT: Chauncey Goodrich.

Trifonas, P. P. (Ed.). (2000). *Revolutionary pedagogies: Cultural politics, instituting education, and the discourse of theory*. New York: Routledge Falmer.

Tyack, D. (Ed.). (1967). *Turning points in American educational history*. Waltham, MA: Blaisdell.

Tyack, D., & Cuban, L. (1995). *Tinkering toward utopia: A century of public school reform*. Cambridge, MA: Harvard University Press.

Vygotsky, L. (1962). *Thought and language*. Cambridge, MA: MIT Press.

Walker, D. (1984). *The transparent lyric: Reading and meaning in the poetry of Stevens and Williams*. Princeton, NJ: Princeton University Press.

Wasserman, M. (1970). *The school fix, NYC, USA*. New York: Outerbridge & Dienstfrey.

Watzlawick, P. (Ed.). (1984). *The invented reality: How do we know what we believe we know? Contributions to constructivism*. New York: Norton.

Weber, L. (1971). *The English infant school and informal education*. Englewood Cliffs, NJ: Prentice-Hall.

Wells, R. V. (1943). *Three Christian Transcendentalists: James Marsh, Caleb Sprague Henry, Frederic Henry Hedge*. New York: Columbia University Press.

Westbrook, R. B. (1991). *John Dewey and American democracy*. Ithaca, NY: Cornell University Press.

Whicher, G. F. (1950). *Mornings at 8:50: Brief evocations of the past for a college audience*. Northampton, MA: Hampshire Bookshop.

Williams, W. C. (1925). *In the American grain*. New York: New Directions.

Williams, W. C. (1934). The American background. In W. Frank, L. Mumford, D. Norman, P. Rosenfeld, & H. Rugg (Eds.), *America and Alfred Stieglitz* (pp. 9–32). New York: Literary Guild.

Williams, W. C. (1951). *The collected earlier poems*. New York: New Directions.

Williams, W. C. (1954). *Selected essays of William Carlos Williams*. New York: Random House.

Williams, W. C. (1957). *The selected letters of William Carlos Williams*. John Thirlwall (Ed.). New York: McDowell, Obolensky.

Williams, W. C. (1963). *The collected later poems*. New York: New Directions.

Williams, W. C. (1974a). *The embodiment of knowledge*. R. Loewinsohn (Ed.). New York: New Directions.

Williams, W. C. (1974b). *Imaginations*. W. Schott (Ed.). New York: New Directions.

Williams, W. C. (1992). *Paterson* (Rev. ed.). New York: New Directions.

Wirth, A. G. (1966). *John Dewey as educator: His design for work in education (1894–1904)*. New York: John Wiley.

Yeats, W. B. (1933). *Collected poems*. New York: Macmillan.

Zilversmit, A. (1993). *Changing schools: Progressive education theory and practice, 1930–1960*. Chicago: University of Chicago Press.

Index

About the Author

Martin Bickman, Professor of English at the University of Colorado, Boulder, was educated at Amherst College, the Harvard Graduate School of Education, and the University of Pennsylvania. Throughout his career he has been active at all levels of education, from reading classes in Boston's inner city to high school in rural Kentucky. At his home institution he has received the Boulder Faculty Assembly Teaching Award, the Faculty Teaching Fellowship, and a lifetime appointment as President's Teaching Scholar. He is author of *American Romantic Psychology* and *Walden: Volatile Truths* and editor of *Approaches to Teaching Herman Melville's* Moby Dick and *Uncommon Learning: Thoreau on Education*. He lives in Boulder with his wife, Louise, a clinical psychologist; they have two children, Sarah and Jed.